FLOATERS
The Professor and the Captain

Roheryn Press

Books by PJS Martin
FLOATERS: The Professor and the Captain

Coming in 2022:

THERE IS NO AWAY (a Rainey Collins cozy
environmental mystery)

FLOATERS
The Professor and the Captain

by PJS Martin

Roheryn Press

Homer, Alaska

First Published in the United States of America by
Roheryn Press, 2021.

Copyright (c) 2021 PJS Martin

Cover art by Jen DePesa

ISBN 978-1-955881-01-2 (paperback edition)

Library of Congress Control Number: 2021912526

This is a memoir. The events and conversations in this
book represent the best of the author's ability; readers
should recognize the effect time has on memory. A few
names and details have been adjusted to protect the privacy
of individuals, and not all stories have been told.

To JRR Tolkien
for a life of wonder

To Pet Rescues
for saving lives of wonder

CONTENTS

1 Joe and Paula Interlude

Floater: (n) an object resting or moving on the surface of a liquid

1987

Anticipation was the best. I always assumed reality would match it. My heart settled down as my pursuit neared its end. I looked out over Acapulco Bay and out to sea but continued chewing on a fingernail. Exhaling deeply, I walked back to the bar and asked, "Por favor, cervesa? Tres Equis?"

The bartender kindly did not smirk at my terrible accent and handed me an icy cold bottle. He said in perfect English, "On your room charge, *Señora?*"

I blushed and said, "Yes. Oh, *sí,* yes, *sí,* please, *por favor.*" *Paula, you have got to work on your Spanish.* I took the cold beer and searched for a seat out of the tropical sun. Finding one, I dropped my novel on the table and sat facing the ocean.

The only other guests were an older couple, two tables over. Based on the number of Texas lone stars on their clothing, belt buckles and jewelry, I suspected I knew where they came from. They turned to me when I sat down and the man said, "How ya' do there, young lady?"

I replied, "Very well sir. How are you both? Such a beautiful spot, overlooking the ocean like this."

"Yup, sure is. Ya' know, they don't start until later in the day."

My head tilted. "Start?"

The couple's eyebrows raised in response. The man gestured with his hand, "Yup, ya' know, the divers? The show don't start—couple of hours yet. No need to be antsy. Relax young lady and enjoy that beer."

Ah, they must have noticed the state of my nails.

He pointed to my seat, "Good ya' got your table early. These seats fill right on up."

I nodded with a scant smile. "I don't know if I'll be here for the show."

Their eyebrows were up again. The woman jumped in, "Oh, gracious, I thought that's why everyone came here. The cliff divers, that's why we came down here, all this way, to Hotel Mirador—all those years watching the ABC Wide World of Sports—we wanted to see it for real. In person. Imagine, jumping off those cliffs. And what a view from this hotel." Her Lone Star earrings clinked as she giggled, "It's just like we are right next to them divers."

I turned to look at the cliffs. My eyes had passed over them in my focus on the sea. Thin, steep fingers of rock reached out from the hotel's elevation a hundred feet above the ocean, extending out and down, into the Pacific. I said, "Yes, they are really high. I'm sure the show will be amazing."

"Well, young lady, where will you be, if not watching the most famous sport in Acapulco, probably in all of Mexico?"

As I started to frame my answer, looking back out to the ocean, I suddenly held my breath. Rising above the horizon was a ship, a ship steaming into the Bay. She was close enough for me to identify her blue hull color and white house rising above her decks. My objective! My smile stretched and I could feel the flush on my face. Success was in view. I stood, pointed, and said loudly enough that the bartender looked over, "There, there, do you see it?"

The man looked and asked, "What? What is that?"

"That's a ship. A research ship. From Woods Hole Oceanographic." My smile stretched and I continued,

"The merchant sailors and the scientists are coming into port for a few days." I quickly drank the beer, grabbed my book, and turned to go, "Sorry, but I have to get to the dock." With a wide grin, I pointed to the ship again, "That's why I'm here. A sailor on that ship is who I came to see. My husband is arriving."

I turned my back on them to politely ignore the question I knew I would see on their faces. I needed to be on my way. I had no time to explain how it worked being married to a US merchant sailor.

I was vibrating as my goal was close. My rush to leave my university and fly to Mexico had worked out. I made it to Acapulco, found the hotel, saw the ship, and I was going to get to see him for the first time in six months.

I still had one more challenge: to find the dock and get myself there. I went searching for the concierge.

One of the joys of hotels is that assistance is just where you'd expect it to be. I explained my problem to the uniformed man at the desk with the phones, next to the hotel's entrance. He said, "*Sí señora*, there is a taxi right here. This taxi can take you to the dock but there are no cruise ships scheduled today."

"I am not looking for the cruise ship dock, but the commercial dock, for big ships?"

His helpfulness slowed a bit as he digested my request, "The main port, in Old Town?"

"Yes, I think that is what I want, the one that large ships come into."

"Large yachts *Señora*? Private ships? That is not near Old Town."

"No, not yachts. I am looking for the commercial ships, the cargo ships."

A certain reputation surrounded unaccompanied women visiting cargo ships. I appreciated that the concierge worked to keep any judgement off his face as he said, "Ah, okay, Old Town."

3

He walked out to the road and spoke to a taxi driver then opened the car's door. I jumped in, hoping my directions, the concierge's translation, and the driver's interpretation would land me somewhere close to the ship.

The hotel was carved into the rock face, on the ridge that separated the Pacific Ocean from Acapulco Bay, towering above Old Town. Flowering purple bougainvillea lined the narrow streets and their scent floated in the air. The purple-lined road twisted and turned as we drove down, losing its color as it lost its elevation. The quality of the atmosphere also changed: diesel engine exhaust replaced sweet flower scents. A poorly operating sewage plant added its tang, and, as we reached the flats of Old Town, a whiff of sea breeze laid over the fumes.

Another hint I was getting close.

The taxi stopped in front of a ten-foot rusty iron fence with a half-open gate and a guard shack. The driver pointed and said, *"Puerto, puerto."*

I handed him a handful of pesos and he nodded okay. I thanked him, got out and nearly tripped over the uneven pavement as I approached the gate. The guy standing in the shack barely looked up at me as he gave a limp wave. I took that as permission to enter.

Beyond the giant fence, I walked through a corridor formed by piles: oily equipment, wooden crates, and burlap sacks. Then, the space opened into a dusty, concrete courtyard whose far end edged the sea.

There she was, just ahead of me. The *R/V Oceanus*.

Deep blue hull, white lettering of her name, and white structures rising three stories above the deck, she was nearly two hundred feet long. I stood with a silly grin on my face and ignored the forklifts zipping in front of me.

Now to find him.

There was an empty steel ramp from the ship to

the shore, blocked at its base by a uniformed Mexican soldier standing tall. I did not think this guy would just wave me past. As I watched, another soldier in a shiny white uniform with gold braids came down the ramp. He said something to the soldier at the ramp's base; they exchanged salutes and walked away. I looked back up at the ship and my heart skipped. There was Joe, striding down the gangway.

I kept myself from jumping up and down like a kid even though I felt like doing so. I did fling my arms open wide until I was gathered in Joe's tight embrace. My face just tucked up under his freshly-shaven chin, his scent replacing all others. This was the finish to my race.

Joe released me and said, "You found me!"

I laughed, "Of course, we always do!"

After more kisses, hugs, and burbles of pleasure, Joe said, "We finally cleared Customs—"

I jumped in, "That's what those soldiers were doing!"

Joe continued, "Yes, 'research ships' are sometimes euphemisms for something less than legal. They took special care with us."

"I imagine the laboratory on the main deck was pretty convincing."

Joe beamed at me, "Exactly. And when he saw all the biological samples from the last dredging operation, he passed us through. I think he was disappointed." Joe looked around, taking in the condition of the port, and said, "I hope you didn't have too much problem getting here today."

"No, I figured it out." I did not want to bother him with the details of how I put together a quick international trip to Mexico while in the middle of my semester. He didn't need to know the favors I called in to cover my class.

He hugged me again, "I love that you are capable and competent. I never worry about you managing."

5

Hearing my favorite complement, I blushed and tightened my hug.

Joe said, "I hate to say this my love, but we only have two days together—"

I burst out, "Two? Wasn't it originally going to be four?"

"Yes, but science got their act together sooner than expected so we sail again in two days. Well, the morning after the second night that is."

I hugged him, keeping my face tight against his broad chest, trying not to think of the tradeoffs I had made to get here. I quietly responded, "Two nights it is then." I silenced the heavy sigh that was trying to move through my lips, and I forced my posture to stay straight.

We reached out for each other's hand at the same moment. Joe said after a moment, "Was my hotel suggestion okay? One of the scientists had suggested the Mirador and I thought it sounded good; I remembered those ABC Wide World of Sports shows. I hope I didn't lead you to somewhere horrible. Is the hotel in a better neighborhood than the port?"

I laughed, "You chose a beautiful hotel, well above Old Town, overlooking the sea."

Joe said, "We might see the cliff divers—"

And we both continued, "If we have time."

We hugged and went hand in hand to find a taxi. With only two days before he had to sail again, two days to reconnect after a six-month absence, two days to enjoy our married life, our time together was precious. No time for conflict or disappointment. Time to enjoy Hotel Mirador's lovely room. Maybe even time for the cliff diver show. A bit of time before we each went back to work. A bit of time before we had to separate again.

2 Fate, Ebb, and Flow

Float: (v) to move in a fluid manner

1980

I was living in a hovel, but a San Francisco one. Not in the pretty part of SF, with the Victorian townhouses and stamp-sized, perfectly manicured front gardens. No, my 5th floor studio apartment was in the old, seedy, red-light district, locally known as the Tenderloin. Its buildings dated to just after the 1906 earthquake and fire. That was also about the time of its last fresh paint, though scattered graffiti provided a touch of color to its grimy palette. Random neon lights added more color at night. If you felt safe enough to stop and stare you could see decorative details under the grime. Fire escapes muddled any design consistency. This was not a tourist destination. The Tenderloin sat between Union Square's high-end shopping and the Mission District's old, industrial, warehouses. In the '80s, the fringe resided in the Tenderloin; they might be poor immigrants, the nearly homeless, sailors who lost their ships, working prostitutes, or the occasional college student needing a cheap place to live. I was in the last category of the fringe.

SF was my escape from suburbia. I could have found cheap housing in the East Bay, but I had enough of identical developments set on quarter-acre lots.

Growing up outside the city limits of Buffalo, our street had small, four-bedroom Cape Cod houses, lawns front and back, driveways on the right, single maple trees near the street, and sidewalks dividing the front lawn. For a change of pace, a few houses planted a second tree. Or cut down their tree and paved over the lawn for parking. Our house had two maples trees, plus a honey locust in the backyard. Ah, Mom, pushing the limit on neighborhood design!

As a kid, the lack of diversity—natural, architectural, ecological, human—any kind of diversity, bothered me, though I didn't have the words to explain my reaction until later in life. The artificial simplicity bored me. It didn't feel real. There was nothing to discover. It felt too regular: regular lawns, regular blocks, regular lifestyles. All too predictable. And just enough room between the houses to minimize interaction. Set the family in a box and keep all others away. Seemed like an odd way for humanity to exist, carefully separated into single-family units with carefully controlled methods of contact. Later in life, as a biologist, I began to understand why this arrangement rubbed me wrong. *Homo sapiens* are social apes. Social interaction matters. And in my suburban neighborhood of Eggertsville, New York, the social network was almost nonexistent except for the kids on the block after school.

San Francisco's urban landscape may have been an artificial creation, but it certainly wasn't predictable.

I always wanted a "real life." Whatever that was, it needed to feel authentic, where adventure was possible, where uncertainty existed, where I needed a certain level of competence to thrive. Was it the world of a crowded, chaotic city? Or a natural landscape where people were visitors? Either could work. When I went off to college, I wanted more than after-school TV and walks between lawn patches. I wanted a dog to share life's experiences through the eyes and nose of another species. I wanted the full realm of possibility with limited amounts of boring bits.

I moved to the San Francisco Bay area to attend UC Berkeley and live an urban adventure. For $250 per month, I could afford a spot in the fabled City by the Bay, though in an apartment as dingy as the Tenderloin's exterior. Sadly, the landlord prohibited dogs, delaying my dog-ownership dream, but the city fascinated me. Even in a cheap apartment in a tough part of town, San Francisco held its magic with an authentic place to explore.

The ancient apartment building had an elevator. As I lived on the 5th floor, the elevator should have been useful. It wasn't. It was agony being locked in a tiny box with peeling linoleum while the concentrated, old urine smell burnt my nostrils. In the stairwell, four of the five flights were relatively odor-free, though the ground-floor landing was particularly nasty with old pee. A fast, smelly elevator would have beat out a slow, scary flight of steps, however, the elevator wasn't fast. And sometimes it got stuck. The stench of urine while waiting for help? In a place where help was scarce? No, the steps were the choice.

In this dreary apartment building, only once did any organization risk the stairs (or the elevator) to post flyers on residents' doors. I was amazed it happened even once. But one Friday, there it was. A yellow paper announcing, "New weekend bus service to the Marin Headlands." Door-to-door advertising by SF Muni, even to hovels!

I had just given up men. They were just too disappointing. My expectations weren't even very high—a second date, a return phone call, something more than a grope in the dark. I was tired of the disappointment. Who needed people, especially of the male gender, after all? I thrived on independence. Books, a comfortable chair, a goofy dog (never a cat), that would suffice. I didn't need a male partner to travel and explore, though, at the ripe old age of twenty-two, I feared becoming Eleanor Rigby, waiting at the window, looking out at the world, alone in a room without disappointment and without escape.

The SF Muni bus service would provide a momentary escape from the solitary room. I packed a lunch, a sweater, and a red scarf.

Somehow, I had missed the news story about the serial killer.

Murdered people had been found in the park north of the city. Why, on August 25, 1980, hadn't I heard of the Mt. Tamalpais Killer when I went up alone to hike? Why had I followed a random ad on a yellow paper stuck on my apartment door when the Sheriff's office was warning people not to go up to the area alone? Why did SF Muni suddenly start advertising in my apartment building? I was an avid newspaper reader but somehow missed Marin's biggest news story of the decade as I took a nearly empty bus to the land across the Bay.

I didn't tell anyone I was going. My cousins were in the East Bay and my mother was back east. I called Mom frequently but, if I thought she would worry, I didn't talk to her about it. Why have an unsolvable conflict?

I had a lifetime of experience sliding around others' anxiety. Mom's tendency to worry was minor compared to her mother's ready apprehension about most any activity. Nana even worried when someone was sleeping. I learned not to engage with the worry. There was no end to Nana's fear-filled abyss; she carried it with her and never let it empty. I chose to avoid it, glide around it, and take care in picking up a phone call. If I had to engage, then laughter could help. Logical discussions never succeeded. When her fear level became ridiculous, like the time she yelled at my brother Tim to come in from his rowboat on Lake Chautauqua so the shark wouldn't kill him, laughter helped the whole family manage not falling into her abyss.

For the Marin Headlands adventure, even though she had never been to the area, Mom would have just worried all day after trying to convince me it wasn't safe. I stayed away from that phone call. I cannot imagine what the conversation would have been like if she had been current on the West Coast news. Of course, I might have listened to her in that case.

The Marin Headlands were north of the Bay, northwest across the Golden Gate Bridge. They overlooked the City and the entrance to the Bay. Further north was the Golden Gate National Recreation Area, Mount Tamalpais State Park, Stinson Beach, and then the Point Reyes National Seashores. The Headlands were a landscape of former military bunkers converted to parkland: grassy slopes dotted with California oaks and shrubs. Trails crisscrossed the bumpy topography. The hills could drop straight to the sea and they rose higher than the frequent, thick fog. The fog could encase the City in a fluffy, white blanket.

I perched on one of those high hills, a short walk from where the bus dropped me off, in the middle of the Headlands. There I sat. Quietly. I soaked up the peace; no city traffic, no sirens, no horns. No urban smells, no human smells. As authentic as San Francisco was as a human habitat, it was also exhausting. Here the wind filled my ears, along with the occasional song of a non-pigeon bird. I forgot the concentrated urine smells as I took long, deep breaths.

Overlooking the Pacific, the fog formed over the City as the cool waters and cool lands caused the moisture in the air to condense. While I thought of the mechanics behind San Francisco's distinctive weather event, all thoughts of the human presence disappeared. Shivering in the breeze off the fog bank, I soaked in the quiet and tucked the scarf around my head.

There I sat, surrounded by steep hills and scrub oaks, golden grass and deer trails. Something caught my eye. Movement, racing up the hill. Too tall for a deer. It was a man, trotting up the hill. He advanced through the brush, the steep slope, no trail in sight, flying along on a 45-degree angle, strong legs moving him, agile and effortless. I was impressed. I did not know then that he had seen me in my red scarf from below, and he was rushing up the hill to meet me.

The red scarf had pulled him up. His hill climb had pulled me over.

When we converged, he said, "Is this trail as tough as the one I just came up?" Sweat was pouring down his face.

Laughing, I said, "No, not at all. I watched you. Was there even a trail there?"

"There was, but maybe it was for deer."

We laughed: big, hearty, warm laughs. In only moments he didn't feel like a stranger. We wore similar clothes: jeans and flannel shirts, though he had the addition of a worn, holed, red shirt layer. His voice … I asked, "Are you from Massachusetts? The Boston area?"

"Yes. How did you know?"

"You have an accent. Those *r* s"

"Pahk the cah."

Laughing, I replied, "Yes! I'm from the East Coast too. It's nice to hear the sounds of Back East. I'm not yet used to California. The weather is always good."

"Exactly! Where's the rain? Storms? No rain for six months? Not normal."

"People can plan outdoor events …"

"Yes, without a rain date! Crazy!"

"You'd think there'd be more hot dog stands and ice cream shops."

"I miss soft serve ice cream—"

"Too much healthy eating going on."

"Not natural." More laughter. My cheeks hurt from smiling.

The conversation wasn't that funny. The chemistry of mutual attraction was producing silly, slap happy people. His crinkling laugh lines, his large, strong hands, his rich, deep voice added to the attraction.

Joe said it was his only vacation day, so he had pulled out a chart to go exploring. He was a student at California Maritime Academy and, between cruise, jobs, and classes, this was his first vacation day in over a year. I explained about the bus. We talked about the hikes we'd like to take and the places we'd like to visit in California: Yosemite, the redwoods, north to Point Reyes and Stinson Beach.

Joe unfolded his map to show me some of these places. What he unfolded was a nautical chart, showing water depth, aids to navigation, and the coastal lands. It included lands only close to shore. The inland was blank. With a map of only shoreline routes and elevations, Joe was exploring the unknown.

He didn't know exactly where he was going but he was going there anyway.

He said, "I think we could drive up to Stinson Beach today."

I looked at the chart, impressed that he could imagine road connections in the blank interior.

He asked, "Do you want to go up?—We could drive together?"

"Well, I have to go back by the bus and the last bus is at 4 this afternoon."

"I'd drive you back to the City." He paused, looking down, "If you want."

Well, he's clearly a confident explorer. Was he also competent? Breathing deeply, I replied, "Sure, let's do it."

We spent the day exploring the Headlands then, north, up to Stinson Beach, a wide sandy bar just south of Point Reyes National Seashore. We chanced upon a burger and soft-serve ice cream cafe on the beach, barely believing our luck. There was an oddly laid-back squirrel laying in the sun that ignored people; we laughed 'til we cried, saying the squirrel had been Californized. The joke was not funny, but

13

the chemistry was making us giggle.

Leaving Stinson Beach, Joe let me drive his car back to the City. I loved driving and was impressed this guy handed the keys over. His car was a green 1968 Ford Fairlane station wagon—not exactly a model eliciting strong reaction by car enthusiasts—so he may not have been concerned about damage by an unfamiliar driver.

Not wanting the day to end, we explored the California Academy of Sciences in Golden Gate Park until the museum closed. On the way back to my apartment, he suggested we stop for a drink. Not knowing any good bars, I offered, "Let's just pick up a six pack and go back to my place."

And life changed.

Later, he explained he had headed out that day to try and overcome his shyness and talk with a woman. I silently wondered why someone would pick a lonely trail in an unpopulated park to try and meet someone new, but by then I knew enough about Joe to know the answer. It was a classic Joe move, improbable, uncommon, a touch antisocial, and, sometimes, just sometimes, wildly successful.

Later he also said the most foolish thing I ever did was driving off with him that day. Maybe he was right. But that trust led to wildly successful years for both of us.

Had I learned of the Mt. Tamalpais murders before that August 25, I would have skipped the Headlands and would not have met Joe. Had I learned that the Marin County authorities warned people from entering the area alone, as there had been three murders (and would be four more), I would have never been there. Should that random SF Muni flyer not made its way to the 5th floor in that ratty apartment, life would have been much different. If Joe had not decided to explore using only a nautical chart, fifty miles away from his college, to overcome his shyness and talk with a strange woman on his only day of vacation, our lives would have taken different paths. Odd thing, random chance.

I do admit I was a touch relieved when the Mt. Tam/Trailside Killer was arrested in May of the following year.

Twenty-four hours after giving up men, I met him—the love of my life, the center of my world. Eleanor's fate wasn't going to be mine. That day my life transformed from lonely years into a romantic adventure. Like *The Hobbit* on the day the dwarves came to see Bilbo: adventure arrived.

A year and a half later, while we were both still students, he asked me to marry him. I said yes, followed by, "Promise me you'll never bore me?" He committed to that as well.

Had I never heard the phrase "Be careful what you ask for?"

I was in my third year at the University of California Berkeley as Joe finished up his final year at the Academy. We waited on wedding plans to see what Joe's employment situation would look like after his graduation as it was hard to plan a wedding when the groom might be out to sea.

A year and a half of being engaged and we had not set a wedding date. This pleased my mother. She was certain that if I got married I'd never finish college. I could not convince her that life for women was different compared to hers in the 1950s.

When I mentioned my mother's comments to Joe, he looked at me in confusion and said, "Of course you are going to finish." He shook his head and continued, "You are too smart not to finish. I'd never get in your way. I don't understand your mother—of course you will get your degree."

My cheeks flushed. Positive encouragement and unwavering support were magic qualities I was unused to in my life before Joe. I soaked up the encouragement as I gave him a big hug, hiding my teary-eyed face from him.

I was living in an all-women cooperative house just off campus in Hoyt Hall, and, luckily, had a single room so Joe could "stay over." This was not sustainable as sooner or later someone would notice a man was a frequent inhabitant in the all-woman hall. Joe delayed the inevitable by showering in the solo bath at 4 a.m. He'd then head out, invisible to my housemates.

Nearing his graduation, Joe and most of his classmates were tense, searching for a ship. The US shipping fleet had shrunk as did its job opportunities. They had spent four years in a maritime academy, training for a specific profession, but jobs were in short supply. Rampant anxiety was not surprising.

In April 1983, about three weeks before Joe's graduation, he called me at Hoyt and asked, "Paula, looks like I can get a job—in Kwajalein. I'd be running a security boat for the US military all around the atoll."

"Great!" I had no idea where Kwajalein was, but I thought a supportive response was best.

"The other problem—it'd be for a full year."

"Sounds like having a job for a full year would be great."

"Well, yes, but, a full year job means I'd be away from you for a full year."

"Oh." I froze a bit as I processed that. "… well, that's the nature of the work." I strove to breathe deeply. *If I was to be a sailor's wife …*

I sucked air in, envisioning a whole year without Joe. I knew long separations were possible, I just hadn't expected one this soon or this long. *Paula, deal with this. Make this work. That's the bargain you made for life with a sailor.* Life had arrived and payment was due. "Okay, a year, we can do that. Maybe I can come out and visit? Where is it by the way?"

"It's one of the Marshall Islands, a few thousand miles southwest of Hawaii."

I was going to have to brush up on my geography.

"Kwajalein is a US military security location, on an atoll, limited access in areas. I don't think they will allow visitors so that may not work."

"Okay then." I paused again, glad he could not see the sadness on my face, "We will just have to write each other—mail delivery is allowed, isn't it?"

Joe laughed, "Yes, that should work out, as long as I don't share any secrets."

"I'll try not to wring them out of you." I held back for a moment then heartily continued, "Okay, sounds like we can manage."

"Paula, one more question. Do you want to get married before I go or wait a year?"

Oh. I blinked at the thought. "When would the job start?"

"Immediately after graduation."

"So, we'd need to get married in three weeks?"

"Yes."

I wavered for a second. Did I want to plan a wedding in three weeks? Or did I want to wave goodbye and not see my fiancé for a year? Not wanting to see the relationship fail, there was only one answer, "Let's do it before you go."

We had a backyard wedding hosted by my dear cousins, Joberta and Bob, who also provided scattered flowers and abundant beverages on short notice. My Hoyt Hall friends showed up, enjoying the first wedding among their college cohort. I asked my sister to be maid of honor and she, along with my brother and mother, flew to California for the wedding. Joe's family and my grandmother were unable to travel. Dress white uniforms, used just the day before in the Academy graduation ceremony, served as wedding outfits for Joe and many of his CMA buddies as a bunch of newly graduated midshipmen filled in for critical functions: Dave photographed the day, Mike stood up as best man, and Jesse officiated.

Jesse had picked up the necessary license via mail order from the Universal Life Church. He needed it for his summer job as captain of a dayboat out of San Francisco where he conducted weddings at sea, or scattered ashes for funeral services at sea. For the wedding, I double-checked to make sure he had at hand the non-funeral, ash-free words.

My wedding "dress" was a simple white blouse and matching skirt I found at a small boutique in Berkeley. On the day of the ceremony, I opened the door to the neighbor-girl Joberta had asked to serve food at the wedding. She was wearing my white outfit. Exactly the same. White blouse and matching skirt with white embroidery. I tried to ask if she bought it from the Berkeley boutique, but I could not speak. I was frozen: my wedding dress was going to match the wait staff's outfit.

Ah, one of the problems of planning a wedding in three weeks.

I could have lived with the sailors looking spiffier than me on my wedding day but having the bride match the server? I was petrified at the thought.

Joe noticed me standing there frozen, holding the door open, "What's wrong Paula?"

I mumbled something as I gawked at her. Finally, I turned to him and pointed at the neighbor kid, and stammered, "She's wearing my dress."

Joe calmly replied, "Why don't you ask her to go home and change?"

Ah, a solution! Joe was a great problem-solver. My brain started again as I took his advice. She headed home to find more colorful clothes.

After that, and the drama of my young cousin Erica, the flower girl, running off to answer the phone during the start of the ceremony, it was a fun, relaxed, and joyous day.

Ironically, the Kwajalein job fell through. But the wedding and marriage did not.

We had a three-day honeymoon. Days Four and Five were spent with Joe walking around repeating, "I need a job. A job! I need a job." This was not setting the stage for great conversation in our married life.

On Day Five, after listening to Joe's rant over breakfast, I headed back to class. Berkeley was on a ten-week quarter system and getting married on the eighth week of the quarter meant there were only two weeks before final exams. I couldn't afford to miss any more class. I got back to Hoyt Hall about 4 p.m. to a message taped to my door, "*Joe called. He has a ship. Will be back in two weeks.*"

I smiled, happy and relieved that his mantra worked. And that I wasn't going to have to listen to it anymore.

My Hoyt Hall housemates had been chatting among themselves about the Joe message. At dinner, one tentatively asked, with the others leaning in, "Joe's gone? Didn't you just get married?"

"Yes, he's gone for a few weeks." I started wagging my fork at them, "He had to sail. He started a job, on a US flagged ship, and the ship will be going out to sea. He'll be away for a while." I forced my voice to relax, "This is how it works for a sailor's wife." I lowered my fork and finished, "We will be apart, but our relationship will be just fine." I nodded my head and returned to my meal.

Quizzical looks flew around the table, but silence settled. I think they expected a married couple to live together for more than a week.

Later I realized that was the first time I explained

how it worked being a sailor's wife. Over the years, I'd have lots of practice.

For the next two decades of marriage, Joe and I lived together occasionally: a month here, a weekend there, a three-month stint twice a year in-between his sailings. Our marriage was made up of honeymoon sandwiches: the time apart was the crusty bread and the time together was the tasty middle. Some years we had mostly bread, which could get stale. Most years we had a balance, enough to keep it fresh.

Over the twenty years since the wedding, my 45-year-old head became topped with strands of silvery gray mixed into the auburn. I was often caught smiling for no apparent reason. Neither tall nor short, I only occasionally needed help to reach the stuff on the top shelf. My glasses gained some thickness over the years, as did my waist. Round would be a reasonable adjective to describe my basic shape. In my younger days, voluptuous would have been a kind description though Rubenesque might have been closer to the truth. Over time, add 50 pounds and those curves widened out. Sitting at a desk studying added to the widening.

Education was my road to financial independence, a dream since I was six years old. That was the year I started watching my mother figure out how to support herself and her kids so she could leave my unbearable father. Later, I watched my grandmother use finances as one of her tools to control my mother. I was sure I did not want those bindings.

As a kid, I had mentioned to my mother that I'd like to be a professor. I then had years of reminders from her how impossible that goal was. She was convinced that it was the rare person who could become a tenured faculty member. I learned not to mention my dream to her unless I was in the mood for a critique.

At UC Berkeley, I earned my first degree in entomology. I continued at University of Massachusetts Amherst for my second and third degrees in entomology, M.S. and Ph.D. I always wanted to study living creatures and teach biology, but I didn't want to spend my days with enzymes and test tubes, or in high school classrooms, or in corporate laboratories. I wanted to study life in its actual setting. I needed something that would hold my interest. To teach students who were interested in the topic and not forced to sit in my classroom. I would have preferred to study more dramatic forms of life: whales or elephants or even snakes. But, as a first-generation college student putting myself through school, I was anxious to get a job from my education. And the possibility of employment would help silence my mother's criticism. Or at least minimize it.

Insects had so many practical implications that a job would be possible even if I never reached my lofty goal of being a professor. My Tenderloin apartment had introduced me to pest control as a potential profession. Or there was biting fly management, invasive species regulation, water quality monitoring, biocontrol scout, or other practical jobs that let me look at living things on a regular basis, even if they were just insects. One way or another, I planned to succeed.

The professor gig came through, but not in entomology. My first job was based on my experience at UMass, where I team-taught the first UMass environmental science course. That set the stage for someone with three degrees in insect science to spend her career in environmental science, teaching and building interdisciplinary programs. Teaching combined with loads of field trips to explore the world of living things—I could not have imagined a better occupation. It held my interest. As my career progressed, work for me remained in the classroom and the field. I was lucky to be a professor at Juniata College, a small liberal arts college that valued the student experience. I chaired the environmental science department I created, helping my students and my faculty towards their goals. I could see success all around me and I was content.

For Joe, over our twenty years of marriage, his 48-year-old head topped by blonde hair now held a touch of gray. Laugh lines still cornered his deep brown eyes, visible behind his glasses. His mustache, a nearly permanent feature of his face, was still whitish blonde. His tall and large frame continued to be most often clothed for comfort and function. Khaki pants and polo shirts, some stained with his latest project: house paint, lube oil, or fish guts. Joe was confident in his ability to problem-solve and generally had a few projects running at the same time. When we first met, solid and strong described him. He too added 50 pounds yet solid and strong still applied. His legs were still muscled to move him quickly and assuredly. His kind, warm eyes were ready to laugh and his deep voice easily carried across a room. I always imagined that voice would carry well over the deck of a ship at sea.

Joe was one of those people that men and women both appreciated. Men liked his sea stories. I think they also respected his ability to fish, drink, and fix things. Women too enjoyed his sea stories. They also responded to his kindhearted, masculine demeanor. And it didn't hurt that he'd fix things for them.

My family adored Joe. I sometimes wondered if they liked him more than me. I know my grandmother did. At a Christmas dinner in my first married year, Nana said, as she passed Joe a third helping, "Paula, don't you do anything to drive Joe away."

I laughed, "Nana, of course I wouldn't—"

She intruded, sternly, "You do whatever he wants."

Odd, coming from a woman who did not do anything anyone else wanted. "I don't think I can promise that much Nana."

"You got a good one there. Do what you need to do to keep him." Nana liked men who ate. And who fixed things.

I felt like I won a blue-ribbon prize at the fair. Or maybe the prize fish—requiring proper care and feeding for the rest of his life. I never managed to keep a house plant going for more than three months and I still felt guilty over those guppies that did not survive my inattention. I was glad that Joe told me, "Paula, if we ever somehow find our relationship broken and you want to fix it, just send me the red scarf. I'll come back to you." Joe's romantic heart gave me a safety net to keep our commitment going.

I wanted my marriage to succeed even if Nana had the same goal.

Over the years, Joe teased, "I'll tell Nana on you." I know he was especially sad when she died.

In our two decades of matrimony, Joe's career success mirrored my own. On ships at sea, Joe served as a ship's officer, ranging from Third Mate up through Captain, the ship's Master. After his first job in California, he shifted to a mate's position with Woods Hole Oceanographic then to captain on cargo ships, including the *M/V Strong Texan*, a 261-foot heavy lift ship. The *Strong Texan* was mostly under contract to the US military and would carry anything from helicopters, food supplies, to nuclear waste.

Dreaming of adventure, I asked Joe if a captain's wife could sail along on a trip or two. Preferably on a trip without nuclear waste.

He said, "You are welcome to, but you won't want to."

I squinted with tilted head and said, "What, do you think the quarters would be too small for us?"

"The bunk is not quite a twin-sized mattress, but that's not the issue. The *Strong Texan* is nothing like a cruise ship—"

"I get that—"

"There is cargo everywhere—"

"It might be fun, morning walks on the deck—"

23

His laughter stopped my dreaming. "Paula, no one walks on the deck more than they need to. The *Texan*'s a heavy lift ship. She has two big cranes built into her main deck. At any moment gobs of grease fly off those cranes. Random things get hit including anyone on deck. Nothing fun about that experience. The crew regularly lubes the crane cables to protect them from exposure to salt water. That sends extra grease flying around. Nope, not enjoyable. And our port stops aren't like the Woods Hole days—we get in and out as soon as possible, no time to explore."

He saw my discouraged look begin to fade as I started to work on a solution and then he gave the final detail to end my dream, "Plus, the cook believes in deep-fat frying everything, including the Christmas turkey, while boiling the green out of any greens."

I never asked again.

Working cargo ships let him move his license. It also meant Joe had to swallow a variety of captains, management companies, crews, and ships, all of varying quality. When he was a month or two out at sea, I'd hear his frustration in emails or phone calls. He kept persevering to his goal: Unlimited Master. Captain on any ship, of any size, in any waters. I used to joke that we were in a competition: would he make Unlimited Master before I made tenured Full Professor? When he pointed out the salary differential, I realized it was in our best financial interest if he won that competition, so I was not disappointed when I lost the race. Hitting the top license was his dream and he succeeded though we both missed the research ship port stops.

We'd meet in ports—airports and harbors—in hotels, on docks, or at bars, around the world. We might not have many Acapulco-like trysts with him working cargo. We did get a trip to Hawaii together so he could oversee security arrangements for a nuclear waste cargo on the *Strong Texan*.

Most of our time together was on his vacations

off the ship. He'd come home to me. I'd work during the day and he'd spend his three-month vacations doing a variety of different things. He rebuilt our house. He remodeled his sister's home. He went fishing including drilling holes through thick ice to try and catch the fish. He'd fix his truck. He'd golf, bike, canoe or conduct whatever outside activity that fit the season and place. My colleagues would get to meet the mysterious husband. They didn't fully believe he existed until they had physical proof of the "Joe" from the Joe-stories. Together, we'd have dinners and picnics and walks in a park. And then he'd sail again, and I'd return to my solo life of books, classrooms, study, and field trips.

Twenty years of marriage and we continued happily. We still laughed more with each other than with anyone else. We still lit up when we met each other no matter where. We were "home" when we were together.

We never did have children, partially because we never had a huge yearning to raise kids. The rare moments where I felt my biological clock ticking coincided with Joe being far out to sea. That was fine. Joe and I were comfortable in our roles as Aunt and Uncle, or Godmother and Godfather. I never wanted to be a single parent for more than half of every year. Joe never wanted to be an absent father, nor even an absent dog owner. We had our students and crew to "parent." It was enough.

I'd keep my friends up to date on Joe's activities, giving him a presence in my life even when he was out to sea. Joe's sailing colleagues told me that Joe talked about me all the time. We figured out a virtual relationship even before the invention of the internet.

We'd write to each other and we'd call when possible. We even had marine-radio calls, where the marine radio operator would patch the radio signal from the ship to the telephone landline. The operator had to be an active participant in the call, to switch between speakers.

I'd pick up the phone, "Hello?"

"This is the Miami Marine Operator, with a call from *RV Oceanus*, collect call for Paula Martin. Will you accept the charges?"

I hugged the phone with both hands and said through my smile, "Oh, yes, please."

The operator continued, "Connecting you to the *Oceanus. Oceanus*, come in please, over."

I heard his voice and my heart filled, as he said, "Hi my love. How are you? Over."

My tongue stumbled in my speed to respond, "I'm great! Great! Great to hear your voice! How are you my sweets? Oooh, do I have to say *over*?"

"Yes, if you can say that when you are done speaking the operator will know when to switch to me. Everything is fine here. I'm calling to let you know the ship should be back to Woods Hole two weeks from today. Over."

I smiled even more, "That's great my love. I'll be there to pick you up. Err, Over."

"I love you dear. Over."

"I love you too Joe. Over."

"Miami Marine Operator, this is *Oceanus*, Over and Out."

There was not much privacy, with both the marine operator listening as well as the sailors in the radio room, but I always felt lighter knowing he was alive and well.

Our virtual marriage, in the early years, included old-fashioned, handwritten letters mailed from around the world. My heart would race when I held the envelope with his handwriting. One of my favorites had a line from a letter he sent while he was at sea on his last Academy cruise: "*If my love for you, my wife to be, outshines the brightest star at this very instant, how bright my love must shine as it shall continue to glow forever."* I looked forward to mail delivery in those days.

Later, the invention of email changed our communication. The technology gave us more frequent connections, but we lost a touch of romance. I lost the joy of seeing Joe's handwriting show up in the post. Our email text became a bit mundane, filled with the day's details, little room for the feelings that emerged when pen met paper. I missed the tactile pleasure of brittle airmail onion skin paper that I knew Joe had labored over. No stamps from faraway places were needed. Emailed electrons did not provide that allure. Over the years, moving from university to university, house to house, I kept few sentimental mementos. I did keep the stacks of letters from him, tied up in a red ribbon.

He sailed around the world and I stayed on the land, relishing that I was not "Brandy"—that "fine girl" whose sailor loved the sea more than life ashore. My sailor kept coming home. We trusted each other and we coped.

Over the years, Joe told me about his sailor colleagues whose marriages failed over the strain of the sailors' absence. We worked to minimize our marital stress as we both pretended not to worry about the other while apart. We each had our own independent streaks. We could problem-solve life's challenges whether together or apart. Plus, we were childless, thus eliminating a major source of friction. We had a warm, loving, drama-free union, though hours spent together were few. I never talked with him about the hard parts of the separation because I didn't want to pressure him to stop sailing. I refused to be one of those complaining wives sitting ashore as I had every intention of making my marriage a success. I figured I had to cope with his career path. The solitary isolation of sailing suited him. Why make him choose?

I also never talked with him about the hard parts of living apart because of time. We had so little time together, why disrupt it with pointless conflict? My life of frequent honeymoons and personal independence kept me from being bored. And I had the added benefit of maximum flexibility in my career path.

I had a choice of graduate schools and then a choice of faculty employment offers. Geography wasn't a limiting factor. It didn't matter if I lived near the sea or in Pennsylvania—Joe flew off to meet his ship and then flew home to meet his wife, wherever I was. In our two decades of married life, geography wasn't destiny.

Geography was about to matter.

Joe told me that he was getting tired of blue water sailing. "Commercial cargo ports are the dregs. And time at sea—it's tough Paula. Hard on the body, getting slammed around. You don't know what it's like, walking down a stairwell and having the ship move under you, slamming you into a steel bulkhead. Smashed shoulders. Smashed knees. Smashed head. I love sailing but being beaten up for months at a time is getting old."

"What is the alternative for you? I'm thinking that working in a hardware store isn't going to do it."

Joe laughed, "What, my dreams of being a clerk at Home Depot are dead?"

I became still, not entirely sure if he was joking. Joe's uncommon approach to life could be surprising.

He continued, to my relief, "I guess you're right, no Home Depot for me. I wouldn't be able to put up with the corporate crap anyway. No, what's next is going to the top of the field."

I peered at him. *Top of the field?* I sputtered, "Wait, I thought the top of the field was being an Unlimited Master—legal to be captain on any ship, in any waters. You know, the license you worked for years to get?

The one that's hanging on the wall of your bridge? The one that took you away from Woods Hole?" I clearly remembered Joe's years of effort to get that big license. My eyes narrowed as I looked at him.

"Yeah, I used to think so. Not today though. Not anymore Paula. Not with ships managed by company suits who aren't out there. Managers living at home every night, phoning in the orders while the captain and crew deal with the weather and the seas. The captain used to be independent. Now, the office tries to conduct day-to-day ship operations. The office thinks it can tell the captain what to do, sending an email filled with orders—totally detached from the ship's reality."

I nodded at this, remembering multiple phone calls about shore-side supervision filled with Joe's frustration and aggravation.

He continued, "Now the captain is treated like middle management, answering to the bosses on shore. It's like the captain has become a bureaucrat. No, today the top shipboard job is pilot."

"Pilot. Like Vince and John."

"Exactly."

John and Vince were friends from the Academy, in the 2D division (2nd Deck) with Joe. Most of 2D from the Class of '83 spent their careers at sea or aboard ships. It was a salty bunch.

John became a San Francisco Bar Pilot, like his Dad, Cap't Al. All commercial ships coming in or going out of San Francisco Bay, up into Richmond, across to Oakland or north on the Sacramento River, all have a San Francisco Bar Pilot aboard.

In Alaska, ships enter the waters in an area much larger than San Francisco Bay, extending from Icy Bay, through Prince William Sound, to Kodiak and through Cook Inlet. Foreign ships had to have a SouthWest Alaska Pilots Association (SWAPA) pilot aboard. Vince was a pilot with SWAPA.

Pilots know the local waters, driving the ship around shallows, through dangerous currents, and up to the docks. They direct the tugboats and the bridge crew. Their goal is to safely dock the ship, without too much smashing of pier or denting of hull. And to safely drive the ship back out to sea, without any hitting of rocks or spilling of oil. Most ports across the world require ships to take aboard pilots—ports tend to be paranoid about damage from ships. Pilots protect the harbor's infrastructure; they work in independent partnerships, answerable only to the state, thus escaping middle management hassles of corporate shipping.

I understood why Joe wanted to be a pilot. The independence suited him. But if Joe was a pilot, a local expert on the local waters, he'd be geographically bound.

He asked, "Paula, what would that mean for you, if I got a pilot's job?"

I told him I'd figure out my next career steps when he landed a pilot's job somewhere. When we knew the location. When we knew his pilot schedule: always on call or two weeks on, two weeks off or some mix. I was not ready to 100% commit to whatever geographic location he landed in, without knowing more.

I felt some excitement about the new potential to change up my career path. I had already reached my major academic goal: being a tenured professor. I had some slight trepidation about giving that up, but the possibility of change was interesting. Plus, if we were living together full-time, I could get a dog. Joe had not wanted a dog when he was gone for long periods of time—he didn't want to be a stranger to an animal every three months. He thought both he and the dog would be uncomfortable with the strangeness, therefore I had put off my dog dreams until we had more time together. My career decisions, and the dog, would all wait to see where Joe settled.

Once again, we were waiting on Joe's job selection to move us to our next situation.

As Joe explored the way forward to a pilot's position, it became clear that becoming a pilot had no easy path. The biggest hurdle was not the dozens of exams, the charts to be drawn from memory, the hundreds of dockings and undocking before being licensed. It was not the challenges of climbing pilot ladders up the side of ships in nasty, horrible weather. Nor learning to give orders to foreign crew whose command of English went no further than "port" and "starboard," on a ship the pilot had never seen before. The biggest hurdle was not figuring out how to protect a ship from unexpected currents, hurricane-force winds, or random patches of ice. No, for Joe, the hardest part of becoming a pilot was getting into a pilot association.

Each pilot association had a different set of rules, of minimum qualifications, of maximum ages. For Pennsylvania, you should not have too much experience because they wanted to train you. For Alaska, you had to be a member of one of the three marine pilot associations, voted in by membership. Florida gave a statewide exam. Galveston held interviews. San Francisco scored the person's shipping experience, with an ever-changing set of preferred characteristics. Joe struggled to match his experience with a pilot organization. Any pilot organization, anywhere. I was back to the days of listening to "I need a job. I need a job."

While he worked his way over the first hurdle to becoming a pilot, in March of 2003 Joe took a shore side job in Juneau, Alaska. It gave him the opportunity to persist on finding a match with a pilotage organization since he wasn't out to sea for months, as well as providing an income. The Juneau job made it easier for him to prepare for pilotage in Alaska, in case Alaska ended up being his pilotage home. And it gave him a taste of the shoreside alternative to pilot: Port Captain.

The job he took as Port Captain was an office job, nine to five, five days a week, with other State employees. They required him to wear a tie though he escaped having to wear a full suit. He was home every night after a day in the office. No deep-sea sailing. No more three months at sea and three months at home. Just home to office and back again.

Joe was now the voice of "the office," the guy with the tie, who was home every night, who sent emails filled with orders to the captains on the ships at sea. He was working the job he had always railed against when he was ship's master.

Once again, Joe had made an unusual choice.

To add to the challenge, his job was 5,000 miles from where I was a tenured associate professor.

It took two decades, but the Martin married lifestyle had hit a snag.

For the first time in our married life, we were both at home every night—just not the same home. Nor the same town. Or the same state. Or even the same time zone. Not even close to the same ocean. We also had extra expenses from the additional household but less income—port captain did not pay what ship's captain paid.

No more regular honeymoon sandwiches. This did not appear to be an ideal situation.

I had gained tenure, the gold ring of academic professor life, and was up for promotion to full professor in 2005 for the diamond to top the gold. Tenure was a restraint to keep faculty at the institution where they earned it as the job security tenure provided rarely transferred to other universities. I did not have any idea about what my future employment situation would look like but, until Joe's path became clear, I intended to hold on to the gold ring.

While our geography had not aligned, our timing had. I had applied for a sabbatical leave to take a year off from campus and write an interdisciplinary textbook on "Water." Juniata College had approved my leave and I could write anywhere. I could use my sabbatical and Joe's shoreside job as a chance for us to live together for an entire year. An entire year!

This would be a first in our twenty-one years since sharing wedding vows. We could practice life together as that might be our future if Joe got a piloting job. No time outs for ships, no months without each other, just week after week after month after month of living together. Our marriage wouldn't have any intermissions, no more stale bread, just all rich filling.

I hoped my relationship skills would be up to the task.

I would escape the conservative, small-town predictableness of central Pennsylvania for wild Alaska—living in an authentic landscape, where wildlife weren't habituated to humans, or where the built environment wasn't an imposter. If it wasn't New York City, then Alaska sounded spectacular for an authentic experience.

To add to the adventure, we would live in tight quarters. Our home for the year was a 33½ foot boat, forcing us to be shoulder-to-shoulder or butt-to-butt. Could be cozy and romantic. Could also be crazy. I stuck with my optimism.

Later, during a bad day in that year together, we tried to decide who was to blame for the boat decision. Joe wanted to blame me as I thought living on a boat had to be cheaper than the monstrous Juneau rents. Plus, I thought the boat was "romantic." I wanted to blame Joe as he always wanted to own a boat, though I didn't understand why someone who spent his working life at sea wanted a floating home. Somehow, buying a boat as a live-aboard seemed like a logical choice.

What were we thinking, buying a boat to live aboard in Alaska as a sensible decision?

3 Testing the Waters

To Float: (v) to propose a plan

Fall 2003

Before committing to a long-term relationship with Alaska, we thought we should live through one of its winters. I could use my winter break from school, the winter before my sabbatical year started, to get a taste of the dark. I envisioned an experience like a NOVA program. *"The sun gets lower in the sky, the days get shorter and a gentle snow begins to fall, heralding the start of a quiet winter season in the Alaska marina."* Later, when my optimism had drained, when I was less in denial, I envisioned the Fellowship of the Ring trying to cross the Misty Mountains in a blowing blizzard and making no headway.

My cell phone played the theme to *The Lord of the Rings*, signaling a call from Joe. I answered, "Hi sweetie pie." I loved that my cell phone told me who was calling. No more being embarrassed by answering a call from my boss with a greeting of "Hi sweets." That had been mortifying.

"Hey my love, how're ya doing?"

"Great. And you?"

"I'm at the lumber store buying marine plywood."

"Excellent. For the all-important toilet installation?"

"Yes. But I was way too optimistic to think I'd get it all done this weekend. I had more tear-out to do. There was more rot to pull out before the new lumber can go in. I should get the toilet finished next weekend."

"Good. You're cutting it a bit close though. You know about my toilet expectation. I'll be happy to live aboard this Christmas if the toilet is in place."

Joe laughed, "What, you're serious? You won't live aboard without a toilet on the boat? The marina has a porta-potty at the top of the ramp. It's a big one that they pump out frequently."

I snorted, "Sorry Joe. I have standards." *He was joking, wasn't he?* "A porta-potty down the dock and up the ramp just won't do. Even if they pump it out every single day. I don't want to have to put on my winter clothes to pee in the middle of the night. Unlike you, I cannot just pee over the side."

The Fellowship crossing the ramp to pee in the middle of the night, then getting blown off, dropping into the depths, ending their quest ... no, no, not ideal. *He must be joking.*

"Joe, think of the toilet as a wifely demand— you're quite good at fulfilling those!"

I could hear him smile as he said, "You sure are demanding. But I'll get it done for you. I can even empathize since right now I am living my life around toilet stops."

"See! I knew a toilet was a basic need. Thanks for getting it done sweetie."

"It's not done yet."

"I have the utmost confidence."

* * *

Two days later, Joe called, "I'm on a run to get more marine plywood."

"Problems?" I asked.

"That #$%@#@# marine surveyor. Did he even look at the boat? The rotten wood is everywhere."

"Is it going to sink?" Life on a sinking boat without a toilet during the winter in Juneau? Adventures were one thing, but I had a practical streak as well. I wanted to escape the mundane but not into misery. I silently wondered if the boat was insured. And did Joe's life insurance cover drowning at home?

"No, no. It's just that the plywood inside the boat is now just rot. The fiberglass hull is fine. It won't sink. But the wood in between the fiberglass is rotten. The walls—they hung carpet on the walls to hide the rotten wood. I should have realized that carpeting on the walls wasn't just for aesthetic purposes."

Carpeting on walls as a good aesthetic? It was a good thing I was always around when we bought a house.

At least Joe had carpentry skills. That gave me security that he could solve the problems he found.

"What's the new lumber for ... the head?" I loved getting to use nautical terms. I felt like a member of the secret society of seafarers even though I became nauseous when a boat moved too much.

"No. It's for the aft cabin, around the water tank. The otters pooped and peed on the deck, looks like in the same place every time. The liquid soaked through, rotting out the wood in the cabin."

The boat had an otter problem. This was different.

"Oh. Ummhh." I was speechless. "Well. Who would have thought?" I paused again. Otters are peeing on the boat. I missed this in my Wildlife Management class. "Well ... Okay." Carpeting on walls, rotten wood inside fiberglass layers, otter pee— —I could only shake my head. "Hey, maybe I can take some pictures of the otters. At least there will be some benefit of having otters pooping on the deck."

"Yeah. Right. Benefits." He continued, "I'll have some kind of alternative plan in place if need be."

"Hey sweets, I am pretty flexible."

"I know. That's one of the many things I like about you."

The call ended with us cooing to each other, and

the traditional smooching sound to close out the call. I continued my toilet optimism.

* * *

With Joe out to sea or away in Alaska, the telephone was how we made basic decisions. Our tones were essential clues.

Hearing my special Joe-tone on my cell phone, I answered with a silvery greeting.

He replied with a low throaty update, "I went into the marine electronics store with my list for the boat."

I followed with upbeat enthusiasm. "Great! Moving the project right along!"

His voice flattened out and tightened up as he spoke of the problem. "Everything on my list was expensive. The first item alone was $1500 for a generator. It powers the batteries off the 110 line and supplies 110 power when we are off the dock. It'd give us power for a TV, the computer and lights and everything we'd run on 110. But weren't we saying we'd forego the TV?"

I modulated my response with a touch of lightness. "Sure, we can easily live without a TV. What else do we need 110 for?"

His tautness loosened up, "We could switch the lights over to 12-volt. The refrigerator can work off either 12-volt or 110."

I calmly asked, "How about hot water?"

He replicated my straight-forward tone, "That could run off either 110 or the engine."

My voice went taut as I thought about life aboard without 110 power, "I need power for my laptop ..."

Joe's voice went back to his appealing throaty-ness, "But I bet you can get a 12-volt inverter ... you know, a car charger?"

We both lightened up and said at the same time,

"Car charger!"

Our problem-solving lead us back to our normal tones, overlaid with a touch of relief.

"Sounding like we can get by without 110 while we are off the dock? How about heat? Isn't that from shore side electricity now?"

"Yes, but when we sail the engine will supply the heat."

"Great. So we can get by on the 12-volt system?"

"Sounds like. Okay, we'll live without the generator. I am going to have to buy four deep cycle batteries and a new marine starter battery. That's gonna cost another $1,000."

"No problem. It is after all a B.O.A.T."

Joe laughed, "Right. Bring On Another Thousand."

He got a bit more serious, "I'm looking forward to you being up here this Christmas so we can make all these decisions together."

"It should be fun, like building a house together."

"Yeah. A small, cramped, expensive house."

The winter break would be a useful preview. I never expected to learn about the interior workings of a boat. How much of an expert was I going to become in the year ahead? Was living with Joe going to be all about fixing the boat?

At our next call I brought him up to date on an old friend from grad school. Russ was quoted on the front page of the *USA Today* and the *New York Times* in his role as a medical entomologist for the Army in Iraq. He was talking about leishmaniasis in the troops, or, what the *USA Today* called "a skin rash." Calling a parasitic disease that can kill you a "skin rash," well, the *USA Today* did keep it simple.

Joe said, "I wonder how his wife Sue is coping with his army tour?"

I paused with a sad smile on my face. *Joe understands that separations can be tough for people.* Then I said, "You and I ... we've been managing life apart from just about the day we met. Russ and Sue, they've been together all the time, and have three little kids. His deployment must make it tough on them. I'm glad you and I have found a way to manage our time apart."

Joe enthused, "Absolutely. Attached at the heart, not at the hip."

"It's good for both of us."

* * *

I was sitting with friends in Pennsylvania, describing my plans to live with Joe. I could see one of them bite her tongue. Her words escaped anyway, "Paula, I have to ask. Why are you doing this?"

"What, the year on a boat in Alaska, writing a book, living with my husband? Doesn't it sound romantic? Adventuresome? Exciting?"

"I understand living with a husband, but this is new for you. Are you really ready?"

I worked to maintain an even tone. "After twenty plus years of marriage, I thought I'd give it a try. Plus, if Joe ends up as a ship's pilot, living together will be an option in the future."

"You don't hear that phrase from many wives ... living with your husband is 'an option.'"

I turned away from her. "Maybe more marriages would succeed if it were."

Another old friend, Page, upon hearing of my sabbatical plans with Joe said, "Don't do it! Don't wreck a good thing!" Page had sampled a few marriages herself.

"Page—"

"Paula, really, go, live with him for a few months, or even six, and then go elsewhere. Live with your Mom, go to friends, anywhere. Just don't take the chance!'"

I chuckled, "Page—"

"No, seriously Paula. You and Joe have a great marriage. I've gone through too many bad marriages; I know how miraculous a good one is. Don't risk it by living together!'"

I refused to take Page seriously. How could I admit that I might wreck my marriage by living with my husband?

A colleague, Henry, listening to Page's suggestion, asked, "Of your twenty years of marriage, how long have you actually lived with Joe?"

"A bit under nine years. I get a fraction of time together for every year of marriage. Sort of the opposite of dog years."

Henry chuckled at the image and then his forehead creased as he slowly said, "Maybe Page is right."

I pasted on a smile and walked away. I expected they were wrong. Anyway, I wasn't looking for marital advice from people whose marriages were shaky. With luck, in a year, I wouldn't be one of those people.

* * *

What did it mean to be a close, happy, married couple? I had no model of that from my own family. I was the first female in three generations to make it beyond seven years of marriage. No clues there. I knew geography or time spent together weren't the final determinants. I knew similar hobbies weren't necessary as Joe was the only one in the family interested in sweating for athletic reasons. Was it just chemistry? Shared values? Ability to laugh together?

My favorite examples of well-married couples in literature were not helpful. Aragorn and Arwen almost left each other before being married. When they did finally get married, it was good for over 100 years, and then Aragorn chose to die, leaving Arwen bereft and alone. But could I really expect it to last forever? I hated their ending, no matter that her grief was ordained at their start. Another example from literature: Jane Eyre and Mr. Rochester. They had so much strife and grief before they married, I always thought their life afterward must have been joyful simply for the release of pain. A void of pain made for a poor romance. Frederic and Catherine start off well in *A Farewell to Arms* but end poorly. Returning to Tolkien, Beren and Luthien endured nonstop pain and agony throughout their partnership, paired with constant love. Sam and Frodo, they were a love story of sorts that did extend to forever, though it took a lifetime to get there. In *Outlander*, gosh, even the passionate Jamie and Claire had a marriage trapped between painful adventures and loss. And these are my best examples from literature. Happily ever after?

Literature might not be the best model. After all, a good book needs conflict and drama. My satisfying married life would have adventure that would require some amount of drama but not long-term pain, much as it had been for twenty years. In my personal life, I was not a fan of conflict.

One of my least favorite memories of childhood was the argument between my divorced parents that ended with my sister Lisa having to run upstairs to call the police. My father had ripped the phone out of her hands while he was also trying to drag my brother Tim out the front door. My most favorite memory of law enforcement was that calm, steady officer who came to the house and removed the threat.

Even with my parents' marital failure, I did want to believe in enduring devotion. Maybe the key was to keep the partnership moving through the storyline, find a way to make it through the drama, with the least amount of pain and conflict.

Winter 2003-2004

On the call a week before my scheduled arrival in Alaska, Joe's tone was flat, "Things are not going well. Luckily, your Mom's in the hospital—"

My anger flared but I kept it out of my voice, "What does that mean? I thought you liked your mother-in-law?" From the tone of his voice, I knew he was not happy. The conversation sure wasn't making me happy.

"Paula, of course I love your Mom. What I mean to say is that you should stop and help take care of her before coming up here for Christmas. That will give me more time to finish up the boat projects."

Breathing again but still constrained, I snapped, "Oh, good. I'll let Mom know how 'helpful' she's being. That she doesn't need to worry that she's taking me away from you." I wondered if sarcasm transmitted over the phone lines?

He did not pick up on the snap or ignored it on purpose. His voice held more energy. "Definitely a good thing, you visiting your Mom. She'll appreciate it and you can take care of her and see the newest *Lord of the Rings* movie while you're there. I really am looking forward to you getting here Paula, truly. I just need a few more days to prep the boat for you."

I breathed more deeply and decided to take this at face value and not be insulted that he was delaying my visit. I lightened up. I was glad he caught on to my *Lord of the Rings* enthusiasm. Living apart as much as we did, details of the other's life could escape. I knew I was not great at remembering his favorite bicycle manufacturer. "Yeah, it's opening this week and I've been waiting for a year. And Las Vegas has those comfy theater seats." *Mom would appreciate the visit.*

"… and, by the time you're up here, I'll have the boat in shape … really, I will. The toilet will be up and running."

"Okay then, it should work," I said, and hoped it was true. The toilet project had been going on since he bought the boat. *Joe had the skills for the work, but did he have the time?*

I managed to change my flight reservations without spending too much money. I finished up for the semester, glad to put away the red pen and walk the grades to the Registrar. I was free. Time to travel to Alaska for three "practice" weeks with Joe on the boat, time to see if I could stand living on the boat through a bit of an Alaskan winter. First though, Las Vegas to see Mom and catch a movie.

Mom spent her first 65 years living in Buffalo. Her health began to deteriorate, and Buffalo winters weren't helping. My brother, sister, and I got together and helped fund her to spend a winter away from the cold. We suggested somewhere warm and dry, thinking she'd choose Tucson or Phoenix. She chose Vegas, explaining, "Hey, if it's three in the morning and I can't sleep, there's always a bingo game going on."

How practical of her.

She did so well during that winter (health-wise that is … finance-wise the bingo parlors and blackjack tables made out) that Joe and I invested in a Las Vegas condo for her. Lisa bought her a car. And Tim provided for her as well, explaining, "Hey, I'm giving her the only grandchild." She had all three of her kids pitching in for the next phase of her life, as she left Buffalo and moved to Vegas fulltime to become "Gammy Vegas."

She had been enjoying the warmth and the sun of Vegas for two years. My siblings and I would fly into town for a "Mom visit" that we layered with casino, show or restaurant visits. I was glad Joe had suggested the travel change as her health had again taken a downward turn.

* * *

Las Vegas flights must be unique. I always felt

bad for their flight attendants. On the way in, there is a wildness, a sense of expectancy, voices are louder, gestures grander. Big dreams filled the air. Going there, passengers loosened up, detached from their customary demeanor, prepping for a shameless world. These folks were pushing their personal edge, flying to the land where "what happens in Vegas stays in Vegas."

On my flight to Vegas I eavesdropped on the two guys next to me.

Aisle seat said, "She bought this huge piece of furniture. Said we had extra money."

Window seat replied, "Yeah. Right. 'Extra' money? Whose 'extra'?"

"Exactly. MINE. We have two joint checking accounts, but one is mainly mine and the other's hers. She's going back to work this year so hers will start to have some cash added. I could have done a weekend golf expedition with that cash. Jeesh."

Loosening of behavioral constraints shows up in more than one way on a Vegas flight. I'm pretty sure I'd be running screaming from that miserly relationship. It makes no sense to be generous to yourself while stingy to your partner. How can you be mean and rude to the person you share your bed with? Sounded risky.

Mothers, however, take a free pass when it comes to being rude. I think it comes from years of parenting—they expect they can say whatever is on their minds, as long it's "for your own good." The difficulty comes once the child starts to age. By the time you hit, say, your forties, you figure you know what's good and that Mom should just keep out of it. We know what we want, we know how to behave, and we can actually survive without advice on how to turn on a light bulb. Mom often disagreed.

I might be lucky. When my Mom disagreed, she did so subtly. Eyebrows raised just a touch. A slight widening of the eyes. Her head turned away with a pinched look as she held in the words, the advice, the correction. She could usually hold in the words, until they sometimes just burst out.

I knew when Mom had a negative comment by what she was not saying. If I came out dressed for going out to dinner and she didn't comment on what I was wearing, that meant she didn't like it. If she offered jewelry, that meant she didn't like it but thought there was hope through accessorization. Her opinion had to be pretty bad for her to actually say, "Is that what you are wearing?"

Mom was in the Summerlin Hospital, getting over pneumonia; one more "gift" from her COPD. This was not her first go-round for hospital stays.

Lisa frequently flew down from Central Washington to stay during Mom's hospitalizations. My sister had a miraculous system of packing a half-filled, small carry-on that would serve her for weeks at a time. And she always looked great, even on Week Two of a trip. I had never figured out either of those skills: packing light and always looking great. But I was glad she had been able to fly down and see Mom so often, both for Mom's sake and for my sake. It reduced my guilt for not visiting more. I hadn't been out to see my mother for six months.

For this trip, it was just me visiting Mom in the hospital. As I entered her room, she quickly said, "Don't touch me Paula—you might get sick."

Had her health regressed? Did something happen that I didn't know about? Was I out of the loop? "But, I thought you were feeling better? What's happened? Aren't they ready to discharge you?"

"Yes, but, you never know. And you with your asthma. It's nice to see you, but no kisses. Don't take the chance."

Whew. Okay. No kisses for Mom. "You have a nice room here, Mom—a single and everything."

"All the rooms in this hospital are single." She sounded a bit smug. Summerlin Hospital was Mom's kind of hospital, where all the rooms overlook the Las Vegas Strip, fifteen miles away. "It has a great view. But I'm ready to go home."

"I bet you are. It's been two weeks."

"The hospital people are very nice, but I'd like to sleep in my own bed. It gets exhausting here."

"Exhausting?"

"Yes. They wake me up every few hours to give me a pill or take a test or something or another."

"Ironic, isn't it?"

We both laughed. Mom and I mostly got along pretty well.

Mom's big concern was whether they towed her car.

"I parked it just outside of the Emergency Room."

"I know, I walked past it when I came in. Isn't that parking area supposed to be for thirty minutes only? And you've been here two weeks?"

"I know, I know. But I wasn't feeling well when I came to the hospital. I didn't want to walk too far."

"Okay, that makes sense. But the question is Mom, why did you drive yourself to the hospital if you were feeling that poorly?"

"I didn't want to ask anyone for help. You know the ladies in the condo complex, none of them are doing too well themselves. I didn't want to ask them to bother."

You mean the ladies you lunch with? The ladies you go to shows with every week or two? The ladies of your card club, your book club and your social club? I didn't say any of this out loud, but she probably saw it on my face.

"You know, Paula, you know I don't like to ask people for favors."

"Okay Mom, I understand. But try calling a cab next time. The hospital is only two blocks from the condo."

"They take forever to get here."

I stayed quiet then, hoping she might get a clue on what my silence meant--my optimistic dream of how communication worked.

The car was miraculously not towed when we brought her down. Mom commented, "I kept asking the people in the ER and they told me not to worry about it, that they would tell security. I guess they did tell security. I didn't have to worry after all. How nice."

I got Mom settled into the condo and did her shopping and errands. The errands seemed endless and minor. "Could you put that magazine on the 2nd shelf by the TV?" "I like the glasses and mugs right-side up in the cabinet, if you don't mind?" "Would you move that trashcan to the left of the desk?" I worked on my patience—she was always polite in her fussiness. What really drove me nuts was her constant flow of information.

"The light switch is on the left side of the door."

I found I had to hold in the words. What, am I an idiot not to know where the light switch is?

"The garbage can is under the sink."

In a 900 square foot condo, I could find the garbage can all by my 45-year-old self. Plus, I just emptied it this morning.

"Just turn the dial all the way to the left to get the stove to light."

I wondered if she thought I'd just arrived on Planet Earth and had never seen a gas stove before?

This has gotten worse with Mom over the years. Her kids moved away and anything we learned while she was not around didn't count. Plus, she thought we needed to be reminded of anything we had learned from her.

FLOATERS

It was annoying being a 45-year-old 8-year-old.

She did sometimes realize how silly it was. "I guess you know where the dryer is. I am just trying to be helpful."

I said, "Thanks Mom." *Could she see me roll my eyes?* I even more appreciated Lisa's visits.

While Mom napped, I escaped to *Lord of the Rings, The Return of the King*. Finally. The last of the trilogy. It had been a long wait for the adventure to end. I arrived early to get my favorite seat, a recliner in stadium-style seating, with a rail at my feet, balancing the popcorn on the left with a large diet Pepsi on the right. The movie was three hours long. It was too short at that. Even with its multitudes of endings: Frodo and Sam passed out at Mount Doom; Frodo waking up and joy bursting from the remaining Fellows; Aragorn's Coronation; the return to the Shire; Sam's wedding; the Gray Havens departures; and, finally, at the actual end, Sam returning home. I cried. Okay, I cried at each of the multitude. Sadness and joy at the story. Sadness and loss at the story ending. The movie I had anticipated for years was done. Seen. Finished.

I cried for myself. What would fill that void of anticipation? I had loved the books for decades and each annual reread gave me a touch of its initial glamor, but never quite provided the same enchantment. Never again could I have a first read. Now the movie would never be new again, and I would never have the allure of seeing it for the first time.

Later, the special extended version of the three films helped, for a time.

Joe called just before I left Las Vegas, "The toilet isn't ready yet."

I was glad Joe couldn't see my flushed face. Before I could figure out how to respond, he continued, "But don't worry, I have a plan."

"A plan?"

"Yeah. We'll stay at the Breakwater for two nights."

The Breakwater Inn, just across the street from the harbor, was the Juneau hotel he first lived in, before buying the boat. I was relieved that Joe seemed to be taking this "wifely demand" of a functional toilet pretty seriously. I started smiling, thinking of his concern for me on the boat. I have so rarely made any "wifely demands" other than those midnight ones, I appreciated his focus on my comfort.

Just before I left Vegas, Mom asked, "Paula, how's the boat?"

I made the mistake of answering honestly.

"You have no toilet? How are you going to live on a boat with no toilet?" Mom looked pretty upset; she didn't even bother to hide it.

"Don't worry Mom, Joe will get it in."

She glared at me then finally calmed down as her vision of Joe the Capable Man returned to her. "Well, yes, he will. He is dependable, isn't he. And he's good with fixing things." Mom liked Joe too. "But is it a good idea to stay on a boat? In Alaska? In the winter? Won't it be too cold? It doesn't sound right to me."

"It will be an adventure. And Joe won't let anything happen." I loved having Joe as the trump card. He was handy and capable and therefore he was magic to Mom. Magic for me too. Magic to minimize the concerns she tried to push onto me; magic to end the conflict before it had begun.

Mom was not going to understand the attraction of Alaska: the landscape, the wild, the real world. She lived her whole life in houses or apartments that melded together with the neighboring houses and apartments, all laid out carefully, block by block. She liked it that way. Plus, she was afraid of birds. She was the only person I ever met who was scared of sparrows. Crows. Even chickadees bothered her. And their nests. And especially their feathers. No, Alaska had too many birds for Mom.

"You are the plucky one. Call me and let me know how it's going. My social club will want the updates. They think you are the funniest."

Great, the senior citizen, cribbage-playing ladies of Summerlin think I'm the funniest. Maybe I could get a lounge show at the casino.

* * *

As poorly behaved as passengers might be flying into Vegas, it seemed to be worse flying out. Passengers were mostly dispirited, depressed and hung-over. Their dreams shattered, sometimes messily. Folks were not at the top of their game. The wild expectancy was replaced by the mundane. I felt for the poor flight attendants who dealt with this misery each day. I was happy to get off the plane, even if it meant sitting in SeaTac for three hours before going on to Juneau.

SeaTac at least had a brew pub that sold Juneau-brewed Alaskan Amber. I gave it a try. The pub was running a special, with a dollar off the large size, "Perfect," I thought, and opened a book.

Then the beer arrived. In the biggest mug I'd seen since the Munich Oktoberfest. Huge. A foot high. I laughed. The tables were packed together, so I grinned at the couple next to me, saying "I had no idea!"

And the woman frowned, "I'd be under the table if I drank all that!"

"Well," I felt the need to explain, "I have a three-hour layover." I slowly turned my back and returned to my book.

A single woman in her forties sat down at the table next to me. We smiled at each other—that friendly connection that said, "No, I won't start drooling and screaming or steal your purse."

She asked the waitress, "Do all your beers come in THAT size?"

I turned away and controlled my eye twitches.

Two guys sat down next to me, chatting that they were looking forward to a cold brew. I didn't even look at them. It didn't matter. One of them asked the waitress, pointing at my beer, "What's that?"

"A large." She sounded like she had heard that question before.

"Oh. I'll have a medium."

Second guy, "Make mine a small."

I would have liked to hide behind that big beer. It was tasty though.

If Joe was there, we'd re-live the San Francisco deli story, where he was embarrassed by the size of his sandwich when the table next to him said, "We'll take one of those and split it three ways."

Everybody in the pub was on their cell phones. People alone, people in groups, couples, every table had a cell phone out and then I remembered I had somebody I could call—Joe. He wasn't at sea, he was ashore! I smiled and rang him up.

We had a short conversation, laughed over the giant Alaskan Amber experience. And shared our eagerness to be together in just a few hours. Like the *Lord of the Rings* movies, I loved the anticipation. Our physical separation was soon to end, and we'd return to the intimacy impossible when apart. *What would happen when I had more than a year without separation? Would I still be so happy to see him?*

I'd been eager to start my sabbatical and live with Joe. But the more I thought, the more I talked to friends, the more I wondered—could we still be happily married while living together? God, I hoped so. That had always been the question Joe and I danced around. Well, the music was about to end. We'd face the walk off the dance floor and see how it went. But, first, a taste of Alaska in the winter. After I finished the giant beer.

Turns out, the beer was a bad choice.

Leaving Seattle, the plane bounced. For the entire trip. Never-ending turbulence. My motion sickness visited in full force. I hoped to keep the dinner and large beer down. Or at least get off the plane before I lost it.

The stop in Ketchikan was especially bad. The wind bashed the plane and, even while sitting on the runway, I could feel the sway. Experiencing turbulence while on the ground? Not desirable. I looked out the window to rain blowing sideways, in thick sheets, heavy blankets. The rain sometimes blocked out the shine from the runway floodlight. I tried not to think what take-off was going to feel like. I kept my eyes closed in an attempt to settle my queasiness.

Leaving Ketchikan, the plane filled up. I imagined the people were escaping the weather. I sat in the middle seat on a crowded flight and I had no desire to use the airsick bag with such close neighbors. Before the beverage cart blocked the aisle, I made it to the back and into the relative privacy of the "toilet." Puking on planes had never been my favorite activity; experience had not made it better.

I was shaky- and pukey-feeling as I left the plane in Juneau. My blood shot eyes searched the crowd. Joe should be standing to the side, out of the traffic flow, watching for me. There! My heart beat faster and my smile broke out. Through the crowd our eyes met, and his smile broke out. Then I had the comfort of his hug. I relaxed into his arm and closed my red eyes. Home again.

Joe asked, "Love, you okay?"

"Yeah—now I'm good."

"Rough flight?"

"Ketchikan … "

"Say no more. How's your stomach?"

"Better now that I've emptied its contents."

"Oh, poor love. Here, let me get your bags."

We made our way through baggage claim, the crowds of holiday travelers, and out to the car. Dark and rainy—blackness from overcast skies, water, snow, and ice. The city was not in its most picturesque condition—rainy and gray, with piles of slushy, dirty snow. The white-sided mountains were barely visible through foggy, ragged clouds. It was dark even though the sun was up. Neither National Geographic nor Tolkien prepared me for slushy, icy, gray Juneau. There was no gentle snow, no white fluffy layer covering the ground. Nor was there a magnificent, powerful blizzard, blowing snow into my eyes. Just slush. With icy spots. No color. No brightness. Dull and miserable. When the overcast sky blocked the view of the mountain, it reminded me of Buffalo. I left Buffalo for a few reasons, dull and gray being one of them.

Well, Juneau might not be pretty, but neither was I. Too much nausea, too much turbulence, too much beer.

Joe kissed my head and held my hand, to be sure I didn't slip. We chatted about work and the series of upcoming holiday parties.

"Are you okay?"

"My stomach is better, but my head is pounding."

"Do you have pills?"

"No, I don't. How about you?"

"We can stop and pick some up."

We stopped at his office and he ran in to get the industrial-sized bottle of ibuprofen off his desk. *Why did he have such a large bottle of painkillers on his desk?* The question dissipated as we arrived at the Breakwater Inn.

Old home days. The Breakwater was built into a hillside and its lower level, tucked under the upper balconies, housed the studio apartments for long-term rentals for people who could cope with small and dark spaces. Joe had been one of those people. He had lived in a ground-floor efficiency in the Breakwater for his first six months in town and I visited him here for a month last summer. For a two-night stay, we would enjoy the upper floor that held more air and light and a bit less moisture.

I started to apologize for not being up to using the king-sized bed in the best possible manner, Joe stopped me, "Paula, there is no need to apologize."

"I know but …"

"Just stop it. I love you and I'm glad you are here. Now, rest."

Another hug; worth the trip, without a doubt.

I mentioned I had to rinse off my pants before they were stained from the vomit splash.

"I can do that for you. I have experience after all."

I laughed, "Yeah, but I want to WEAR these clothes again!"

"You know we could chart our relationship around the times you've thrown up."

"There was that time in San Francisco …"

"When I washed your clothes and shrank your wool suit and sweater."

"When you accidentally locked me into the public bathroom at the parking lot."

"Yeah, I'm still shocked I did that—just trying to protect my sick love while in a public garage bathroom in the Tenderloin. Do you remember the time driving back from the D.C. airport—I had to pull over so you could puke. And that limo ride in Seattle …"

"Oh, don't remind me … I'm still embarrassed about that one."

"You don't need to be."

"Thanks, you are sweet." Paused, "I think though I'd rather find some other means to track our life together—the times your wife vomited is just not a romantic benchmark."

"Sure, no problem." He never brought it up again.

* * *

Joe's boss threw a potluck Christmas party for everybody in the Alaska Marine Highway administrative offices.

Marsha, one of his co-workers, informed Joe that he should bring a dish.

"Me, cook something? I don't think so."

Marsha asked, "Isn't Paula here?"

Joe frowned, "Yes, she got here last night. So?"

"So, she can cook tonight and bring it tomorrow."

Joe just laughed, "We'll make a stop at the liquor store." We weren't even living on the boat yet. Even if we were, there was no functional stove on the boat. And even if there was, I rarely cooked for potlucks— I figured that was the purpose of bottled wine. Way less stress.

It wasn't fair to call Juneau gray and dark and wet. It did have other attributes. When the sun appeared, or at least when the clouds thinned out and allowed a hint of sun, Juneau could be spectacular. Sadly, this did not seem to happen very often.

Dramatic topographic layers framed the city. The outer frame was the mountains: tall, steep, rugged edges, topped by ice and snow throughout the year. The lower mountainsides were coated with spruce, trees tipped in white for winter. These mountains were all sharp angles, meeting at the flat plane of the water and nearshore. The shorelands were filled with swamps, meadows, or human structures. The steep slopes left few areas for humans to easily build upon, leaving only the flats for development. Water poured off creeks on the mountains, puddling below, forming an aquatic frame. The water seeped and flowed over the land, ran off under Egan Drive, and entered the Gastineau Channel and the Inside Passage. Gastineau Channel was narrow and separated Juneau from Douglas Island. Douglas Island had the same framed layers: swamps and human dwellings on its narrow flatland, then jutting mountains rising immediately upwards. Egan Drive was the one main road, running north and south, mostly parallel with the water. A ride along Egan Drive felt like moving through the center of a picture, with mountains holding you tight against the watery edge.

Joe and I drove up Egan and then into the residential neighborhood in the Mendenhall Valley, a valley carved out by a local glacier. We were glad the house was well lit as the grayness soaked in most of the ambient light. We arrived and the wine was welcomed.

The administrative folks were friendly. I had met most of them last summer. Strangely, I got a half dozen offers from these people to live with them. I understood that Alaskans were friendly, but move-in offers? That was a level of neighborliness I'd expect to be shown to fire or flood survivors.

Joe's boss offered, "We have an extra room. You two can stay with us over the holidays."

Lora from softball told us, "I'm house-sitting so you two can have my apartment."

Another coworker said, "My couch pulls out into a double bed—you and Joe would be comfortable."

I now knew more about their living arrangements than I ever expected. I politely replied, "Thanks for the backup plans but I'm sure the boat will be fine."

Lora continued, "Paula, really, feel free to use the apartment. It is just sitting there."

"That will be a great option, thanks Lora." I

hadn't been on the boat even for a night and these folks thought I wanted off?

Lora pulled Joe over. "Now Joe, you take care of her, do you hear?"

Joe and I said in tandem, "Of course I will." "Of course he will." Did my mother call Lora? Did she reach out to all these people? Did she magically take over their brains?

Fred was the ferry terminal manager. His wife Chris saw me from across the room and yelled, "You're really going to live on the boat?"

Laughing, I nodded my head yes.

Still yelling, "You're crazy you know."

"Hey, what's the problem? Joe's promised me the toilet will be installed tomorrow."

Even louder, "Crazy!"

Why were these people warning me off the boat? My normal optimistic self was getting suspicious, especially because these were Alaskans warning me off.

I took Joe aside and asked, "I don't get it. These are Alaskans … adventurous, capable, competent. After all, they live in a temperate rainforest! Why are they concerned about me living on a boat?"

Joe answered, "It is exactly because they are Alaskans. Most of them HAVE lived on boats."

"Oooh." I stared at Joe. That wasn't the answer I wanted to hear.

Well, ignorance was bliss—I hadn't lived on a boat yet, I hadn't even seen it yet, so I had nothing to worry about. Anyway, there were a bunch of people willing to take me in. I went back to the party to collect phone numbers.

* * *

The morning after the party we were still in the Breakwater Hotel. Joe asked, "What do you want to do today? I don't have to go into work."

"I want to visit the boat. I'm dying to see it." Joe had emailed me pictures, but a picture of a boat in a shed just didn't tell much of a story. It was like the blind man and the elephant, feeling only part of the whole. Plus, Joe kept sending me pictures of his work on the boat: a torn-out head, a torn-apart aft cabin, a salon covered in tools. Those parts were not leaving me a pleasant sense of the whole. Or even a pleasant sense of the parts. I wanted to see the real thing, and I hoped it looked better than the pictures implied. *Maybe Joe had put it all back together?*

Joe smiled, "Let's go."

The boat lived in the Aurora Harbor, just across Egan Drive from the Breakwater. Aurora was one of three city-managed harbors and the only one with rows of boat sheds. The harbor had eleven floats, lettered A through K, each float with slips for thirty-two boats. The boat sheds were in the middle three floats, E through G, and each boat shed housed two slips, protecting two boats per shed. There were three ramps that connected the land to the docks. We crossed the street and cut through Aurora's parking lot, to its southernmost ramp. Our boat was in E-25.

I paused at the top of the shiny, gray aluminum ramp, and looked down, a bit dizzy from the 45-degree angle. I turned back to Joe, "You actually carried plywood down this ramp?"

He laughed, "It was high tide when I did that. Now it's low tide. Juneau has a big tidal change."

I knew that, but it was one thing to abstractly state that the tide in Juneau has a range of twenty feet. It was a whole different feeling to be peering down a steep ramp at low tide. I felt like a ski jumper without skis. *People walked down this thing? In the rain? Or when it was icy?*

"Just hold onto the handrail and use the cleats."

"Use the cleats?"

"Put your toe on the cleat. It will stop your foot from sliding."

The cleats were raised slats on the ramp. Okay. My toe was pointing downward—almost ballerina-like, but the cleats worked against the downward pull of gravity. I could see I would need to schedule grocery runs around the tides.

I managed not to ski jump.

On the docks, we passed three floats before coming to E float. Boat sheds lined the right side while uncovered slips were on the left. The sheds looked like tall garages. There were two human-sized doors with glass windows on each side of each shed. The man-sized doors led to an interior dock, so you could walk to your boat, protected under cover. At the opposite end of the shed was the boat entrance. In place of a garage door that real garages would have, there were two giant canvas curtains. The curtains were large enough to cover the entire width of the boat slip. The curtains could be opened or closed to allow boats to sail in or out of the shed. The shed was about as big as a two-car garage though much taller.

We reached E-25. The broken glass in its man-door window was covered with a piece of plywood. No one had painted the door in recent history. Nor the shed. I surmised that both had once been painted, based on bits peeling off. This was not a cheery, welcoming entrance. It would have been fitting in a crime thriller as a place where the killer dumps the body. Or, the part of town where no one walks at night. *Paula, think about this as a neighborhood where appearances are unimportant—they have better things to do then paint the garage.* I always preferred the empathetic perspective, plus it helped me be willing to enter the door to E-25.

Joe unlocked the padlock and held the door open. "Watch your step," he warned. I stepped over the high threshold to get my first view of the boat.

FLOATERS

There she was, the *MV Pilot Project*. Home.

I took two steps on the dock then I carefully lifted my leg to miss stepping on a hammer. I hopped over an open toolbox. I managed not to trip on scattered pieces of teak while listening to Joe apologize, "Sorry sweets, this is a work in progress."

I nodded while searching for a place to put my feet, "It's okay."

Then I stopped and steadied myself. And gawked. About ten feet from the shed door was the "step" that led to the boat's deck. The "step" was an uneven, industrial-sized chunk of Styrofoam, topped with an irregularly-shaped piece of plywood, covered—in part—by a carpet remnant. Large nails held the carpet onto the Styrofoam, though half of them were about to fall out. I shuddered to think that might be the same carpet on the walls inside the boat. Early '70s shag in a yellow-brown tone was a ghastly design concept. Did they have leftover carpet from the boat project and decided to use it on the step? I could not imagine who came to that decision and I was really hoping it wasn't Joe. If it was, designing homes together would be a serious challenge in our future. I tried to regain a positive focus. *Paula, just stop. You'll never know how that step came to be. Or at least you don't want to know. Give it up. Look at the boat.*

I turned to my left to get my first full look at the *Pilot Project*. The boat style itself was classic. Joe would call it a 33½ foot trawler yacht having a full-displacement fiberglass hull, flybridge above the main salon, teak decks and trim. The interior had a salon, V-berth and aft cabin. She was powered by a Ford Lehmann diesel in the engine room below the main deck, moving a left-handed screw. I'd call it a 33½ foot boat with three rooms and a half bath, a boat you could drive from the upper deck (flybridge) or from inside. A boat with a wide, flared bow—this was no bullet-shaped speedster. A boat with a square, broad back end, with room to picnic. Its outside floors were worn teak, with black, rubbery trim embedded around each piece of wood. It had stainless steel railings and a varnished wood railing in the front, with lovely cedar twirly-Qs.

"It's beautiful." I meant it—no sarcasm, no snark. The aesthetics of the carpeted Styrofoam step, the chaotic mess on the dock, and the peeling paint of the shed, all of that didn't matter. The *Pilot Project*: her lines flowed, spacious and graceful. She was lovely. And her decorative curlicues added a joyful, romantic touch. I was a bit breathless at the thought, *I was going to get to live aboard her!*

I stepped up on the Styrofoam step, carefully, as it wobbled, and then up onto the boat's worn exterior teak deck. I walked around the bow. A sliding wooden door with failing varnish and brown paint gave entryway to the boat's interior.

I tugged the door open and descended two steep steps into the salon. Immediately to the right was the sturdy wooden ship's wheel with lovely brass accoutrements. On the dashboard was an old, glass-enclosed compass. Above the dash, there was a black plastic hood, like the vision test apparatus at a DMV office. I later found out it was the radar screen was in that hood.

Turning to the left, I found the salon: a narrow cabin, lined with windows. Everywhere was teak—warm, smooth, and golden. I just wanted to run my hands over it. I rubbed the smooth teak handrails in the ceiling. Golden, detailed teak framed the windows and doors, along with the cabinets and counters. Even the step treads were teak, steps into the salon and the ones down into the two cabins. The salon floor was teak parquet, smooth, and finely joined. It was intact: no broken edges, no holes, no cracks. The space glowed amber yellow.

There was a three-burner stove, a tiny sink, a tiny refrigerator, and a tiny countertop—a kitchen dollhouse. Just behind the tiny kitchen, there were cushioned benches for sitting, one on each side of the boat. To the back (the stern), there were two more steep steps down to the back room (the aft cabin). Between the shape, the teak, and the glow, I could see why Joe loved the boat when he first walked in.

The salon had room for six to sit cramped together and three to stand shoulder to shoulder, but no one would be able to pass each other without intimate contact. The salon was the living room, kitchen, dining room, computer room, navigation area, steering area, and engine controls. It was also the workroom where Joe fixed things. And it was where Joe slept. One small, multiple purpose space. I had no idea such a thing was possible. I would soon discover whether such a thing was at all desirable.

The largest room was in the back, the aft cabin, two steps down from the salon. At the base of the stairs, immediately to the left was a bathroom, the head, and straight on were two tiny doors with a ceiling slider leading to the back deck (the stern). It took only three shortened strides to go from the stairs to the back-deck access. Turning around to face towards the salon, I looked again at the door to the head. The door looked like it belonged in a hobbit dwelling: polished and curved. It glowed with its gleaming teak. That was the only glow in the aft cabin.

There used to be teak stairs from the aft hatch leading to the stern. There also used to be teak cabinets, walls, bulkheads with teak veneer, a bed, a closet and a floor, the deck. I knew that because Joe had told me. All those bits were either gone or piled on the dock or stacked in Joe's car. He had to remove them to rebuild other sections. Having the salon as my example, I could almost imagine how lovely this space used to be. It was a work in progress, mostly work and minimal progress.

As Joe had removed all the teak woodwork, the aft cabin had unfinished fiberglass bulkheads with old glue stains, water stains and nasty gray (but dry) bilge where the floor should be. Old, stained fiberglass was hideous, with long, dried drips of some former liquid running down the walls. There was nothing cozy about the space. The cabin had no curtains, no seating, no comfy bed, just a bunch of tools. With stained fiberglass that looked like it had bled. The "big" room was now Joe's workroom, his staging area for the rebuild, and, most importantly, the staging area for the toilet installation. I was glad there was currently no seating in the aft cabin—I didn't want to spend too much time looking at the glue-stained walls.

Turning again to the front of the boat (the bow), I saw another space that dropped down from the salon, and I said to Joe, "That's a nice sized closet in the front, plus it has a few more closets off it. Great."

"Paula, that's not a closet. It's the forward cabin—the V-berth. See how the two bunk areas at the bow form a V?"

Bunks? I thought they were tables to hold the dozen Rubbermaid totes sitting on them. Okay, bunks. Then I noticed all the carpet on the walls up there. Well, at least the salon was free of 1950s shag wall carpet. Suddenly I could see a positive aspect to carpet on walls—it hid the dreadful old fiberglass.

"And see the door in there? It used to lead to a second head, but it was in a horrible condition, so I pulled it out."

His back was to me so he couldn't see my scrunched-up face. *It was more horrible?* The head off the aft cabin, the one where he pulled the old toilet, the one with no veneer on the walls, and hideous fiberglass, was in better shape than this one off the V-berth? Chilling. I was glad I didn't see it before he pulled it.

Then I nearly choked when I realized what this meant, "Wait … you mean we used to have two toilets? And now we have none? 'Cause you pulled them out?"

He tensed up and sharply replied, "I pulled them out only after having nasty dirty foul toilet water leaking onto my feet."

Okay, I now knew why he was tense.

He continued, "And we do have one—I bought a new one. We have a $1,000 toilet. And a $1,000 MSD. They just aren't attached yet."

This seemed to be a sensitive subject, so I chose to deflect, "An MSD?"

Joe enthused, "Marine Sanitation Device. It kills all the germs in the dirty toilet water—making it safe, and legal, to flush it over the side."

I smiled, trying to share his enthusiasm. Usually the technology of sanitation hid behind ceramic tanks, flush handles and sewer pipes. It was all a bit closer to the surface here. I was holding my enthusiasm for when the toilet accoutrements were functional.

I asked, "When are they going to be hooked up?" I was visualizing trying to reach the porta-potty at the top of the ramp at 2 a.m. with snow and wind and at low tide. Ski-jump ramp conditions with a full bladder. Or, like Gandalf and the Fellowship trying to force their way over the pass. "Can it be installed soon please?" The visual disturbed me.

"How about today?"

"Excellent!" Joe did like to please me.

I spent the day occasionally handing Joe tools while I sat in the golden glow of the salon. He hammered and screwed and lugged the toilet and the MSD around. I supplied occasional encouragement. Six hours later, I finished reading my paperback and started a second, and, voila, he had finished!

Never had I stood over a toilet with such anticipation. Would it flush? Would it leak? Would the MSD work? He hit the switch, and, a flush! Success! Marvelous technology! Amazing husband! It was all good. Joe and I hugged.

"We can sleep in the boat tonight!" And I wouldn't have nightmares about finding the porta-potty.

"Great. But, Paula, don't flush the toilet too often."

I frowned, confused. "What, does this $1,000 toilet have a limited number of flushes? I'd think the rest of the boat would rot out before we'd run out of $1,000 toilet flushes."

"It's not the toilet Paula."

"What is it—the MSD? I'd think a $1,000 MSD ..."

"No, no, not the MSD. It's the electric."

"Electric?"

"Yes. The toilet macerates everything. Breaks it down. Think of a blender."

"Blender in a toilet?" A new visual, got it. Wished I hadn't gotten it.

"Yes, an electric blender."

"You've obviously hooked up the electricity since the toilet works. So, the issue is ... ?"

"The batteries."

"You've hooked it up to the batteries."

"Yes."

"And so?"

"The batteries aren't being charged."

"Oh." I paused. The midnight ramp climb was appearing before my eyes again. "Every flush could be our last?"

"Yes."

"Well." I worked to keep my facial muscles from communicating, "Okay, let's not test it again then."

"Good plan."

"And let's follow the California drought rule, 'if it's yellow' ..."

"Let it mellow."

In unison we laughed, finishing together, "And if it's brown, flush it down."

Well, he installed the toilet. I got what I asked for. I didn't define how long I wanted the toilet to work though … maybe I should have been clearer?

* * *

It was my first morning on the boat. I woke up to chittering, growling, and barking. Joe was quietly sleeping. What was the noise? I heard splashy, splishy, squishy footsteps.

Otters!

I woke Joe up and we tried to see the creatures, sneaking around inside the boat so they wouldn't be scared off. Joe went for my camera and handed it to me. I quickly snapped a shot of two otters—heads both toward me, heads ear to ear. They were sitting on one another or in some sort of intimate contact. After the flash, they jumped into the water.

I happily turned to Joe, "I got them!" Then I looked at the camera. "Oh. No. I'm an idiot. No film."

Joe, in his best Jacques Cousteau voice, said, "And de adventuring wildlife photographer es challenged by zee wily ot-ter."

We both laughed and went back to bed. After all, my headache was gone.

4 Surveyor's Report

Floater: (n) worker shifting to various tasks

Spring 2004

I was nursing my cosmopolitan. My plan was to limit myself, trying to make one drink last. Or maybe two. Definitely not three.

I was still getting over the transition from living with Joe to life at the College: boat to classroom. Our normal pattern had Joe leaving home to head to a ship. When his time at home neared its end, we each prepared for our different solo phases. Both of us refocused. Both prepared for the alternative lifestyle that happened about twice a year. But this year, I left Joe. I left him to head back to my college. He stayed in place. I felt unsettled, as though I should be somewhere else.

Boat life had been surprisingly solitary, hidden away in a boat shed, with occasional social forays with Joe's colleagues. In my college life, I had to work to find some alone time. From the students in class, my student advisees, and all the various colleagues, I had people around me all day. I closed my eyes envisioning the quiet on the boat and started smiling.

Not wanting to appear asleep at the bar, I opened my eyes and twirled my stem, enjoying the wonder of wonders that was Mimi's, a rare and special martini bar in downtown Huntingdon. Neighborhood taverns thrived in Central Pennsylvania. Yuengling Beer was the beverage of choice and upscale meant drinking your beer in a glass. Mimi's verged on being an oasis of sophistication in central Pennsylvania's sea of simplicity. Juniata College faculty and staff would show up at Mimi's sooner or later, often on a weekly basis. That was one reason I tried to limit my intake—getting drunk around co-workers was always a bad idea, no matter what kind of bar it was.

My other reason was the person who took the seat next me: my boss's wife, Bonnie. She was wearing her pearls and cardigan sweater set, looking steady and prudent. Unlike me, she was still new at sitting at a bar without her husband. Normally Jim would be with her, but Jim was busy at the college for the evening. I thought the pearls helped boost her confidence. No, it should not be a three-cosmopolitan night. Bonnie was my friend and I didn't want to embarrass her while she wore her pearls and experienced bar life sans husband.

We chatted about Alaska and Joe. She missed him. So did I. It had been a month since I left him after the Christmas break. I had four more months before I could return to Alaska on my sabbatical—I had to finish up the semester.

"So how was it, Paula? Living on the boat at Christmas time? Was it great? Are you going back?"

"It sure was an adventure."

"What happened?"

Oh, where should I start? "Did I tell you about the otters?"

"Otters? Sea otters?"

"No—river otters. I know, funny! In Southeast Alaska, mussels grow on the marina piers. The otters eat mussels. And so the otters hang around the waterfront. And they like to socialize, especially when they jump on the decks of boats."

"Socialize?"

"They lick, play and bite other otters, as well as, well, more intimate contact. Plus, they seem to like smelling and rolling in each other's spraints."

Bonnie started twisting her pearls, "Spraints?"

"Sorry that was the biologist talking. Spraints is the scientific term for otter poo, otter droppings, you know, otter crap. Spraints are black and fishy smelling. Wet and squishy. That's one reason Joe and I named the otters 'Squishy' and 'Squashy.'"

Bonnie was staring at me. "And the other reason … I'm almost afraid to ask … ?"

"It's the sound they make. When the otters start walking on the deck, the sound can only be described as 'squishy.' Plus, when they are 'socializing,' intimately, squishy sounds—"

"I get it. I get it." She brought up her hand to stop my otter sex description. Bonnie's cringe was strong and I was afraid her pearls might break. She continued, "So, you had to clean up spraints?"

"No, gosh no, I didn't. Joe did. And he was getting tired of it. I guess coming home from work in the dark and stepping in black, smelly, squishy droppings wasn't very appealing."

Her eyebrows rose.

I continued, "At first, the spraints covered the boat shed dock and the boat deck. Joe solved the problem by fencing his half of the boat shed. The otters couldn't get onto the dock or the boat decks, voilà!" I smiled thinking of his clever fix. "However, the otters could slink through gaps, so Joe kept finding more openings to block. Finally, the otters moved to our neighbor's boat, the other boat in our shed. They took full advantage. In three weeks, the otters coated the other boat's decks with nasty, smelly black spraints. Joe saved me from spraint cleanup."

"Were your neighbors mad?"

"No, they weren't. They understood the battle. Being practical Alaskans, they wanted to know if the fence worked. They were making tactical plans of their own. However, a fence would have made it tough for them to get onto their boat. Just before I left, they tried a different solution."

"What, otter repellent?"

"Well, you could call it that." That would be a nice name for it.

"What keeps otters off?"

Bonnie wasn't going to like this. I know I didn't. "Nail boards."

"Nail boards? Are we talking emery boards?"

I laughed, "No, not for fingernails. Apparently nail boards are a typical Alaskan method to protect a cabin from bears. I heard a long-time Alaskan call them 'unwelcome mats.' Take a wooden plank and nail dozens of large nails through, close together, so the sharp points stick out. Then hang the planks where you want to block the wildlife. Sharp ends out. That kind of nail boards."

Bonnie dropped her hand from her pearls and slapped the bar, "The otters get pinned by the boards!?"

"No, No! When they jump on them, the sharp points make them quickly jump off again."

"Uggh. Wildlife torture devices ... sounds mean."

"A bit, but they work. No more otters for the neighbors. I do though have these visions of otters with wounded paws. Not pretty. No more spraints though."

Bonnie and I both paused, returning to our drinks. I was thinking about the trade-offs people choose to make in life, wanting to live close to nature yet wanting it on their terms, spraint-free. I didn't want to think about what was going through Bonnie's mind.

Even just a few weeks on the *Pilot Project* revealed a few of the tradeoffs I was going to face: cold quarters, tight space, and uncomfortable furniture.

When you sit with the Provost's wife at *Mimi's*, the world stops by to say "hi" to her. I got a little overflow, "Hey Paula, how are you? How was your time with Joe?"

"It was a bit surreal. After all these years of marriage, to be the one waiting for him to come home for work before dinner, to be the one to meet him at work for lunch, to have a husband on a regular work schedule—it was odd!"

The group laughed and someone said, "Welcome to normality. Did you get tired of it?"

"No!" But it was only three weeks.

The crowd around Bonnie increased. And therefore, so did my overflow. A new face popped up, "Paula! How was Alaska?" I chose not to tell the otter story. "How was the dark?"

"Juneau wasn't too bad. It is far enough south there was always some sun every day, though the cloud cover did a good job of hiding it."

"So how bad was it?"

"Sometimes as little as five and a half hours of 'daylight'—or whatever light could pass through the clouds and fog. By 9 or 9:30 a.m. it was as light as it was going to get, and dark again by 3 or 3:30 p.m."

"Sounds depressing."

"It was okay. I probably slept longer everyday than I do in Pennsylvania. Plus, we had a happy light."

The overflow was staring at me.

"A happy light—you know—a full spectrum light designed to help Seasonal Affective Disorder (SAD)?"

Now they were nodding. With academics you must give them the big words.

"Tracey, one of our friends who moved to Alaska from California ten years ago, she gave the happy light to Joe last winter. During her first Alaskan winter, she studied for her bar exam while sitting under the happy light. Tracey passed the bar so she figured the light would help Joe through his first winter."

"Do you think it helped?"

"I enjoyed my three weeks on the boat—it didn't hurt." I couldn't tell them that Joe had rigged the light as a boat shed ceiling light—it took something away from the romance of the concept.

Bonnie looked at me, "A happy light ... what a life Paula. And you are still looking forward to your sabbatical, actually living with your husband?"

"Yes, in most ways." Pausing, I waved at the bartender, "Could I have another cosmo please?"

A voice from the overflow, "Ohhhhh, trouble in Paradise?"

"No, no. Joe and I are still good. But living on a boat in the winter is not like living in a house in Huntingdon. Central PA is colder than Southeast Alaska but my home here is warmer than the boat. On windy days it is a huge difference."

"How cold was the boat?"

I paused, suddenly realizing my similarity to Pippin, the "fool of a Took" in the Mines of Moria, when he dropped a pebble down a well to get a measure of the depth. Sometimes it's best not to know and keep the monsters sleeping.

"I was wondering that myself one day while I shivered. Wanting to know the answer, I went out and bought two thermometers—one for inside the boat and the other for the shed. That was a mistake."

"A mistake?"

"Yeah. Because now I could put a number to my shivers—I could quantify it and compare it to the temperature I'd normally set. I felt much colder having a number." I looked to the overflow. "How low would you set your thermostat?"

"If I was really trying to save money, I'd put it

at 60° F.”

Someone in the back said, “Me, I never go lower than 65.”

“The boat’s warmest was generally closer to 60 than 65. But when the temperature dropped outside, or when the Taku winds were blowing off the glacier, ripping up the Channel at 50 knots, blasting across the marina, and through the cracks in the boat shed and its broken window, then the boat temperature dropped. We went through days of 40°F—inside the boat.”

Voices from the outskirts yelled, “Forties!”

“Yeah. Forties. Not cozy. I wish I hadn’t known.” I preferred a carefree vision of my world, but I could not ignore the stark realities when the numbers neared the temperature at which water froze.

I continued, “But blankets were warm. Slippers were necessary. And I appreciated Joe even more than usual.”

“You ‘appreciate’ a husband who has you living on a nearly freezing boat?”

I nodded at them, “Yes! A husband who didn’t complain when I stuck my icy feet and hands up against him. He’d even warm them up without me asking. He didn’t even flinch too much.”

“Yeah, you have a good one there.” Was there a hint of eye rolling from the overflow? A touch of sarcasm? I ignored it.

Someone who knew me well said, “Ah, not quite the escape you hoped for.”

“Well, cuddling became a survival trait.”

“What—you and Joe need an excuse?”

I blushed.

Bonnie looked concerned. “Paula, Joe usually takes such good care of you. Why didn’t he get another heater for the boat?"

"He had three." Two of which were donations from friends who were concerned that Joe would freeze to death. "But only two of them could be on at any one time."

The overflow raised its eyebrows.

"There is an amp shortage in the marina."

The crowd of eyes were questioning me. They didn't get it.

"The Juneau City Harbor only provides twenty-amp electrical service in the Aurora Basin marina. If we turned on all three heaters, even if everything else was off, we'd pop the breaker. Even with two heaters on, we had to be careful. We could keep the fridge, the hot water heater and two heaters on, but if we turned on the coffee pot—pop! And then you had to jump off the boat, leave the shed, go out in the snow or the rain and switch the breaker back on. Do this a few times, especially when you are in your 'jammies, and you quickly remember to count your amps. It took me four times. At least when Joe was on board, he made the run to the breaker box for us."

"Not quite like living on land, is it?"

"No. Not quite." Not even close. I waved to the bartender—that third cosmo was calling.

* * *

Getting the finances to work for the sabbatical year was a bit tricky, especially as Joe and I were paying the mortgage on Mom's condo. The Port Captain job did not pay as well as his sailing days. Plus, I would take a 50% hit on salary for the sabbatical year. With all the uncertainty of Joe's job and with money being tight, we decided to sell our Pennsylvania house.

I moved into an apartment in Huntingdon, just around the corner from *Mimi's*, for the few months until my sabbatical started. That reduced costs, though it meant I had to empty the house and figure out what went into storage and what went to the apartment and move it all without Joe's help. Even without the house, we were still going into the red each month between Mom's condo, Joe's Alaska travel, and the boat. We were consuming our savings. Retirement wasn't looking good but at least we had the money to fund this part of life's adventures. We thought it would ultimately work. When Joe became a pilot, his pay would be better than state employee wages and professor wages combined. We were operating as Mr. and Mrs. Optimism.

Joe called. Apparently, the Port Captain job was nuts. He was on a rant. "I have to fly down to investigate a drinking and sexual harassment allegation on one of the vessels. Between crew members. And the captain is not being cooperative. What, is the guy an idiot? If he doesn't know what's happening on his ship, then he's useless. If he does know but is hiding it, then he's worse than useless. Paula, I just don't get these guys. They don't take responsibility, the basic responsibility of being captain. Pitiful."

He continued to rant for a while. I commiserated. Life as Port Captain revolved around managing more than 800 people on ten ships spread across the state. There was always another crisis showing up in Joe's office. He had to do crisis management yet had little power to prevent the crisis from arising. All I could do was listen to the outburst; he sounded seriously stressed out. Maybe he needed more time with the happy light?

At the next call, his mood had brightened. SWAPA was going to vote to bring in a new pilot trainee; the vote would take place in April. At the end of the call, I wanted to shout and jump up and down as my mood had also brightened. Then I stopped. I didn't want to jinx it. I didn't want to hope too much. If I created the dream, imagined the life, and if it didn't happen, I didn't want the disappointment. Again.

Joe's earlier attempt to get into the San Francisco Pilots did not work out. The SF Pilots rejected his application as he was five days short of the required sea time over a five-year span. We had already built the San Francisco pilot life in our minds: one week of work and one week off, biking, hiking, restaurants, friends. All the charms of the Bay Area. The dream disappeared because Joe was short five days. Poof. Vanished. Gone.

Part of the thrill of challenge, the push to reach the next goal, meant the risk of failure. But I hated the taste of disappointment.

His goal held big opportunities for both of us. He'd have more flexible time and he'd be home most every night. He'd make more money and work independently, free of any corporate control. We could live together and end the challenges of living apart. I could explore a new career phase, with a university where he was piloting or maybe as an independent writer or consultant. Or as a volunteer at a local nonprofit. And it would be a way out of the growing repetitiveness that came with the gold ring of tenure. We both saw success if he reached his goal, but we both had to brave potential failures to get there.

I discovered my own personal nail board. I had to bounce off and not let its spikes of disappointment stop me.

It was good that I had found the right perspective. Two weeks after the good news phone call was the bad news phone call. Joe told me SWAPA was delaying its vote. We were again in a waiting game. With an uncertain timeline. I used my mental defenses against the sharp disappointing bits.

SWAPA was not out of the realm of possibility. Vince suggested Joe travel to Homer to shake hands with the pilots, so the people who would vote could see his face and have a sense of his commitment. Schmoozing was in Joe's future.

Even with the pilot job uncertainty, I still wanted to spend my sabbatical year with Joe. He'd be Port Captain and drive towards his pilotage objective. I'd enjoy time with my husband, experience boat life, and work on my sabbatical project. We'd be together as he worked toward his goal that would affect both of our lives.

At that point, I had not realized how much I played the role of Ms. Optimism, floating along with Joe's job possibilities. Bilbo hadn't known what would emerge when he left Bag End to join the dwarves. Would he have changed his mind if he did? Would I have?

5: Taking the Plunge

Float: (v) to move through a liquid

Start of Summer 2004

My mother was worried. I could hear it in her voice on the phone. "Paula, driving on the Alcan, all by yourself. It just isn't a good idea."

"Mom, I'm in a car that's nearly new. The roads are paved." *Mostly paved.* "I like to drive. I won't overdo."

"Paula, you'll be all alone."

"Mom, I'll have a cell phone. And I have a new copy of the *Milepost*. It tells me exactly where everything is along the way for every single road I'll be on. Gas stations, hotels, restaurants, it tells me everything; I'll be fine."

"But you'll be driving 4,000 miles."

More like 5,000. "Mom, I promise I'll take it slow. No more than 300 miles a day. And about half of those miles are with the college class before I head north. Don't worry."

"I'm going to worry."

"And I'm going to go. I'll keep in regular phone contact with Joe." This was my ace in the hole—I had a husband and if "he lets me" then Mom, a woman of the 1950s, won't keep pushing. "If you are worried and cannot get through to me, just call Joe. He'll know where I am every day."

"Well, I guess I can't do anything."

Exactly. I ignored the guilt that tried to come along with her disapproval. However, it was tenacious. I kept finding a few bits that hung on.

* * *

During the academic year, I searched for opportunities to teach beyond the classroom, especially where I could escape rural Pennsylvania. I managed this with most of my classes and a few unique programs, many with heavy doses of outdoor exploration. Field work provided a great learning environment and maintained my enthusiasm for the job. I had committed to three special courses during my sabbatical year, even though they reduced my time with Joe.

The first, the 2004 *Remote Field Course*, I'd finish before heading to Alaska. Forty students, with me and three other faculty, exploring the environs of the Southwest. The class discussed the day's events around an evening campfire. I led students through questions of conservation biology and land use by walking them through national parks and federal lands.

Students learned aspects of geology, biology, anthropology, and environment plus a good dash of practical skills. There was the New Jersey student who learned to pump her own gas. There was the Pennsylvania student who learned that it was necessary to stop at the toll booths on the highway. There was the football player who learned that hydration could prevent collapse on a desert trail. And it was more than just the football player who learned about hydration, but, no one died, and only one was hospitalized.

After two weeks enduring random situations created by eighteen- to twenty-year-olds, I was ready for my sabbatical. My solitary drive to Alaska sounded great, as did leaving forty students and the other faculty to drive back to Pennsylvania without me. I headed north.

I skipped my visit to Mom in Vegas. I convinced myself that after two weeks around people that I needed alone-time. And that I had just seen her a few months back. More likely it was that I did not want to revisit the Alcan drive argument and I took the coward's way out.

Two years later, after Mom had died, I regretted that decision, lamented the loss of time with her, even though she would have worried at me all the while. I would have faced the conflict if I knew how few of her days remained.

When your mother is gone and no one is there to nit at you, the void is forever.

* * *

The treacherous Alcan. The Alaska Highway. The myth, the legend, the dream. Wilderness a thousand miles from a toilet. A road filled with broken-down vehicles and blown-out windshields. Drivers fending off attacking bears while fixing a flat. I might have listened to Mom's concerns if any of that was reality. The Alcan might not have the amenities of the Eisenhower Interstate system but it was no longer a rough bush track. I had done my homework. I had read *The Milepost*, the "Bible of North Country Travel," the guidebook for the Alaska Highway. Its *Travel Planning* section said extreme road conditions were a thing of the past. No more cars stuck in the mud. Few shattered windshields, except for a few dings. Flat tires were rare. Flush toilets were still a bit scattered. The biggest danger was getting stuck behind a slow RV convoy. Part of me was sad, but I did enjoy the comfort of a smooth ride. Inaccessible toilets would be my biggest peril.

As I drove north, I called Joe two to three times a day. I knew I'd have dead cell phone land ahead and I wanted to get my "Joe time" in. The first few calls weren't so much fun.

Me, "So, how's it going?"

"This place is insane. Absolutely @#$!%$&*#@ insane."

I concentrated on calm thoughts, hoping they'd

transmit through the cell phone ether, "What's up?"

Joe described the latest stupidity in his office. Maybe it was the boss' boss telling his office what to do based solely on political buddies. Maybe it was his own boss who kept changing expectations, and everyone stayed in flux. Maybe it was just a random hit of a captain mouthing off via email. I wasn't tracking the details. Joe was fuming … angry and irritated and not enjoying life. And I was not either, with my "Joe time" filled by Angry Joe. I was not a fan of Angry Joe. I kept using the calm voice. If the ether transfer didn't work to calm Joe down, maybe it would work on me.

I reached the land between cell phone towers, the quiet zone. Southwest Montana seemed to be the land of fly-fishing adventurers scattered among cattle ranches. My first overnight camping stop in Montana was at Clark Canyon Dam Recreation Site. The Upper Beaverhead River flowed out of the dam and supported a variety of fishers hoping for trout. Mowed lawns surrounded the run-of-the-river reservoir, which meant good parking for campers. I saw run-down RVs scattered about at the edge of the lake, close to fishing poles and fire pits. It was always odd to sleep near strangers, separated only by a stretch of grass and a car door. I channeled Mom as I picked a spot close to the spillway: room for a quick U-turn to escape in case of emergency. I wasn't sure if the RVers engaged in evening entertainment that I'd need to escape from, but I chose to be cautious. Mom would have approved.

Like most US dams, this dam was designated for multiple purposes. Clark Canyon Dam was a multi-million-dollar project producing water for farming, a lake for recreation, and water storage for those rare southwest Montana floods. Based on the farms I drove past, I suspected the dam's water grew feed for cattle. I was sure the golf course on its southern shore appreciated the regular and cheap water supply. Would the product of the alfalfa fields ever cover the cost of the dam? Alfalfa is not a high-priced crop. It would take hundreds of years of alfalfa sales to come close to the cost of the dam. The real-world economics were not the final reason to build this dam. The vote-catching ability of new dams made them priceless. Did the displaced wildlife find a new home? Or did their populations shrink as the human/cattle population swelled? I suspected I knew the answer to this question but was happier not being sure. As a place to sleep, once I cleared my mind, it was quiet and relaxing. It was probably too early in the season for an all-night RV beer party.

The next day, I left the Interstate north of Missoula. Behind me was the traffic, the convoys of heavy trucks, and the nearly identical intersections. No longer would I wonder what enchanting combination of brand name food and gas retailers would appear at the next exit. McDonalds and Shell? Burger King and Petro? Conoco and Hardee's? Sinclair and Subway? Or, please, no, a Dunkin' Donuts? I had a hard time driving past Dunkin'. From this point until I hit the outskirts of Anchorage, the roads were at best two lanes, no more "controlled access highway." And the stores were local: unique, small, and dusty. The bloated, standardized growth following Eisenhower's Concrete Dream was behind me and I felt connected to the world again.

Joe's job had either gotten better or he was toning down the anger for our calls. I liked to think he heard that overly calm voice of mine as not-a-good-thing. I preferred those calls.

After I drove through cell-phone-dead-land, I also appreciated the phone messages he left, "Hi sweets. I know you can't get this now, but I just wanted to say, 'I love you,' one more time. So, there it is! All my love forever. Bye my sweets."

He never left a rant in the messages. Just one more thing I loved about him.

During the hours and days on my drive to Joe,

I imagined what life with my husband would be like. Idyllic days, wandering through beautiful hiking trails hand-in-hand. Relaxing days, sitting on the deck, overlooking spectacular vistas, discussing the day's events. Adventuresome days, cruising local waters, exploring islands and bays, identifying the local critters. All my fantasies were about what we'd do together: more little honeymoons. More time to share an extraordinary world. It never crossed my mind to consider the basics: the daily chores, laundry, shopping, cooking, or getting to the gym for a morning shower. Or the tight, dark quarters on a boat in a boat shed. Nor what life would be like with a captain, a man now wearing a tie at work and managing ships from ashore.

Joe would have enjoyed the drive north. One of my colleagues, Neil, had suggested Route 93, up through Montana and into the Canadian Rockies, before connecting with the Alaska Highway in northern British Columbia. Neil grew up in Wyoming, in a National Forest inholding—a patch of private land surrounded by national forest on all sides. He knew the beauty of the wild lands, though he did talk about keeping a rifle at hand, as the beauty had a dangerous edge to it. I had always wanted to see the Canadian Rockies, so I took his advice, though the route added a few hours to the trip—easy price to pay to fulfill an old dream.

In Canada, Route 93 wove between mountain ranges of the Rockies. First was the Columbia Range with the Columbia River to the west, and the Goat Range with the highest peaks of the Canadian Rockies to the east and north. Route 93 ran west of Calgary and Edmonton, entirely bypassing the Great Plains and most of Canada's northern cities. No flat landscapes for this trip. Important rivers watering the Great Plains arose on this eastern flank: the Red Deer, the Northern and Southern Saskatchewan Rivers and the Athabasca. Here, less than 400 miles by flight from the Pacific Ocean, the elevation break of the Rockies forced all the water off the mountains' eastern flanks to wind the long way around, more than 2,000 miles to an ocean, some through the northern plains to the Laurentian Great Lakes and then the Atlantic, and others north, to the Arctic Ocean. From creeks I could step over, these waters traveled the world and I felt like a tiny part of those odysseys. My 2,700-mile trip kept me daydreaming about other travelers, whether human, animal, or water.

Once over the border in Canada, I picked a spot to both stretch my legs and plant the car for the night. In May it was easy to find camping sites because it was still cool, and the campers had not hit in force. Most campers appeared around the same time as the hordes of mosquitoes as summer's temperature animated both.

I slept in the car as protection. Protection from the voice in my head, Mom repeating, "You're all alone. It's not safe." I tried to ignore her, but her voice did travel. I found I could best quiet it when I slept in the car with locked doors. *It was warmer that way.*

My first stop in the Rockies was at Kootenay National Park, which bordered its more famous cousin, Banff National Park, and nearby to its less famous distant relative, Bugaboo Provincial Park. The parks shared views of ice-covered mountain peaks. At the foot of the mountains on the Kootenay side appeared a geological phenomenon that pulled in people from around the world: hot water.

Radium Hot Springs emitted the naturally heated water and the Kootenay National Park provided a public spot for soaking. I wandered into the building after paying my entrance fee. The green speckled cement walls matched most 1950s public institutions. I followed the signs to the women's locker room, though I could have followed the smell of chlorine. *Just like my high school gym. At least I don't have to put on an ill-fitting, one-piece, royal blue gym uniform.*

I changed into my swimsuit before following the

instructions plastered on each wall: "Shower before Entering." The large, shared shower had a dozen rusty, stained shower heads, and was warm and humid, thick with chlorine. They were taking their disinfection efforts seriously.

From the dingy shower, I exited the building and stopped, frozen in awe. Steep canyon walls surrounded me. And at their base was a network of pools. The Canadians had built a huge, outdoor public pool system, broken into different baths with varying degrees of hotness. The Radium Hot Springs powered the swimming baths. The surrounding mountain walls still had snow high on their ridge tops.

It was a hot tub fantasy in the midst of icy alpine heights.

I floated, relaxed in the heated water, and looked up the mountain cliffs. I saw a big-horned sheep walking on a thin scrap of rock. *How did they do that without falling off?* I had to hold onto the handrail walking into the building. Wildlife viewing while swimming. This no longer reminded me of high school.

Later I thought about the name of this mountain range: The Goat Range. The name was a mirror. Swimming in heated water while looking at wildlife on icy cliffs—my childhood dreams of the incredible Canadian Rockies were coming true.

Radium Hot Spring's name did not, however, quite fit the dream. The name's origin was from the radioactive element whose decay product, radon, was found in low concentrations in the waters. In the 1920s, the radiation was a tourist attraction for people seeking healing from hot water spas. The name became tarnished with time and knowledge.

Another detour I considered taking also had a unique name: Head-Smashed-In Buffalo Jump World Heritage Site. I was tempted to see the historic site, where bison were herded off cliffs as an efficient hunting mechanism.

Instead, I continued north.

I reached the spine of the Canadian Rockies. At the south end was Banff and to the north, Jasper. I took time to visit both. First was Banff. After days on roads with few people and little development, I found Banff to be surreal—an alpine tourist shopping haven. Restaurants, ski lifts, gear stores, gas stations, all nestled between endless gift shops. And mountains arising above it all. I ate and escaped.

The next stop, Lake Louise, was home to a classic, high-end ski and spa retreat. There was an enormous parking lot to hold hundreds of cars, buses, and RVs. I joined the crowd walking to the Lake. We all stopped, caught as though trapped on glue boards, as we reached the lake shore. Imagine a mirror reflecting alpine glory. Then add a tall mountain resort to the reflection. That is Lake Louise. I imagined Tolkien's Mirrormere in the Dimrall Dale looked much like this, but without the hotel.

The trail led around the eastern end of the Lake, guiding visitors towards the resort. The crowds moved erratically with kids zooming around groups of adults and the adults moving at drastically different speeds. At any moment, a group would randomly stop for a photo opportunity, which made my walk rather stop-and-go. I'd been alone in a car for too many days to fully appreciate this sudden immersion in humanity. I returned to the giant parking lot, found my car, and fled the crowds.

Between Lake Louise and Jasper lay the Icefields Parkway—a road running in the valley between ice-covered mountains, connecting Banff and Jasper National Parks. The traffic thinned out and alpine heaven was all around. White mountain tops. Blue skies. Green trees. Sharp air with the smell of green. I hadn't realized how invigorating truly fresh air could be. I cut my day's travel short and camped in its midst at Rampart Creek. The stream ran fast over fist-sized cobble and car-size boulders, and its sound sent me to sleep, silencing the Mom-voice in my head.

I stopped in Jasper where the railroad dominated; trains delivered tourists from the east, like a land-based cruise ship. Again, I found this reentry to human masses tough to take. I jumped back to my car. The journey was turning me into a recluse.

The mighty Athabasca River arose just south of Jasper, and flowed northeast, draining glaciers of the Columbia Icefield. Those waters joined the Mackenzie River and eventually the Arctic Ocean. While I didn't want to be around people, I was enjoying my connection to the great waters of the North.

With a left turn at Jasper, I started moving west. I joined the Yellowhead Highway, a northern trans-Canada route named for a blonde beaver trapper, Tête Jaune (Yellow Head), who traveled through the region. Today, yellowheads are common (though not often natural) and beavers are making a comeback. I had to start watching my gas gauge as there were long stretches between supplies. As I drove past the massive block of Mount Robson, the highest point in the Canadian Rockies at 12,970 feet, the day was clear. The Mount sat bulky against the sky, with a rock-layered cap and angled, eroded sides. It was the landscape here, not the human scape, that dominated the surrounding world. I had to keep reminding myself to focus on the driving, not the scenery.

The next major fork in the road came at Prince George, British Columbia. *The Milepost* suggested I cut north and east to reach Dawson Creek, the official start of the Alaska Highway. I, however, just could not bear going backwards—Joe was north and west, not east. I eyeballed my route choices. I chose the western route, west on the Yellowhead, then north on the Cassiar Highway. I didn't take a minute to check the mileage difference between the routes and with that decision, I added 200 miles to the drive. Slow miles. Slow with dips and fissures and mounds from years of frost heaves mixed with long stretches of washboard dirt. Calling the Cassiar a "highway" was like calling Tolkien's *The Silmarillion* a children's book like *The Hobbit*. Travel on the Cassiar required constant concentration. My casual estimate of the distance of this route was an error. The good news was that I didn't have to deal with traffic.

On the Cassiar, nearly 100 road miles from Prince George, I had to decide if I was going to take the detour down the dead-end road to visit Hyder, Alaska (population 77) and its sister town, Stewart, B.C. (population 300). This was the only land link to any bit of Alaska south of the Yukon Territory. The pair are old mining towns, on the east and west bank of the Portland Canal, a fjord of southern Southeast Alaska. Gold, silver and copper mining had mostly ended; the towns kept going with forestry, fishing and tourism. I didn't take the extra time for a visit, which was too bad as it meant I missed Stewart's Toaster Museum. How did 500 toasters get to the end of the Portland Canal? What kind of person saved them all? In a museum? And who would stop and visit a toaster museum thirty-six miles down a dead-end road? These questions kept me entertained for miles though their answers would have to wait for some future travel adventure. I felt the need to shorten my distance to Joe.

The Cassiar lies between the glaciated Coast Mountains to the west and the Skeena Mountains to the east. If I was concerned about gas stations before, now I really had to be careful not to get myself stuck.

At the cut-off to Hyder, I stopped for lunch and for gas at the Meziadin Junction Esso, an all-in-one café, campground, gas, and tire repair station. Its interior, once I found a functional door to enter through, was a maze of different rooms built at different times. The various linoleum types clued me in to its construction history. While I chewed on a burger, through the smudged window I watched a man ride up, on a bicycle. Gear covered both man and bike. Boxes and bags hung off both. The sun was

gnt段

shining on a 65°F day, but the man wore heavy layers of old coats and parkas. He was sweating, using an old bandana to wipe his bald head. He reminded me of an overdressed, cargo-laden Uncle Fester. He came in and started talking, to the wait staff, to the bus boy, to the cashier, or to whomever was close to his table.

As I finished lunch, sitting across the room from him, I learned the reason for his loads. He was talking to the room at large while the wait staff walked past him without a look. "Ya-up. Once a year. I come to town. Once a year. Ge't my supplies. Have a meal. Good meals here. Good coffee. Ya-up. Once a year." The six-year old at the neighboring table looked interested. The six-year old's parents were carefully listening too.

The cashier, who seemed to know him, asked, "Any luck?"

"Ge'tting close. Ya-up. Close. I fig'ur next year. Fo' sure, next year. I come to town next year, I be loaded. Plenty of loonies. Close to it. The claim, ya-up, a good one. Heavy gold close. I can tell. Close. Maybe then I stay in town. After the strike. Then I leave my ride."

I looked at his ride: a thirty-year old Schwinn. I guessed the tire repair station here helped him out more than once.

As I left the café, I heard him again, "Traffic. Too much traffic here. Riding no good. Ya-up. Too many people here." There were nine people in the café. I was glad my recluse transformation had not yet reached the stage of being antsy in a crowd of nine.

I headed north, away from the "crowd." No more electrical service on this stretch of the highway. That might explain why the gas at my next fill-up was the most expensive of the trip: $1.90 per liter, about $6 per gallon. The place used a diesel generator to power its pumps, light its rooms and refrigerate its food. It took petro to pump petro—no wonder it was pricey.

FLOATERS

I hoped to get off the Cassiar and onto the Alaska Highway before I stopped again but I could not keep my eyes open. The rough, twisty road was exhausting. Dease River Crossing gave me a place to camp for the night, open meadows surrounded by deep green spruce, bordered by a fast, clear creek. I got out of my car and was greeted by an overly friendly, gigantic German Shepard. The dog, while trained not to jump up, kept bumping my hand with his head and sticking his nose in my crotch. Attention, he wanted attention. And new smells. Dog entertainment, that was my role here. A man came over, following the dog. I nodded at him as I continued as dog entertainer.

The man said, "He really loves people."

"I can see that."

"It has been quiet early in the season. He's been a little lonely."

"I can tell," I said as I brushed the dog hair off my legs. There was no one else around. I'd seen only a handful of cars in the last 150 miles. Looking around, the Dease River Campground was empty.

I stood and chatted with the man while I petted the dog. The dog was happy to have a camper to play with and I was happy to have a dog companion, even a large, shedding one.

The man finally introduced himself as the campground/dog owner and let me know that he had a coin-operated washer and dryer. As clean clothes, sans dog hairs sounded good, I'd get up early and use that laundry.

I slept in a tiny cabin next to the river. No electricity, no heat, but a single mattress and a lockable door. Mom would have been happy (well, sort of). I was happy about the sleeping situation: the comfort of a mattress that let me stretch out. I lost some of the pleasure as I shivered throughout the night. At first light, I got up to a day crisp and cold, and a change in my morning plans.

The cold snap froze the campground's water supply. Ice blocked the pipe delivering water off the mountain stream. The owner said if I waited until lunchtime the pipe would thaw as the sun warmed it up and the laundry and shower would then be available. I declined. I hit the road again and blasted the heater on full. I got warm and blew away the dog hairs at the same time.

May in northern British Columbia: I was beginning to understand the campers who waited for the summer heat.

Traveling the lonely Cassiar, I kept looking to my left. Just over those mountains, over the ice fields and down the glaciers—there was Joe. In Juneau. As the crow flies, assuming the crow made it over the ice fields, Dease River was only 150 miles from Juneau. Yet I had nearly 600 road miles ahead of me as there were no direct, connecting paths. Of all the wilderness lands that humans have intruded through, we had yet to build a road over glaciers. I heard the Chinese were working on one, and the Alaska Department of Transportation was considering one. But for now, glaciers are a boundary for human land road travel—one of the few left on the planet. While the ice kept me separated from Joe for a bit longer, I did not complain. These lands were a mystery. I was glad such mysteries still existed; it would be a sadder world when all was humanized.

Just over the B.C. border, in the Yukon Territory, I finally hit the "Alcan," highway of myth and legend. *Wow. Five or six cars, all at once! A traffic jam compared to the last 500 miles.* I had to wait for more than a minute for a gap in traffic. Mom thought I'd be alone on the Alaska Highway? Not apparently. There was a migratory fleet of RVs, all traveling slowly, moving north at the start of the summer, with the return migration at summer's end. My Subaru Forester joined the migration and entered the danger zone. The RVs moved so slowly that faster cars lost patience and zipped around them. And in the process, the speeding cars flung gravel that dinged windshields and wrecked paint jobs. The lumber trucks screaming around corners were a bigger risk, but no worse than the ones I had experienced in southern Georgia. I could live with a ding or two.

The wildlife did match the myth of the Alcan. At one point, I had to stop for a grizzly bear and her two cubs. Later, there was a herd of bison in the road. And in the Canadian Rockies, there was a sign that said, "Watch for Sheep" and there, right there, in the road, were sheep. The Canadians did know how to organize.

Finally, after 2,300 miles, I made it to the Yukon. With a childhood filled with Dudley Do-Right cartoons, owning a delight in both moose and squirrels, I had dreamed of the Yukon Territory, isolated and wild. I was hoping I would not have more myths destroyed as this was my lifelong dream of what the real, authentic world looked like. I had finally arrived.

The spruce-filled landscape flattened into rolling hills with distant mountains. Spruce tree diversity shifted to mostly black spruce, a species that could live in poor habitats: extremely dry or extremely wet, low nutrients or high nutrients, or even in the presence of parasites. These poor habitats often caused malformed trees: bent, forked, or bulbous in the wrong spots. Missing limbs. Dwarfed. No Christmas tree shapes here. They might be missing branches and have extra needles bunched at their top. These were not majestic trees like the Sitka Spruce. These were short and skinny, bent and ugly. These were survivors. I liked them. They weren't pretty. They weren't "normal." But they could live in conditions no other trees could survive, and I appreciated that. They were their own form of beautiful.

There were few houses, few villages, very few roads splintering off from the Alaska Highway. The First Nations presence felt strong in the area. The name "Teslin" came from the Tlingit word *Teslintoo* meaning "long narrow waters" which perfectly described the seventy-eight-mile-long Teslin Lake. Museums popped up along the road. Some were no more than a single room with displays, others with beautifully-designed, stand-alone buildings with contents much more diverse than the Toaster Museum of Stewart.

Teslin had an Inland Tlingit history and culture display in the Teslin Tlingit Heritage Center. It also had the Northern Wildlife Museum at the Yukon Hotel with mostly stuffed local animals: bear, moose, and eagle. My favorite museum was the George Johnston Museum; George was an Inland Tlingit who recorded life in Teslin in the early 20th century through his photographs. He was also responsible for building the first four miles of roads in the area, so he could drive the car he imported. During his winters, he drove the car on the frozen Teslin Lake, getting way more driving miles than just upon his short road. George Johnston was a good reminder of how crucial the Tlingit peoples were in building the Alaska Highway. Tlingit paths, trails and roads made the base for the Highway, and First Nations guides helped the US Army surveyors navigate the terrain.

The Alcan's creation was a story of cooperation during wartime. The First Nations, the Canadian government, and the US Army all responded to the threat of Japan's bombing of Pearl Harbor by working together to create what they thought might be an essential road for North American defense. While the road wasn't needed for World War II, it did open up a path for snowbirds and Yukon travelers.

Large rivers cut a geographic thrill for travelers, even though the region's mountains did not rise as high as the Rockies nor have such steep roads. The first thrill was in the middle of Teslin Lake where the end of the Nisutlin River formed Nisutlin Bay which then flowed into the Lake. The high bridge over the Bay had seven trusses and was set with the long lake immediately to the left. On the bridge, cars traveled over fast, turbulent water. I tried to ignore my dislike of driving on bridges as I worked to calm my breathing while my knuckles whitened on the steering wheel.

Just beyond was another thrill, the Teslin Bridge, more than a quarter mile long, over the Teslin River which flowed north out of the Lake. On this bridge, they put all the steel truss material below the road level, giving drivers a sense of driving in the air. As a person who was not fond of that airy feeling while driving, I was not enthused. I would have tried to channel Mom, but she was terrified of bridge driving. I had to manage on my own.

George Johnston also reminded me that whether I stayed north for a year or for a lifetime, I would not have the local knowledge that he had, his family had, and his people had. I would always be a stranger in this landscape. I would never have the privilege of this being my ancestral home. It meant I had things to learn about the region, discovering its shape, its history, and its heart. I smiled at the thought. Even if the landscape and ecosystem were a stranger to me, I would still appreciate what I could learn of it.

After hundreds of miles without cell towers, I got phone contact near Whitehorse. Finally, time for a Joe fix. I missed talking to him, well, until the call connected.

His job must have gotten worse. I heard it in his voice, in the tempo of his words, in his controlled tone. Plus, his first words clued me in, "This #@$%&*@ crazy place! It's spinning out of control." He paused, reigning it in, "And, how are you?"

Calm, Paula, calm. I caught him at a bad moment. I was a bit sorry that I had cell phone coverage. Joe had lost his positive attitude and the phone let me both discover it and share it. Were some things in married life better not shared?

I told him where I was, that the trip had gone well, and ended the call. Short calls meant Joe's crazy-place mentality had less of a chance to trap me to join.

I often mirrored moods of those around me,

particularly to create a conflict-free-zone. This did not appear to be a good survival tactic to life with Joe as Port Captain. I wondered as I drove through the endless bent, black spruce, was it my job, my fate, to reflect his mood? It was great when his mood was positive, warm, and romantic, but when it wasn't? I could cope with bits of his misery, but full-time together? Without becoming as twisted as a black spruce tree? Could I stand to live with Mr. Negativity? I started to rant to myself about the burden of married life. I wondered how much more I'd rant when we were living together.

I watched the forests zoom past me and I calmed myself. Joe was my essential bar against loneliness, even when he was out to sea. He was my heart. My guy might not stay home but he always returned. I focused on the positive and figured that I'd deal with the moods when I had to.

Heading into Whitehorse was a touch out of the way, but I could not leave the Yukon without seeing it.

As I traveled toward the capital of the Yukon, the color of the soil had changed. The land was sandy, gray soil, leftover deposits from the Yukon River. The roadside became banks of ancient river silt. At Whitehorse, the road dipped down into the great, broad valley cut by the wide, fast, old Yukon River that drained an enormous area of North America.

Its waters originated in northern British Columbia and continued to collect waters from most of the Yukon Territory as it flowed north. The River turned west and south, draining the central heart of interior Alaska, before joining the sea at its great delta in Western Alaska. It spanned 2,000 miles, draining more than 321,000 square miles of land, before it joined the Bering Sea in Norton Sound, south of Nome.

Whitehorse grew up on the riverbanks. The river was the heart of the city, making it the transportation hub for the region and linking the railroad from Skagway to the riverboats and roads of the northern interior.

I would have loved to spend hours walking along the river, exploring the cafés and bookstores (more than one!) but I had to be satisfied with a quick view of the capital and the river that was its heart. I needed to put on miles.

Whitehorse was rich with car washes and windshield repair signs, along with body shops ready to take the beaten cars and spiff them back to normal. *Who needed a pristine looking car?* My windshield was fine, and I figured the dirt layers protected my paint from the gravel-flinging.

I left Whitehorse and passed out of phone range. The Alaska Highway kept going, north and west, past Whitehorse, to Haines Junction and around Kluane National Park and north towards Alaska. I wanted to drive that way to have a sense of the enormity of the giant Park, but I did not. I headed south. It was time to leave the Yukon to later explore its myths and legends. It was time to leave the Alaska Highway. There was a ferry that would get me to Juneau if I cut south to Carcross and then into Alaska at Skagway, spending time on the other unique Alaska "road": the Alaska Marine Highway.

US Customs was housed in a small building at an alpine station, almost eight miles south of the actual border. The true border sat at the summit of the White Pass (nearly 3,300 feet in elevation), exposed to harsh weather for much of the year. The practical site south was still in the mountains but had some protection from the worst of the weather. I could see a glacier while waiting for Customs. *This was Alaska.* Skagway was my first town, winter population of 600 and summer population over 20,000, depending on cruise ship arrivals. I was a week early from my original plans as I didn't stick to those 300 miles per day I mentioned to Mom. I chose not to confess my error to her. Instead, I called Joe to tell him of the surprise weekend visit. He was happy with the news.

He then said, "But the boat is a mess. I haven't gotten it ready for you yet."

I responded, a bit sharply, "I don't care about the condition of the boat. I haven't seen you in four months and that is what I'm looking forward to."

I was a bit hurt and angry. *He thought I cared about the state of the boat?* I cared about seeing him. Then, suddenly, I flashed back to the years I'd get a call from Joe: his ship was coming in early and he'd be home sooner than expected. I often (okay, always) said, "But I haven't gotten the house cleaned up yet." And Joe would respond, a bit sharply, "Paula, it doesn't matter." I finally got it now that I was on the receiving end.

Joe said he'd set up my ferry ticket to get me and the car to Juneau but there were hours to wait for the ferry. I got a hotel room to catch some comfortable sleep. The room had this great big bed, with a huge, mirrored closet right next to it. I sadly looked at it, wishing Joe would be here to put the bed to its best use.

I called Joe to let him know I settled in. He said, "I'm running out of the office. Have to go to the boat and pack an overnight bag and catch the ferry."

I pulled in my breath and held the air. I tried to keep my disappointment from him that he'd miss my first days in Alaska at the start of my sabbatical. *I'd been traveling to Joe and Joe was traveling away?* I had an ice pit in the center of my chest. I said out loud, "the ferry?"

"Yeah. I thought I'd come up and meet you in Skagway. We could catch an hour or two in the hotel before the ferry heads south."

"Really?! Great! Wow, I'm thrilled." The ice pit melted away. I should have trusted him. I looked at the bed and grinned.

For the first time in my life, I enjoyed setting an alarm for 2 a.m. when the ferry was due. Joe planned to come to the hotel, the Sergeant Preston Lodge, Room #2. I had given him detailed instructions:

"Walk from the terminal straight down Broadway to 6th Street, then take a left. The Sgt. Preston is on the right side. As you face the lodge office, take the boardwalk to the right. It leads only to Room #2." I knew I was being ridiculous with the specific directions, but I didn't want him to get lost. Didn't want him to be delayed.

Yet I also didn't want to sit and wait.

I woke up to the alarm and shook the sleep out of my head as I threw on my clothes and walked down to the ferry terminal. It was two in the morning and crowds filled the terminal: friends waiting for friends, cruise ship staff waiting for passengers, B&B operators waiting for clients, and, at least one spouse, waiting for her partner.

Even after twenty-one years of marriage, waiting for Joe's ship was still a thrill. I bounced with nervous energy, until I saw him come up the ramp. I flung my arms wide and we smiled and enjoyed a tight embrace then walked hand-in-hand to Room #2 in the Sgt. Preston Lodge. The ferry didn't leave for three hours. Tomorrow I'd be in Juneau on the boat, but I already felt like I was at home. I had made it to Joe.

6 Alaskan Logistics

Float: (v) to vacillate

May 2004

I'd like to say it was like coming home: the harbor, the boat shed, the carpeted Styrofoam step, home with my husband. Not quite. To paraphrase Bilbo, this was going to be more along the lines of "There, and back again, and back again, and back again."

Joe carried three of my "critical" bags. He strode down the ramp, hands filled with bags, his eyes straight ahead. I carried one light bag, clutched the handrail, and stared at my feet. Joe was well ahead. I minced my way down the cleats built into the ramp, sure that I was going to roll down the steep slope.

Joe stopped and turned back, looking up at me, "Here, I can take that bag."

"No, I got it." He had three; I should be able to manage my one small one. "I'm just slow—it's pretty steep. This must be really low tide."

He looked at me, eyes crinkling as he worked not to smile, slowly shaking his head, "Ummh, no. The tide has another five feet or so to go down."

I paused, blinked, and looked around. The Grand Canyon trails weren't this steep. I did not remember it being this bad last Christmas but, maybe, I just ignored certain challenges? Clearly, when carrying stuff down to the boat, I was going to have to plan around tide tables.

Joe continued, "The City of Juneau is planning a harbor refit, and this ramp will be replaced with a longer one. That will help."

"Is that happening any time soon?"

"Sorry, no."

I would have to dream of the day when the practical effect of The Pythagorean Theorem, complementary angles, and trigonometry, acted in my benefit. A squared + B squared = C squared. If they build a longer ramp—longer hypotenuse—then the angle becomes less acute, and I would feel less like I'm about to take a header down to the ocean. Walking down a short hypotenuse with a sharp acute angle was challenging, at least for someone who could trip on a nanoscopic bump.

That weekend we joined a BBQ at the Douglas softball fields with much of the same colleagues from the winter potluck. I paused to marvel at the twist: socializing with Joe's colleagues, not mine. Having grilled meat, canned beer, and picnic tables while meeting his colleagues. And meeting them more than once. More than a quick drink at the bar closest to the dock with a couple of the sailors off the ship. My world with Joe had shifted.

Lora gave me a big hug, "You came back!"

I said, "Sure, of course I did!"

"Winter on the boat didn't scare you away. That's great!"

"Hey, I learned I needed warm slippers and a few extra blankets. And Joe let me warm my feet against his legs—I was all set."

Lora laughed and hugged me again just as Kathy and Larry walked over. Lora said, "Joe must be so happy you are here!"

Larry said, "He's been talking about you getting here for weeks."

Kathy added, "And, Paula, if the boat gets too difficult, we do still have a room."

Lora nodded, "Me too!"

My smile was on the short side, "Thanks but I should be fine—ready for the next adventure." This conversation was a bit like talking with Mom; I refused to show fear.

Lora and Kathy looked at each other and then back at me. Kathy said, "Let's make sure you have our phone numbers, just in case."

After the BBQ and with a new stash of phone numbers, we headed back to the boat. Time to move a clean-up project along. Joe apologized that more hadn't been done, and I reassured him that I did not expect miracles. There were so many boat projects. I was just glad the crucial ones were moving along, like getting the battery on shoreside power so it could recharge. No more wondering if the toilet flush would be the last!

As usual when we just got together, we filled the time. The storage space on the boat was a project: to be cleaned, to be emptied, to be drained. Moldy, damp cabinets did not create that homey feeling.

I left anything sensitive to damp in the car, which was most of it. My car was going to be my storehouse, which was good, as it looked like I was soon to be on the road again.

On the boat, I cleaned out three lower cabinets. Bleach was a wonderful invention. Joe preferred Simple Green but I gagged on its artificial pine smell. Cleaning chemicals that induced vomiting were not my first choice. Bleach and soapy water removed the moldy smell, leaving just the odor I was beginning to associate with the *Pilot Project*: a diesel/saltwater scent. Joe didn't think there was a scent at all; I think his nose had been dulled through overexposure.

I handed him a cushion from the main salon, "Here, smell this. Put your nose right up into it."

He did and said, "What, what's the issue? I don't smell anything. What do you smell?"

"Me, I smell diesel fumes. Not overpowering but definitely there. And a bit of sour salty smell too—like a sea breeze that's been trapped indoors for a few years."

Joe laughed, "Fuel and ocean waters. I've spent my life around those, no wonder I can't smell them anymore." He paused and the smile left his face, "Is it a problem for you? We'll be sleeping on these cushions until we get a mattress."

I flashed a quick smile, "No, I'm fine. I'll adapt. I'll just think of it as the new smell of home. How's the pilot job search going?"

Joe's eyebrows squished together and then he laughed, "Pittsburgh, Paula, Pittsburgh."

I blinked at him for a second and then joined his laughter. We had an old rule to reduce confusion, when changing topics in the middle of a conversation, we needed to raise our hand and say "Pittsburgh" as a clue to a topic change. Smiling, with my hand up, I said, "Pittsburgh. How's the pilot deal going?"

Joe continued, "SWAPA has about sixteen pilots. They periodically vote to decide if they want to bring in a new trainee."

"How do they decide?"

Joe shrugged, "Who knows? I'll send in a resumé and then hope they like it. Vince suggested again that I meet up with different members and connect with them."

"Connect? How?"

Joe shrugged again, "Letter? Phone call? Email? Not really sure."

"Sounds like schmoozing is in your future."

Joe did not respond and turned back to cleaning the cabinet. While Joe was charming and people liked him, the concept of forcing a relationship was entirely alien to him. Even repugnant. He did not want to have to sell himself, but it looked like that was the deal.

I cleaned out under the steps at the entrance to the salon. The teak tread of each step would lift off, opening a 2-foot-by-1-foot storage space below. Living in a 33½ foot boat, each little bit of storage space was gold, but also required regular moisture removal, or, if you waited too long, regular mold removal.

Joe worked the forward V-berth, repacking plastic storage bins. The joys of Rubbermaid tubs with tops: no moisture entry, no mold formation! It was handy having him in the forward berth while I went to the aft end to work. When we had to move around each other in the main salon it was an intimate bump and grind. Fun but not efficient.

I moved toiletries into the teak cupboards on the side of the mirror in the head. Well, I tried to move them. I could not lay a toothbrush in that cabinet as the cabinet was not long enough. A bathroom cabinet too small for a toothbrush! The countertop was at least big enough to fit a toothbrush but there wasn't also room for Joe's. We'd have to share. I thought it would be good to use extra bleach on the countertop.

I stopped to gaze upon the door to the head. It needed nothing. Smooth, curved top, all solid teak. Wonderful brass hinges, dark and solid. I stood there smiling as it reminded me of the door to Bilbo and Frodo Baggins' home, Bag End. But unlike Bag End, grotesque, old fiberglass surrounded this beautifully crafted door. Fiberglass walls with brown streaks, bloated fibers, bits of mold that filled the gaps.

My smile disappeared. Was this head the perfect dichotomous representation of the coming sabbatical year and life with my husband? Two, mutually exclusive categories nearly co-existing: charm or revulsion, joy or misery, romantic chats or angry rants. For the first time, my certainty about joyful married life that included living together wavered for a second.

I didn't want to think about it. *Everything was fine.*

I started taking a hard look at the kitchen, *no, no, the galley,* that I ignored last winter. With a year on this boat, sooner or later I'd need the kitchen.

While I didn't like to cook, it was going to get expensive to eat out for every meal. The tiny, smaller-than-a-dorm fridge had space for four yogurts and a quart of milk, which would cover breakfast, especially with the drip coffee maker. Lunch? Peanut butter and jelly worked well but it was going to get old seven days a week. I could cram sandwich meats into the fridge. And the smallest jar of mayonnaise. Sandwiches for lunch would work. Dinner?

I yelled, "Hey, Joe," hoping he'd hear me as he was shifting stuff around on the dock, "I'm thinking about cooking options. Does the stove work?"

There was a three-burner gas stove with a tweensy-tiny oven. That could work for a hot meal or two.

Joe poked his head in the salon and said, "It's gas."

"Yes, and so?"

"I don't know how good the gas lines are. I didn't set up a propane tank to them because I didn't want us to die in the middle of the night."

"Ah, death from gas line failure, no, not desirable."

"Plus, when you burn propane, it adds moisture to the air. We are better off without added moisture."

I was trying to imagine the amount of moisture added to the air from burning propane compared to what was added from living in a temperate rainforest. I decided to focus on the gas line danger: no hot meals on the *Pilot Project*. That did suit my level of interest in cooking but not my financial situation or tasting preference.

Joe continued, "Sweets, it should be okay. I'm looking at a really nice marine BBQ that would fit up on the outside railing on the fly-bridge. We could barbeque burgers and hot dogs up there. Might be a nice way to end the day."

"That sounds great, my sweets."

"It's a nice BBQ. Stainless steel. Runs off propane—outside propane—so it won't kill us."

"Outside, non-deadly propane, yes, that sounds good. What does a stainless-steel BBQ cost?"

"It won't be cheap. After all—"

"Yes, I know, this is a B.O.A.T. Those marine stores have to make their money somewhere."

We both laughed. I was always glad we shared a "comfortable" attitude about money. And even more glad that we made enough to pay for our less-than-frugal ways. Or, had made enough. I was trying to ignore our financial condition.

We had four days together in Juneau before it was time to travel. As Joe was searching for a pilot position, we were going to be spending more time apart. Pilotage trips, Coast Guard exams, and schmoozing opportunities had to be fit somehow around Joe's normal workweek. Which meant travel. He needed to get observer trips in the SWAPA region, in part to prepare for the exams and in part to demonstrate his commitment to SWAPA membership. Plus, he could meet up with SWAPA pilots, the people who had to vote him in, along the way. When you spend thousands of dollars and your precious weekends to train, that might prove commitment to SWAPA voters. I had the freedom to tag along, to be his driver in between airports and ships, working on my manuscript along the way. And

I'd reap periodic library visits.

I adjusted my expectations of what this year of living with my husband was going to be like. As usual, it was going to be unusual. Not quite the full-time immersion into married life that I had expected. Luckily, I enjoyed the chance to further explore Alaska, with or without Joe. I was going to play logistical aid to Joe's weekend travels, traveling around the enormous, road-limited Alaskan landscape.

Alaska is vast. In Michigan, they move their hand to describe the complicated shape of their state. Alaskans do the same. A right-handed fist with an extended index finger and thumb, thumb pointed downwards while elbow points up, forms the basic shape of the State of Alaska. The index finger represents the Aleutian Islands, the thumb Southeast Alaska. Ketchikan is at the tip of the thumb, Juneau is above the knuckle, and Yakutat is where the thumb joins the hand. The mass of the hand is the rest of the state. And that mass is roadless beyond Anchorage, the Kenai Peninsula, Fairbanks, and a link to Canada and the Yukon Territory, without counting ice roads and four-wheeler tracks.

The hand analogy fails because it doesn't include the Kenai Peninsula, over 100 miles long, and 100 miles wide at its widest point. The hand needs a slab of skin near the base of the index figure to represent the Kenai Peninsula. According to the US Geological Service, the Kenai Peninsula is a Cape—a projection of land extending into a body of water. The body of water is the Gulf of Alaska, and the projection of the peninsula created Cook Inlet to its west. The Kenai Peninsula needed to be on the hand-diagram, as the home of nearly 10% of the human population in the state. And it's on the road. Alaska: where having a road that connects to other roads is a big deal.

The Alaska road system extends south from Anchorage to the eastern and southern end of the Kenai Peninsula. The Kenai Peninsula Borough has the state's second-largest concentration of people. That is less than 60,000 people living in a land area equal to that of Massachusetts and New Jersey combined. At the end of the road lies Homer, home of Vince and Tracey, and SWAPA's office. My plan was to leave Juneau and head towards the road system, Anchorage and then Homer, to taxi Joe around between pilotage trips.

Joe told me the day after I left, "Hey, people at work say I smile a whole lot more when you're in town."

I laughed. I'd been told the same when Joe was at sea. Dennis, friend and lab tech from graduate school, let me know, "Paula you are so much more pleasant when Joe is in town." I took Dennis' comment in the best possible light.

I replied, "I'll see you in two weeks. Hopefully, some of the smile can linger a bit."

"It always does, Paula."

I did love that man.

Joe couldn't drive with me because he didn't have the vacation time to take off work. He'd jet to his pilot training location and I'd travel by car to meet him nearby, or to transport him to a more distant port. This gave me more opportunity to explore Alaska, and I didn't have to live on the boat alone. I wasn't quite feeling up to that yet. The boat still had too many hidden storage compartments with too few bleach applications for me to be entirely comfortable. Plus, it was a boat. I preferred being confident in my skill set before I needed them at 2 in the morning.

The ferry from Juneau first stopped in Skagway, just fifteen miles from Haines. The two towns were separated by complex topographies. The Takshanuk Mountain Range, the Lutak Inlet, the Taiya Inlet, and the Ferebee Glacier and Valley all squeezed between these two tiny towns. That made a ferry ride the quickest way to travel between them. Tourists would rent a car to complete the Golden Circle Route. They circle from Skagway to Haines by road, through Whitehorse and the Yukon, and then ferry to complete the loop. My car had to work around the crowded tourist reservations. Instead of being able to get off in Haines, which would have given me a shorter drive to Anchorage, I was forced off in Skagway.

I did not complain. The route was spectacular and it would give me a chance for more time in Whitehorse. Out of Skagway, I drove through a steep, long alpine pass with high alpine lakes and deep green, old-growth spruce. The road paralleled the land the goldrush folks moved through. I only had to drive the car while they had to move 1,000 pounds of supplies up a pass over 3,200 feet high. This was also the land of the Tlingit People who used the areas for trade well before westerners obsessed over gold. Moving across these mountains meant climbing from sea-level to more than two-thirds of a mile high in about 30 miles of trail. And the steepest bit was near the top, with about 1,000 feet of elevation rise in the final half mile. This was steeper than the Aurora Harbor ramp at low tide. The goldrush climbers or the Tlingit people had no handy ramp cleats to prevent sliding off though they did dig steps in the snow. I was appreciative of my car and the paved road.

Before I left Skagway, I called Mom to update her on my road trip. I should have realized that her response was not going to be encouraging.

"Paula! Driving alone in Alaska! That doesn't sound safe."

"Mom. It's fine. There are plenty of good roads. And plenty of gas stations."

"Well, I would hope so!"

"The *Milepost* lists all the stations so I can plan where I need to stop and gas up."

"Paula! You have to plan where you stop and get gas? And you are all alone?"

Dang, I walked into that one. "Mom, it's fine."

"I thought this was supposed to be the year of you and Joe living together."

"It is, Mom, it is."

"Doesn't sound like it."

"Did you expect us to lock ourselves in and not leave the boat? We still have to live our lives."

"You sure don't live a normal married life."

"Mom, you'd be surprised if we did. We never have."

"Paula, you just be careful out there." She paused, "When does Joe get back with you?"

"In about a week."

"You be careful until then—and don't run out of gas!"

Ending the call, I worked not to feel like I was sixteen years old again. Mom had a hard time imagining her children could be competent at something. I reminded myself, once again, I didn't have to live with her worry; it wasn't mine.

I made it back to Whitehorse three hours after Skagway. The Yukon Territory had 35,000 people; 25,000 of them lived in Whitehorse.

I remembered being a kid and looking at a map of Canada, thinking about the big "empty" areas to the north of the Canadian provinces, imagining a distant land with Mounties, Sasquatch, and packs of wargs, a land I hoped to reach someday.

It was a joy having made it.

Walking along the banks of the Yukon River in downtown Whitehorse, I imagined the wilds where all the water had come from. And the wilds beyond.

I sat outside and watched the streets, the tourists, the cafés and bookstore. The face of many buildings had 19th-century-style wood, each bright with a different color. The old paddlewheel steamship, the *SS Klondike II*, was permanently sitting as a National Historic Site, on the river's bank. She no longer moved supplies and people along the river, but she still represented the heart of Whitehorse, the hub of the North.

I took an evening to celebrate the completion of my childhood dream, grateful for the chance to walk the banks of the mighty river, grateful for the mystery and exploration, grateful for the feeling of accomplishment of that little girl's dreams. I found no Sasquatch in town, but I did get to see a giant sculpture of a Mountie, along with a few real ones in patrol cars.

I left the next morning, driving West. From Whitehorse, the ancient river silt lined the roads most of the way to the next stop, Haines Junction. This was truly a junction, with giant signs directing travelers to the correct road: right to head to Tok, Fairbanks and Anchorage, or straight for Haines and a ferry south. Gas was crucial as there might be 120 miles before the next fuel in either direction. Haines Junction had a wealth of gas stations and convenience stores, at least three of each.

The town was the entryway to Kluane National Park, the enormous Park I was sorry to miss on my drive last month. This day, I took enough time for a stop in the National Park Visitor's Center.

The highlight of the Center was an enormous physical map of the region. I wanted to run my hands over the jagged topography, to touch the top of Mt. Elias, to feel like I had been to the highest point in Canada. That was probably why the Center fenced off the map—too many grubby hands. The Center had ecological dioramas of the plants and animals' habitats, providing a display of what people were unlikely to see from the roadside. As with most museums in the North, there was a selection of stuffed animals. Those too were kept well out of reach. The golden eagle was hung from the ceiling; too high to touch but allowed a visitor to feel connected to the wildlife.

The philosophy seemed to be that if you cannot keep animals alive in cages, or have enough wild ones roaming around for people to see and appreciate, then keep them stuffed so people can still appreciate them—and maybe help save them. Such a conundrum. Such an irony. Kill them and stuff them because we love them. Kill them and stuff them to save them.

The other critical component to the Visitor's Center was its bathrooms—inside, heated, with flushing toilets. These were in short supply elsewhere on the road to Alaska. The more traditional, outside, unheated, non-flushing toilets were in the parking lot.

The Milepost should include a special map of flush toilet locations for those people with overly sensitive noses or an aversion to cold butts.

From Haines Junction, I drove along the eastern border of Kluane National Park. Coming down a pass, a lake appeared on the right. At first, it seemed the lake was small; it was immediately next to the road's edge. Then, as I raised my eyes and looked north, the lake became an eternity pool. Unending, on and on to the horizon. Surrounded by mountains on each side, Kluane Lake stretched as far as I could see. Massive. The road sometimes just skirted the edge between the lake and the mountain, and I felt like I could fall into either.

In the forty-five miles along Kluane Lake, there were only two human outposts, Desolation Bay and Burwash Landing. Mountains and the wind-blown lake encompassed the world. This was not a lake for a comfortable little canoe paddle. This was not a lake for a summer swim. As I drove, I imagined I was moving along Tolkien's Long Lake as Bilbo and the Dwarves headed toward the Lonely Mountain. The wind whipped down Kluane Lake, driving white caps on water that never got warm.

After an hour, the Lake ended. I was back in the

land of scraggy black spruce. My next goal was the Canadian/US border, to enter the interior of Alaska. But before I could get there, there were frost heaves.

I think there should be an adventure tour guide entry: Come north and experience a truly bad road. See what the force of freezing water can do!

People paved the road, but they weren't in charge. Geology, climate, soils, and hydrology controlled this road. It was another dose of reality to human hubris. Earth processes are usually slow, but here, where humans are few and climate is extreme, those processes are immediate and obvious. Summers of 90° F to winters of negative 60° F, along with areas of permafrost, made it tough to sustain the human-built without a truckload of maintenance money. The road was saying, *You can travel here but this land is the master.*

As my car ate the miles, my mind rambled. How do people survive here? How did the indigenous peoples survive? How is the moose population doing? The wolf population? The big-horned sheep and the mountain goat? Populations thriving or in decline? What's the role of the grizzlies on prey populations? What behavioral responses do all these mammals show to biting flies? How does the fauna and flora change with elevation? With precipitation and standing water? What's the impact of nonnative species like the dandelions that sprout in any bit of disturbed soil? What are the native pollinators and how do they manage the short summer season? When climate change hits, how will these relationships shift? Prey and predator. Soil and water. Pest and host? The land was a wonder to me, so many mysteries in an intact ecosystem. I hoped humans would not simplify this one.

I hit the US and into Tok. Another place with gas stations, windshield repair options, convenience stores, a few motels and restaurants, surrounded by straggly black spruce. Fast Eddy's, a diner connected to a hotel, had something not available in over a thousand miles on the Alaska Highway: a salad bar. It wasn't a great salad bar, but it had fresh vegetables, most of which had never been frozen.

Tok was far enough away that it was a town without chains: no McDonalds, no Subway, no Arbys, no Taco Bell. Fast Eddy's was ideal, where the restaurant cashier was also the hotel clerk—very efficient when you plan to stay overnight.

Past Tok, nearing Glennallen, home to billions of mosquitoes breeding in the puddles above the permafrost, I called Joe when I hit a cell phone patch.

He sounded good. We reviewed the pleasure of the last weekend that had been a special treat for both of us. I then made the mistake of asking about the job.

Joe responded, "I have to start looking around to find something else that I can stand."

"Bad day?"

"It's impossible to get anything done, to be effective with anything. Nothing I do fixes anything, it's just patch work to solve the crisis of the day. It's like using duct tape to fix a leak. I can't stand it."

While this didn't surprise me, as I never expected Joe to fit well behind a tie and a desk, I had a bad feeling. "When you say you can't stand it … ?"

"I've got to get out of here, get a new job."

I choked a bit and asked, "You're going to leave, leave before next May? Leave before the end of my sabbatical?"

"I can't stand it, even until May."

"You'd leave Juneau and ship out?"

"Anything to get out of this insanity."

I became queasy and my heart pounded so much I felt the thumps in my jawline. My joy for this sabbatical year with Joe disappeared. Poof. Gone. In its place, white hot outrage rolled in, making me instantly sick.

I lost cell phone service before I had a chance to communicate my reaction.

I could live with Joe changing jobs, even Joe hurting his chances to get into SWAPA, that was his career, his choice. I was mad because I had just moved out of the Huntingdon apartment for my sabbatical year. I had sold the house last fall to fund this adventure and keep Mom in her condo. I had adjusted the fundamental structure of my life, our life, to do this sabbatical year with Joe. And now, less than a month into it, Joe didn't think he could hang around?

I did not plan to spend my sabbatical living alone on a rundown boat with a limited number of toilet flushes in a miserable shed with otter poop somewhere in southeast Alaska without my husband.

I liked authentic adventures, but I had my limits.

I spent the next hours on the drive ignoring the landscape and worried at the problem. I rarely shared my anger with Joe and I didn't know how to do that well. We never had angry confrontations in the few months we had at home together. How could I best share my reaction? In a way that Joe would know how upset I would be, yet not worsen the situation?

Joe's tendency, one of his fundamental character traits, would be to dig in his heels when told what to do. On this one, if he became tenacious and quit right now, then my anger could become a permanent part of the relationship. I wanted the marriage to succeed so I needed to find a remedy.

I could not tell him what to do, but I could tell him my reaction if he suddenly quit. I would not be pleased, seriously not pleased. I had sold the house, moved out, sold off a bunch of possessions, all to fund this piece of our life and he was going to walk away from it?

Driving from Glennallen, my mood matched the scraggly spruce.

I still had over a week before meeting Joe in Anchorage, so I took the turnoff to Lake Louise. The Lake was sixteen miles north of the Alaska Highway, down a dirt road surrounded by black spruce. This was not the Lake Louise of the Canadian Rockies. This was the Alaskan version, more than twenty-times bigger than the Canadian lake.

There were signs to resorts and campgrounds, along with an unusual concentration of "For Sale" signs. After bouncing down the rough road, I found a campground overlooking the lake. To my left I saw one of the resorts—again, not the Canadian, idyllic alpine style. This resort had randomly boarded-up windows and chipped paint. It reminded me a bit of the boat shed. It looked beat upon. The large, old, for-sale sign added a depressing mystique. There was no one else here—no one human at least.

I opened my car door and stepped out. And I got hit. Surrounded. Engulfed. Biting flies, everywhere. As an entomologist, I had collected biting flies on three continents, in most kinds of habitats. This was a new experience. I had seen huge numbers of mosquitoes in the salt marshes of the Carolinas, but this onslaught was different. There were more kinds of biting flies all together than I had ever seen in one spot. Mosquitoes, not surprising. Black flies (buffalo gnats or white socks), also not surprising. Add in moose flies, and a smaller type of horse fly, and no see-ums, biting gnats, and Lake Louise Alaska became a special place for biting fly pain. Here were the largest to the smallest types of biting flies, in the millions, and they were all out, starving, and active.

I was no longer surprised at the lack of people— these flies would have sucked them dry.

I jumped back into the car. I had to keep the windows up otherwise the flies would have exsanguinated me. I could just imagine the State Trooper phone call to Joe, "Sir, I have some bad news. The moose flies got your wife."

No. I was a professional entomologist, I refused to end that way.

The only problem with keeping the windows up was the temperature. This might have been Alaska and there might be local permafrost, but the air temperature was 90° F. And the sun wouldn't go down until midnight. And there were no clouds. Hot, sunny, and trapped. I could run the AC, but I knew the engine exhaust would attract even more biting flies to the car as the carbon dioxide would pull them in. There were few choices here. If I turned back, it would have been another hour on that rough road and then another hour back to Glennallen to possibly find a place to stay. If I drove forward towards Anchorage, it might be hours before finding a hotel. Exhausted, I chose to stay and sweat in the car.

I climbed through the car and set up my sleeping bag in the back, and laid down, with knees bent. The windows had to stay closed to keep the flies out. I was trapped by bloodsuckers, cramped, sweating, angry at my husband, overlooking Lake Louise next to a dead resort. I felt like I had entered a Stephen King novel.

I fully understood all the "For Sale" signs. Sometimes escaping from a miserable situation was the only choice. I hoped this was not a portent for my future with Joe.

7 Bounces

Float: (v) to automatically adjust a parameter as related parameters change

June 2004

The drive from Lake Louise to Anchorage was painful. The road conditions hurt. Frost heaves, road construction, and RVs were exhausting. My mood added to the pain level.

I hesitated, but I finally called Joe when I reached Anchorage. I was loath to call not knowing his mood nor how the conversation would go. I had to let him know my reaction to him moving out of Juneau and leaving me at the start of our year together, but I just did not want to go down that path.

"Paula, let me play you this phone message I got today."

Was it a crazed captain or an annoying Coast Guard lieutenant? Some ridiculous part of his current job? No. It was the training director from SWAPA, responding to Joe's first schmoozing letter. He was positive, helpful, and welcoming. I smiled in relief.

My mood continued to improve when Joe said, "I can hang 'til May Paula, I can."

The tightness relaxed and I could breathe again. The anger slipped off. My queasy departed. No major conflict! Joe had figured out how to continue.

My eyes closed. Managing a life together was harder than I had thought.

I hoped to make it to May too.

The next day, Joe landed in Anchorage where I met him at the airport. We chatted about my drive and his week. It was another fine homecoming. I warned him off Lake Louise, at least without top-quality mosquito netting. Then, just a few hours later, I dropped him in Whittier so he could complete a pilotage trip in Prince William Sound.

Prince William Sound is a huge, complex body of water, three times as big as San Francisco Bay. On the hand-map, it lived northeast of the Kenai Peninsula and about 500 miles west of Yakutat, between the flap of skin and the base of the thumb. The Sound is a compilation of islands, bays, and peninsulas, surrounded by ice-covered mountains. Imagine a fjord. Now multiply it by six and jumble it up. Add random islands. Put in three towns and ten times as many glaciers.

Prince William Sound's human footprint is small. Its three towns are spread apart. Whittier is the westernmost, Cordova is the easternmost, and Valdez, the northernmost, lies between the other two. All three are unique.

Valdez has the highest snowfall of any city in the world yet is still an ice-free port. Oil flows down from the North Slope of Alaska, through the Trans-Alaskan Pipeline to Valdez, where oil tankers come to sail it away. On good days, Valdez connects to the road system; on not so good days, new snow or fresh avalanches block road access.

Cordova is a fishing town. A pro-development governor once tried to connect the town to the road system but the majority of Cordova residents were uninterested. They had the Alaska Marine Highway ferries as their main transport link, and they didn't want the hassles that a road would bring.

Whittier does connect to the road system, but via a one-way tunnel shared by the Alaska Railroad. The State carefully controls access to the tunnel, requiring cars and trains to wait their turn, for each direction. This meant driving to Whittier meant timing the opening of the tunnel.

Glaciers have more of a presence than people in Prince William Sound. College Fjord is packed with them: the terminal point for five glaciers calving into the Sound, close to five valley glaciers, and surrounded by a variety of smaller glaciers. Cruise ships love College Fjord. In 1899, John Muir and members of the Harriman Expedition were first to record descriptions of the glaciers. Harriman decided to honor select ivy-league colleges with their very own glacier: Amherst, Barnard, Columbia, Harvard, Vassar, Williams and Yale—all were immortalized with a named river of ice.

Joe needed to learn these names and a million other details of Prince William Sound to prove he knew the waters before he could even start training as a pilot. The most infamous feature that all pilots had to learn was Bligh Reef.

Bligh Reef was named after the First Mate who sailed on Captain Cook's ship that brought the first westerners to the region: Navigator Bligh. This was the same Bligh who became the notorious Captain Bligh of the *Mutiny on the Bounty* some years after his Alaskan travels. Two centuries after its naming, the *Exxon Valdez* ran into the reef, adding more notoriety to the name. Mr. Bligh had a bit of a black cloud hanging over him; I hoped it never shadowed Joe.

Pilots had to be experts on the dangers of local waters, which meant Joe had to become knowledgeable about Prince William Sound. Pilots learn through experience, by sailing on the waters, studying the navigation charts, and observing on the bridge of a vessel transiting the waters. Once Joe had sufficient time at sea observing a particular area, then the Coast Guard would allow him to stand for testing. And once he passed those tests, there were others required by the State. Then he might be allowed to start the intense part of the training: driving ships while under the eye of an experienced training pilot. Assuming of course that SWAPA voted him in. About 50% of the trainees who start the process don't make it through to completion. Joe was just at the beginning, and, even in the best-case scenario, had years to go.

When I dropped Joe off in Whittier, he jumped on the *Aurora*, a ferry of the Alaska Marine Highway, to be an observer on the bridge as the ferry sailed to Valdez and Cordova and then back again. Joe needed twelve observer roundtrips before the Coast Guard would allow him to sit for an exam. He got two of the twelve on his first long weekend on the *Aurora*. This was going to be a long, expensive effort, just to get to the point of testing. All of his vacation days, his weekends, and a big chunk of our retirement savings were going to go into this. Yet SWAPA had not yet voted Joe in. He had no assurance that the effort would pay off.

He was again risking an uncertain path.

While he sailed, I visited Homer to see Tracey, then back to pick him up for the return. For the month of May my life revolved around the map of Alaska, driving, writing at night, planning the next day, planning where and when I could next catch up to Joe. It was great. This was like a concentrated series of honeymoon sandwiches—a few days apart and a few days together. Intense and fulfilling. I was glad this wasn't going to last too long. A rapid bounce between life-with-Joe to life-on-my-own would ultimately wear me down.

Joe's job bound him to his desk in-between weekends and vacation days. My sabbatical gave me the freedom to explore. Our worlds had been transposed. In his blue-water sailing days, I was bound to the usual workweek life and he had the freedom to explore when he was home. This was a marvelous change for me, but, for Joe? I didn't have to ask him. I knew. He showed me most every day: it was miserable for him.

Periodically, I popped into his office. Each time, the post-it notes surrounding his computer screen seemed to be multiplying. I made the mistake of mentioning that and he mumbled, "Wait until you see my emails."

He had Outlook folders upon Outlook folders and as I watched the emails just kept flooding in. It looked like an email spam attack, but it was just regular communications. In minutes there was a whole new list filling the screen. I turned to him, "How do you manage this?"

He laughed scornfully, "Manage? There is no managing. I'm shooting for survival."

I was glad he took every bit of vacation time he had to go on pilot observer trips. The break from the office might improve his chance of surviving the onslaught.

On one trip, I left Homer early in the morning and rushed to make the Whittier tunnel opening. When I got to the tunnel ticket booth, I asked, "When is the next opening?"

The man said, "In about five minutes."

I nodded in relief. If I had missed it, it would have been three hours of sitting here, with Joe sitting on the other side of the mountain.

I passed the ticket agent the fare. He handed me the receipt and said, "Lane 4."

I thanked him and found my way to the spot. Lanes 1-3 had about ten cars each while Lane 4 just had three cars in front of me. Lanes 6, 7 and 8 had a few trucks and large RVs lined up. Once parked, I looked around, smiling at the incongruity of eight lanes of traffic surrounded by wilderness and mountains, no human footprint except for the tunnel. The tunnel entrance was surrounded by a steel A-frame to protect the entrance from snow and smaller avalanches. Nothing would save access from the big snow slides.

Once my lane started to move, I entered the rough rock-hewn tunnel. The narrow passage meant straddling a train track while trying not to hit the tunnel wall. This was worse than a bridge. The 25 mile-per-hour speed limit was too fast for me, but I think the RV behind me was even slower.

I was relieved to make it through the two-and-a-half mile one-way tunnel with no damage to my Subaru. My nerves took a bit of recovery time.

The next challenge was to find parking. Cars, RVs, and boat trailers were filling the lots and street parking nearest the harbor. I drove over to the giant, fourteen-story building and found a spot. Whittier's giant building is where most residents live. The military built up Whittier, first in World War II and later in the Cold War, as a base for military support in the North Pacific. They completed the tunnel in the early 1940s and the buildings in later years, though some structures were destroyed by the 1964 earthquake and tsunami. The City of Whittier purchased all the structures in the 1970s, giving the 200 residents of Whittier a place to live, in the giant building now named Begich Towers. As I parked, I felt the same incongruity as around the Whittier Tunnel: a spot of human development plopped down in wilderness.

I found my way to the ferry dock and smiled as I saw Joe step off the ramp. As usual, our timing was perfect. We kissed and held hands and headed back to the car, just in time to make the return tunnel opening for our drive to Anchorage.

Joe and I continued our tradition of having great conversations on a long car ride. We chatted about future plans and what we liked about Alaska, maximizing our short time together. I gushed about Homer. He spoke about his observer time. Then I had to drop him off at the airport so he could head back to Juneau for a week in the office, while I hung around Anchorage, waiting for his return. I used the University of Alaska Anchorage's Consortium Library for my sabbatical project and I found a cheap hotel.

I learned that I would not recommend cheap hotels in Anchorage in the summer, but it was better than living in the car.

The next Friday night, I picked him up at the Anchorage airport.

He said, "Hey sweets, I pulled some extra time off from work. How about after my observer trip on the ferry, we head down to Homer and visit Vince and Tracey together?"

"Great idea my love!"

Homer, the "Cosmic Hamlet," or "The Halibut Capital of the World," or "The End of the Road." A town of 4,000 with almost as many nicknames. Homer sits on Kachemak Bay, which opens off the southernmost, eastern side of Cook Inlet. The town peers south over the bay, west to the inlet, and southwest to the Gulf of Alaska. The mountain ranges across the bay are topped with glaciers. Ice slowly erodes the mountains. An ancient glacier had carved out Kachemak Bay and left its sediments in a narrow moraine which created Homer's most distinctive physical form: the Homer Spit.

The Homer Spit is a long, thin extension of land stretching out five miles into the bay. It is the southernmost end of the Alaska Highway. The end of the spit is jammed with structures: the boat harbor, the ferry dock, the US Coast Guard dock, a hotel, condos, restaurants, tiny gift stores, fish freezers, charter boat offices, and the Salty Dog.

We stopped in the Salty Dog for a drink and to enjoy the ambiance of an ancient, dark bar, made claustrophobic by its low ceiling. To add to the atmosphere, dollar bills were tacked chaotically to the ceiling, most scribbled with personalized messages. Each year the staff removes most, donating the take to local charities, and, for a time, reducing the fire danger in the bar. As it was summertime, the walls were well covered again.

Two 20-somethings sat at the end of the bar, drinking heavily and speaking loudly. One had hair that was randomly clipped; he was wearing rose-colored reading glasses. The other had a ponytail and was wearing flannels, plaid flannels, mismatched top and bottom flannels—two different sets of pajamas? Both wore XtraTufs: rubber boots, also known as Alaskan slippers. They talked about the fish they had caught, and how they despised acrylic paint as oils were the medium for real painting. Two drunk fishermen at noon talking about art methods—that was Homer. Or at least one of its faces.

After the Salty Dog, we waited for Vince. He was going to take us to his home across the Bay, Halibut Cove, where he and Tracey lived during the summer months. While Joe and I waited for Vince, we walked the harbor, comparing other people's boats to the *Pilot Project*.

"Hey Joe, I don't see any large, carpeted Styrofoam blocks? How do they get up on their boats? Or are we just lucky enough to have a special design just for the *Pilot Project?*"

Joe laughed, "Yes, special, that's us." He seemed to think about it some more and continued, "The wind probably whips down here in the winter. Styrofoam would be blown away; no protective boat sheds here."

"Hey, yes, and no junk scattered on the docks."

Joe laughed, "One of the benefits of bad weather in an open harbor: can't leave anything laying around."

We stopped at one end of a dock finger. Steel-hulled, commercial fishing boats surrounded us, with even larger ones across the harbor. The ice-covered mountains across the Bay were crisp and bright in the sun.

"Does this harbor ice up? What happens to all these boats in the winter?"

"It gets some ice. A lot of these boats get pulled for the winter."

"Ah, could be tough to be a live-aboard down here."

Joe was shaking his head, "I don't think there are any, or at least none that do it on purpose. Juneau and the boat shed, that's a comfortable Alaskan live-aboard place."

"Comfortable," such a relative term.

We caught up with Vince at his boat, the twenty-four-foot *Rhino*. Vince, in his XtraTufs and plaid shirt, waved us over, "Come on aboard. Take a seat inside the house here. Tracey and the boys are over at the Cove already."

As Vince took the lines down, Joe said, "Thanks for the invite Vince."

"Sure, should be fun."

After getting out of the harbor, the water was rough, choppy and chaotic. I was attempting to sit on the padded seat to the left of the driver's seat. It took both my hands and at least one foot to stay in the seat. Joe was standing in the back, calmly using one hand to hold on. Vince's approach to dealing with the waves was to go fast; he explained, "It gets the bounce over with sooner."

Okay.

Vince was enjoying sharing his local knowledge, "This is just the day breeze."

I asked, "Day breeze?" The waves had white caps.

Vince replied, "Yeah, just the day breeze. On sunny days like this, by early afternoon, the heat of the sun moves the air upslope on these mountains plus the cold dense air above those glaciers start moving too. Big pressure gradients form between the land and the sea as the land heats up. Gets breezy, usually calms down at night."

Sunny days bring on large waves? This was different from my East Coast beach experience.

As we neared the southern shore of the Bay, near the entrance to Halibut Cove, the waves calmed a bit. There was a forty-foot ship fishing near the entrance to the Cove. Vince turned to us and said, "Hey, that's my brother-in-law's boat." He quickly spun the *Rhino* to head over. I was barely able to stop myself from falling out of the seat with the sudden change in direction. I looked back at Joe. He was planted, casually holding on with one hand. I realized a life at sea built those strong legs of his, along with extraordinary balancing skills.

Vince said, as he pulled up to the *Creel*, "I don't know if Tracey got anything for dinner, so I'll pick something up for us." He put the bow of the *Rhino* up against the *Creel*'s steel hull then he went out on the *Rhino*'s deck, and yelled up to the *Creel*'s gang, "Hey, have you caught anything good? I could use a couple of nice ones."

The gang tossed two salmon down and Vince popped them into his cooler. Vince yelled his thanks, went back to the controls and we headed back towards the Cove. This time I knew to hold on in advance of his maneuver.

Vince chortled, "Great way to go grocery shopping, isn't it?"

When we got to their home in Halibut Cove, Tracey was standing at the top of the ramp, her long blonde hair blowing in the day breeze, waving us in. We joined her at the top of the ramp and walked along the boardwalk to their home overlooking the Cove. Vince then handed Tracey the cooler with the fish, saying, "I stopped at the *Creel*."

Tracey replied, "Sweet. I wasn't sure about dinner so I dug some mussels. We can have fish tonight and the mussels tomorrow."

Vince said, "Sweet!"

Joe and I looked at each other and smiled. Sweet indeed.

It might have been that weekend that I began to fall in love with Homer: sitting on a deck, eating the freshest of fish, watching eagles and otters, laughing with friends, watching the alpine glow against the mountains at midnight. I soaked up Tracey's stories of her balancing her law practice, her two kids, and her life as a marine pilot's wife. Life did not get much more authentic.

After a few days, Joe had to head back to work, and I stayed on with Tracey. She and I were sitting at The Saltry, the only restaurant in the Cove, sipping gin and tonics poured from a pitcher on the table and chatting with another friend, Dave.

"So, Paula, where are you living now? You seem to be on the move."

"I'm about to settle in one place for a year."

"Oh, a whole year!"

I detected sarcasm here. Since Dave was originally from Connecticut, sarcasm was highly likely. I said, "I'm living with Joe."

"That's new."

"Yeah, we're experimenting."

Tracey pipped in, "Tell him where you are living, Paula."

"In Juneau." Tracey nodded her head, looked at me with raised eyebrows. I filled in what she was waiting for, "On a boat in Juneau."

"What kind of boat?"

"A trawler yacht. 33½ feet. Teak and rotting plywood inside with a fiberglass hull."

Dave took it in stride, "That sounds pretty standard." This guy has lived in Alaska long enough to find rotting marine plywood as normal.

Tracey added, laughing, "They're sleeping on a table."

He squinted and looked pained, "Ooof."

Tracey added to the visual, "Yeah, sex on a table, imagine."

I joined the joke, "Tough on the knees."

Now we had Dave blushing, "And once again the conversation quickly gets out of hand with you Tracey, and now you too Paula." He smiled, shook his head and changed the subject, "We have a show at the East End Bar in two weeks; I'll be on guitar and my bandmate Sally will be on fiddle. Will you be around Paula?"

"Dang, no, I'd love to, but it's time to get back to see Joe."

"Maybe next time … I hope there is a next time. You are a fun addition around here."

* * *

Sleeping on the table was an issue not because it was uncomfortable. The salon table in the "down" position, at the same height as the seating bench, gave enough space for a bed for two, though calling it a double bed would be an exaggeration. While I could barely straighten out my legs, tucked in the bench with Joe on the outside, it was warm and cozy and soft enough with cushions. Plus, Joe regularly gathered me in his arms and moved my cold feet against his legs to encase me in warmth. Those joys and comforts, however, came with tradeoffs.

Table sleeping meant the table didn't work for other things, like writing, the reason for my sabbatical. Or as a surface for tools to fix the boat. Or for making dinner. Or eating dinner. We had only one bench for seating, though if we pushed the bedding out of the way we could fit in a second seat. My food prep surface was limited to the two-foot square countertop. Raising and lowering the table was not simple or quick—usually sailor language was involved—so we kept it low.

If we could find a mattress, we could use the salon for all those other purposes and sleep in the aft cabin. A mattress would solve another problem: the cushions falling off with any "motion" while we were on the salon table "bed."

I was coping with the diesel-scented, unstable cushions as a sleeping base, but if I could find a solution, I'd take it. Joe would still warm me up in his arms, whatever size of mattress we had. Like most boat things, getting a boat mattress was not simple. Or cheap. The mattress had to fit in the aft cabin, which had space for a true, standard double bed. However, it had to get into the aft cabin first. And the only way a double mattress could make it through the tight entrance was if it could be folded. A folding double mattress? The local furniture store was not going to have one. While I had been in Anchorage, I had stopped at an actual mattress store. They had a memory foam that could fold but it would cost $1,500. There were boat parts that could be bought for that price. Though wasn't the mattress a boat part? I kept searching.

I mentioned the mattress problem to Tracey and she suggested NoMar, a small boat canvas fabrication store in Homer. Sure enough, they sold a four-inch foam which would make a reasonable mattress and made a marine canvas mattress cover to fit. And all for less than the memory foam. Finally, an essential boat part for under $1,000!

I was ready to get back to life on the boat, life with Joe, and particularly life on the boat with Joe and a mattress.

8 Staying in Place

Floater: (n) a spot interfering with vision

June-July 2004

I picked up the NoMar foam and drove for a few days, backtracking through Glennallen and Tok. I did not stop at Lake Louise, having learned my lesson. I had a ferry reservation at Haines to return me to Juneau. Joe had finally completed his twelve Prince William Sound Observer trips and no longer needed my taxi service. I could return to the original plan: living with Joe on the boat in Juneau.

Joe was also happy about the mattress as it was another step in the eternal boat project. We hauled it out of the car in the Aurora Harbor parking lot. This took special care because the lot was dirt with puddles of various depths, made up of various liquids. We found a good parking spot close to the ramp, good meaning more gravel and less mud. The worst parking spot was next to the dumpster; that not only had big, deep puddles but also extra fluids from rotting fish. It was best to stay far away from that spot. Especially when carrying a giant piece of foam that could all too easily suck up liquids. I did not wish to sleep with the scent of old fish heads.

We safely completed the transport and Joe said, after sliding the mattress into place, "Looks great."

I replied, "Yes, it does." I chose to ignore the hideous aft cabin walls of stained, gray fiberglass. Or that the person sleeping nearest the hull would be leaning against them. *Paula, just ignore those dried up drips of … of whatever. Ignore it. The drips are stuck there and won't fall on your head when you sleep. And Joe's side of the mattress is closest to the hull—you don't have to deal with hugging the hull at night. Just look at the comfy mattress, Paula, focus, ignore the ick.*

Joe said, "Okay, now we need some sheets 'cause the ones I have won't fit."

I replied, "It's okay love, I picked up sheets in Anchorage. I didn't want to delay our testing of the new boat part!"

Joe laughed. We found the mattress worked as expected.

* * *

The Aurora parking lot was fascinating with more than just legal, registered cars and dripping garbage dumpsters. There was also the waste oil drum, helping to keep oil out of Alaska's waters, if it was emptied frequently and used properly. People often just left open containers of oil, hoping someone else would take on the messy job of pouring it into the drum. Imagine a plastic dish pan filled three-quarters high with oily sludge. And now imagine it outside in a temperate rainforest. Rain happened and muck followed. The oil waste drum was next to the porta-potty and sometimes people used the commode for oil (or other) non-human waste products. People could be pigs, but at least they didn't dump straight into the ocean.

Next to the porta-potty and oily waste drum was the steel bin. Joe loved checking it out each time he passed. Me, I just stared at Joe wondering what the heck was he thinking? This was another example of our differences. The steel bin was the metal recycling spot. Have an old engine that didn't work? Dump it in the steel bin. A broken water pump? Into the steel bin. Mangled propeller? Old batteries? Rusty wires? I saw a scrap-metal recycling loop in operation. Joe saw a treasure chest. While we were both correct, I thought Joe had plenty of projects already on his plate. Refurbishment of someone's trash on top of the *Pilot Project* projects? That might explain all the stuff scattered around in the boat shed.

Boat life with Joe fell into a pattern during the work week. Joe got up about 5 a.m., set up coffee for me, and left after giving me a quick kiss. I stayed in bed until a more reasonable hour arrived. Then coffee, but only after checking the electrical amp demands. With coffee in hand, I wrapped up in a blanket with my computer, writing, or more often, thinking about writing while doing something else.

As the space was so tight, if my computer was open then any books I used had to go on my lap. If I wanted to write with pen and paper, I had to shift the computer around on the table or move it to the bench. My reference books and notes filled the two 2-foot-long shelves of the teak bookcase built into the bulkhead dividing the salon from the aft cabin. Each day when starting writing, I'd pull down the notes I wanted and then when my writing time would end, or when lunch would start, the notes would get packed away again. My writing set-up and take-down sometimes felt like it took more energy than my actual writing.

Part of the day's decision was whether to go to the gym or not. For most people that is a question of whether it was a day for a workout. Life on the *Pilot Project* meant that the decision was also about what the tide looked like, what the weather looked like, and if I wanted to slog through the conditions for a shower. The boat's "shower" was not functional, usable or desirable, at least from my perspective. Joe used it. And then everything in the head got wet … toilet paper, toilet seat, towels, deodorant, makeup, toothpaste, hairbrush, anything not relocated or enclosed in the minuscule cabinet. I found it unpleasant to shower in a tweensy-tiny space where you could barely turn around, especially as the state of the fiberglass walls reminded me of a horror movie. And mold was always a concern. And the hot water was undependable as Joe frequently shut off the hot water tank for a project in the engine room. Plus, water supply could run out entirely once the freshwater tanks were empty. I would only consider showering on the *Pilot Project* as a desperate remedy to filth. I did not plan to ever be so grungy. The gym shower had a dependable, hot water supply in a pleasant, clean shower stall—it was clearly the winner.

I liked adventures but I was discovering my tolerance limits to life on a small, cramped, expensive floating house with mold issues.

I'd walk to the gym, six blocks down from the harbor. While there, I'd decide on the next steps for the day: back to the boat or on to buy groceries. The gym was close to the grocery store, letting me maximize the task-per-block walked effort. As cooking choices were limited, shopping was easy.

The big decision: sandwiches with sliced ham or sliced turkey? Joe had installed the BBQ so I could also choose a meat and vegetable for grilling. But, due to the teeny tiny fridge, I had to be sure to use most purchases in the next day or two. If nothing else looked good the decision would be which restaurant we'd prefer. Groceries were kinder to the budget, but restaurants were the more pleasurable choice, and the more frequent one.

Back to the boat, after figuring out how to stow any purchases, it was writing time. Too often, when I couldn't get any words down, I'd head to the library to read more. When you are writing an interdisciplinary book on water, there is an ocean of information to sort through. Or to drown in.

Some days I'd head to the beach or the glacier or a creek or a lake to let the watery environment soak in. That generally left me flooded with ideas which I sketched out in brief but rarely in depth. My library and real-world stimuli were not helping me to complete the text, but I did enjoy the time.

I learned my writing brain was much like an engine: when it flooded it wasn't going to start. Or it would just putter and fail. Then it was time to switch to reading rather than writing. I had finished my annual read of the *Lord of the Rings* just before the trip and was glad Juneau had a great independent bookstore, Hearthside Books. There I had found *Sten*, a seven-volume science fiction space opera. That would help clear out my brain's nonfiction flood.

Lunch was a sandwich, sometimes shared with Joe as he escaped from his office for an hour. If it was not raining, we'd head to the park next to his office building, down the street from the Juneau salmon nursery. We both enjoyed watching full-grown salmon work their way up a fish ladder, though I tended to focus on issues of turbulence, pressure, chemotaxis and bubble disease—all the aquatic science factors the fish were coping with. Joe mostly thought about catching and eating them.

When Joe got home after work, we'd make the eating decision. We never pressured each other into cooking. Joe didn't expect me to supply food, though he was always happy if I did, no matter what it was. I was always relieved that Joe carried none of the gender-role expectations related to cooking. We would have both been disappointed if he had. In the evenings on the boat, we were both quick to respond to the slightest suggestion to dine out. Our savings account was not responding well nor were our waistlines, but eating out was preferred, particularly with the teensy tiny boat galley and an outside BBQ.

One of the added benefits of eating out was that Joe decompressed from his day as a state employee and that tension stayed off the boat. At least on good days. Boat projects mostly waited until there was a free weekend day. The patterns of our evenings also fell into a pattern: a glass or two of cheap Australian red wine followed by the final routine before sleep. Joe would check the lines if it had been rough and would turn off the salon lights as I went into the aft cabin for a visit to the head and to settle into the bed. I set my eyeglasses on the floor next to me while Joe set his on the shelf at the entrance to the aft cabin. Joe finished turning off the lights then slid in next to me from the foot of the bed. We curled up together, which helped keep Joe off the cold hull and had the added benefit of warming me up too.

* * *

About a week after we got back from Homer, Mom called to catch up. I told her about the mattress success. She told me about her conversation with Chris, a friend of the family living close to her in Vegas.

"I was telling Chris about the boat and the things that needed to be fixed. He laughed and asked, 'How is it a guy like Joe with decades of shipping experience ends up buying a boat that is a wreck! You'd think a master mariner would know better.'"

I was guessing Mom was thinking the same thing.

"Mom, a master mariner has a whole engineering department. Joe's doing this boat himself—and it's coming along." I didn't add what I was thinking, *Slowly, it's coming along very slowly.* But I think she already knew that.

* * *

Some mornings I'd get up with Joe, watching him dress for work. Once he asked, "Hey Paula, would you grab me a shirt and a tie while I make you coffee?"

"Glad to."

His tie selection was limited, as was his shirt collection. I picked a blue and silver striped shirt and held a gray striped tie up against it. I tried a second tie, then a third—very limited choices. I was holding the final tie, blue with tiny Plimsoll marks, thinking it might be okay when Joe came down to the aft cabin and asked, "Paula, what are you doing?"

"I'm coordinating colors and patterns, to have your tie match your shirt. So you don't clash."

His eyebrows raised as he said, "Ooh, that's why

people hold up shirts and ties on TV!"

"Yes." I looked at him, "You never knew that?"

"No. I thought they were looking for stains, to pick the cleaner tie."

"You never considered colors with your tie selection?"

"No, I just picked the top clean shirt and a tie I hadn't worn too often. I might have been careful about stripes, but not colors. This is a new world for me, tie-wearing and shirt-coordination. I prefer the old days of uniforms—well, I really preferred the days when I could just put on whatever was comfortable and clean. Thanks for the match sweets. I probably should ask your opinion for future days. Imagine, holding clothes together to match, who knew!"

I gazed at him with a silly grin on my face. Twenty years of marriage and there were still loads of surprises. My smile faded as I thought, *was that because we had spent so little time together?*

From then on, part of our evening wine drinking included picking out a tie to go with Joe's shirt for the next day. He would never wake me up just to help color coordinate him.

One weekend, we were coming back from a shower/gym/grocery run and Joe mentioned, "When they renovate the ramp, I think they are going to pave the parking area. I hope they don't get rid of the recycling stuff."

I replied, "I would think they will want to have a place to catch most of the waste, especially for the poorer live-aboards who might not have a car to haul it to the dump."

Joe nodded, "I just hope the City doesn't 'yachtify' this place, making it too expensive or too regulated for people trying to get by as a live-aboard."

While I wanted a better ramp and an improved parking lot, I did not want people kicked out of the shelter they pieced together on a boat. The tension of any human development was evident here: comforts and benefits for some, loss for others.

At the far end of the parking lot, down where the lot narrowed and bent, where parking was even more random, the vehicles were particularly interesting. Some had not moved in months (years?) and seemed rusted in place. Flat tires were more common than inflated. In this land of obsolete vehicles, one stood out. It was a white Ford panel van, with an airbrushed sign reading "Boat Repair" and "Experienced" including a painting of an idyllic harbor with pretty boats. Rust and debris maimed the painting as it looked like an axe-wielding monster had been at work. The van's quarter side panels were clearly not original equipment as each had a different color paint. The doors to this "experienced" mobile boat shop were twisted and open. I doubted if they could close. I might have glimpsed a bed in the back, but I wasn't quite sure, and I didn't really want to look too closely.

Later, when Joe and I began to realize the main deck might need work, especially where the otter spraints had laid, I suggested Joe talk to the owner of the Ford panel van. I was such the optimist.

One morning I mumbled, "What time is it love?"

Joe responded, as he slapped on his tie, "5:15 sweets, go back to sleep."

I took his advice.

About three hours later, I woke from a dream. The dream was a new one for me, but the theme was not. I was late for a meeting. Everyone was in the conference room, for a meeting I called. They're all looking at each other while I ran out of the room, to my office, trying to figure out why I called the meeting. As I searched for the agenda, two people came in asking me for stuff. I could not help them either. I was not prepared.

I hated those sorts of dreams. I hated waking up

that way, guilty and agitated at the day's start. My response? Spend an extra thirty minutes lounging in the warm, comfy blankies, giving time for the dream to dissipate. I kept my head under the blankets to block the view of the stained fiberglass walls.

It was the need to pee that drove me out of the blankets, not the guilt from the dream—though that heaviness stayed with me all day. I was struggling with the open schedule of sabbatical. Time to write. Time for Joe. Extra time for life's basic necessities while living aboard a small boat. Then finding recovery time from all of it. I wished the dream would push me to write more but it just weighed me down. I needed to spend time thinking about that group therapy I had at Berkeley.

I hit the head and the toilet flushed—a reassuring sound.

Then it was time to turn on the coffee. I remembered to shut off the heater before turning on the coffeepot, so I could stay in the relative warmth of the shed without having to run out in the rain to flip the breaker.

As the coffee perked, I opened the computer. And stared.

Before we got the mattress in the aft cabin, the computer would go on the cushion pile over the table. Because it was a pain to raise or lower the table each day, the table stayed down, with the bed remaining in the center of the salon. I would write with the laptop balanced on a pillow in front of me on the bed, as I sat cross-legged. This was not a sustainable, comfortable position. I thought I could blame my writing struggle on that as my back would get tired from hunching forward. My legs would get tired from their figure eight. Just two hours into it, my back would be done and I had an excuse to stop writing. With the mattress in place, and the salon back to "normal," the computer sat on the table and I sat on the cushions—still not an ideal writing position as the angles between the table and the seat did not meet any OSHA standards for ergonomic design. Wrists, back and neck started aching, but I could at least get three hours in. Though it might only be three hours of staring at the computer with few words being written.

This was reminding me of my undergraduate struggles, and not in a good way.

At Berkeley, I worked full time, dated Joe, and took nearly a full load of classes. Overly busy and seriously stressed, the quality of my coursework suffered. I struggled with writing papers in a timely manner, such as before they were due, or at least before I'd fail the class. Later in life, as a professor, I had realized how terrible I was as an undergraduate so I tended to be kind to those who also struggled with getting things done. At Berkeley, in the middle of that time crunch, I ran across an invitation for new group therapy sessions on procrastination. I somehow found time to join.

The first session was crowded. And being group therapy for procrastinators, it was also the last time it was crowded. We went around the room introducing each other and discussing our productivity challenges. Most of the attendees were graduate students attempting to finish their theses and dissertations. We talked about what kept us from getting a project done, what kept us from starting, what kept us from finishing. What was going through our minds at those moments? It was eye-opening for me to see I wasn't alone in my struggle to sit and write. Over six meetings we explored how an internal litany of fear of failure led to an inability to work or to complete.

"If I don't get this done, I will fail the class. And if I fail the class, I won't complete college. And if I don't complete college, I won't ever get the job I want. And my future will be pitiful. And my mother will be disappointed with me."

With all that weight hanging on writing, no

wonder I couldn't get a paper done.

I went home that night and sat on my bed in Hoyt Hall and wrote a twenty-page History paper straight through. Twenty pages. Easy. Painless. Enjoyable. Every time my mind went to thinking about needing to pass the class so I could complete the degree, I wrangled my thoughts back to the project at hand. It was a miracle and life changed.

On the final session of group therapy, attendance down to a quarter of the first day, the woman next to me stressed, "This group has not been helpful. I have two-thirds of my thesis done. I've spent eight years of my life on this degree. Two years in London researching the topic. If I don't get it done soon they will kick me from the program. I'd be out. Eight years wasted."

I asked, "Do you have all the research done?"

"Yes. But I can't write it."

I don't think she learned the lesson I did from the sessions.

As I was leaving, I thanked the therapist for the free event and told him that it had made a real difference for me. He said, "You were ready. You were receptive to the idea. You listened. That was not the case for everyone."

That explained the low attendance.

Sitting on the boat, in a shed lit only with a happy light, I needed to again be receptive to the idea of not letting pressures of completion distract me from the work. However, my career status was much different than those undergraduate days. I was a tenured associate professor whose promotion-to-full was already in the hands of the Promotion and Evaluation Committee. Whether I completed this book or not was not going to make a huge impact on my future career status. There was no large push for additional career success.

Life's pressure at this moment was not about what

my future would look like but about managing stress: Joe in working mode, living on a damp boat, in a dark boat shed. Did the lack of a strict deadline and the lack of pressure to complete the work reduce my drive to write? Did relationship and environmental stress affect creativity and productive writing?

I wondered if there was an Advanced Group Therapy Session, for next-level procrastinators?

* * *

Walking down the ramp, I was carrying two grocery bags and Joe was loaded up, carrying a case of wine and four bags. Joe said, "It's so much easier when you are here."

I would have responded but I was too focused on not tripping down the ramp.

Joe continued, "I used to do these grocery runs without the car—walking those six blocks with a grocery load was a pain."

My husband was sure tolerant of pain if he didn't think this activity was difficult.

He continued, "And having you take a few bags is really helpful, thanks love."

I would have responded but I didn't have the lung capacity—even going down the ramp could be exhausting.

We made our way to the boat shed and I dropped my bags to unlock the shed door. Then I carefully stepped over the threshold and over to the boat. *No spraints to tiptoe around today, yeah!* I put my bags on the boat's deck and then I slowly stepped onto the wobbly, carpeted Styrofoam block then up onto the boat. I went around and opened the teak door leading to the main salon. Joe, with his arms filled, just stepped aboard; he didn't use a single handhold. He balanced his load and brought it all aboard and down, into the salon, dropping the case of wine and groceries onto the salon bench. I silently marveled at him the whole way. *What an amazing combination of strength and balance to haul that load. How can he do that?* I took a deep breath and enjoyed the sight of my husband.

Later, we were having our evening wine, a Lindeman's Shiraz, $8 per bottle when bought by the case. It was a deal, as long as Joe was there to carry it. I brought up a topic that had been in my head for a while, "Joe, I'm over forty—"

"No, that's impossible. I'm sure you're only twenty, at most."

I smiled, "You are the sweetest. However, I am over forty and I never expected to get this far in life and not have a dog."

Joe's smile left his voice as he said, "Well, I've been out to sea. I didn't want to come home to a dog that didn't know me."

I nodded in agreement, "I know, I know. Exactly. I know that is why we haven't had one. And that's why I haven't asked. But we are going to be together all this year. We are living together. If we get a dog, it will have time to get used to both of us."

Joe turned away, headed to the forward cabin to grab another bottle of wine, "We can think about it."

I dropped my head and sighed. I wasn't sure how much thinking he was going to do.

With Joe as a state employee, weekends were the center of life, especially when no pilotage trips were scheduled. We had a Juneau Saturday without rain— a magical combination. Joe suggested, "Let's go hike the downtown trails."

"Sure," I replied, though I silently wondered what kind of trails might be found downtown.

The city part of the City of Juneau was crunched: buildings tight against each other and narrow streets tight to the mountainsides and to the waterfront. The State had built large, boxy concrete structures to house government offices, oddly similar to prison architecture. Being married to a state employee made me unduly sensitive to that symbolism.

Beyond the government buildings, a few roads continued up the hillside and the residential neighborhoods appeared, which were also scrunched together. Streets were even narrower. Color diversified as older houses were painted in an enormous variety of hues. Cranberry anyone? How about lavender? And let's put a lime green in there. I felt an appreciation for these residents; they did not fit a traditional mold. They might be state employees during the week, living in the world of bureaucratic white and black mixed into gray, but at home they let their colors show.

The end of the urban appeared suddenly, leading into a narrow canyon that led to a trail. The drizzle started. I bundled my head in my red scarf.

I paused, "Wow, now I can really tell that Juneau is in a temperate rainforest."

Joe peered at me, "What, all the rain we have didn't give you a clue?"

"Hey, I grew up in Buffalo—plenty of rain. But here, these trees, this ground, everything is covered in an extra layer of green. Green moss. On green bark, coated with green algae. Oh, and, look, a giant slug! Buffalo does not have this."

We watched the giant slug for a while as it crossed the trail.

I said, "I really don't care for slugs."

Joe looked at me, laughing, "An entomologist doesn't care for bugs?!"

"Bugs have a nice crisp exoskeleton, generally holding in all their interior gooey things. These slugs, well, their hydro-skeleton lets the gooey things become more obvious."

Joe continued laughing at me. I joined him, "Yes, I know, I'm not being logical. But, look at it. It is leaving a mucus trail. A path of slime. No, nothing appealing about a mucus trail."

Joe said, "So I finally found an animal you don't care for ... mosquitoes, ticks, tarantulas, spiders, worms, horseflies, these are all okay, just no slugs, anything but a slug."

"Exactly!" I poked him, "Nice that we still have things to learn about each other."

Joe took my hand and quietly said, "Yes, one of the many joys of living together."

I sighed and tightened my hold on his hand. We could find romance while slug-watching.

The trail ended in an open area, with a fast-running creek pouring down a mountain and across the valley, and an old, red, mining facility built into the mountain. It had been the Alaskan Gold Mine, until 1944. Today, it was the Last Chance Mining Museum. There were people panning for gold in the stream, looking for their chance.

Joe said, "The mines were largely worked out, but the stream still might have a bit of gold. There are people I know from work who come up here searching for it. They say the stream water may still erode off gold from its resting spots."

"People are rather optimistic."

Joe replied, "Gold fever."

"Well, it's a nice day to spend outside."

"I was up here in the rain a few months ago and there were still people here."

"Gold fever. I hope it's not catching."

The hike back was even nicer than the hike up—all downhill. Joe was always his most relaxed while hiking, engaged in the present. For me, I was also engaged in the present, mostly trying not to trip on something as I wondered about the surrounding ecosystem.

Geology formed Alaska in ways beyond the elevation and waterways. The ores and oil deposits formed its current economy while the landscape formed the household, trading, and subsistence economies of the ancestral peoples. The land and human connection was close and obvious here.

Juneau's shape originated from the mountains. The rise of the mountains created the fjord of the Gastineau Channel. The ice sheet on the top coalesced in the large Mendenhall Glacier. The glacier scraped down the mountains' slopes. Grit and sand and silt came down, especially with the meltwater and rain-water, into the Mendenhall Lake and River. This sediment flow built a river delta fan at the base of the mountains and into the Gastineau Channel, creating wide flats along the seaside, with eagles at rest above. Eagles were especially prevalent near the city dump: all those good smells.

After the hike, sitting in a pub on Douglas Island, I was mesmerized by the landscape across the Channel. The mountains went straight up. Okay, almost straight. Certainly steeper than a 45° angle of repose. Streams of water were free-falling off the mountainside. In other places, with less extreme elevation, those would be creeks. Here they were waterfalls. There were multiple creeks falling off the mountain. It was though the mountainside had suspenders of waterfalls, had fringes of waterfalls, was decorated with waterfalls.

Spruce covered the mountain. These were Sitka Spruce, or, in the Tlingit language, *shéiyi* their needles *ghítghaa*, and when large and old, they were named *seet*. Spruce tips, fresh in the spring or dried or frozen then boiled in the winter, was a common vitamin-rich food for the locals. I used to think of spruce trees as Christmas trees. I now knew better.

Tall trees, up to 180 feet, imperfect with growth in response to neighboring trees, rocks, cliffs, wind, rain, and snowstorms. They were a deep green mixed with pale green lichens hanging off their branches. With broken branches and asymmetrical growth, they leaned off the mountainside while growing toward sun. Hiking among them risked scrapes and bruises, from the deadfall at their feet. Tall and straight with complex branches, the trees created their own boundary: *Here be spruce.*

Spruce covered the mountainside except where it had been scraped. Glaciers, avalanches, or human-made clear-cuts reduced the mountainsides down to gray rock or yellow scrub. Staring into the forest was relaxing and energizing at the same time. What was out there? What might I see? How did it all work? How did it all survive? What's in there? Real, wild, old-growth spruce trees served a wide variety of living things in ways I could barely imagine. This was better than people-watching on the Las Vegas Strip.

"Thanks for the hike suggestion today my love, it was great. I loved getting out into a new forest, a new habitat, a new place."

"Sure love, glad we had the time. And it was nice to hike with you again with the red scarf."

"You noticed!"

"Of course. I'll always notice you in that scarf."

My skin flushed nearly to the color of the scarf.

During the hike, we had walked past stands of Devil's Club, shrubs taller than Joe, with huge leaves over a foot in diameter, clustered at the top. I would have thought they were Dr. Seuss-like plants but for one aspect. They were coated in thorns. Trunk, branch, leaves, all with dense thorns. My appreciation for wilderness and wildlife was changing; they were still a joy but getting up close could be problematic.

Southeast Alaska had Devil's Club that could leave a bleeding trail. Homer had Pushki that could leave a blistering rash. Pushki was also a tall plant with huge leaves, but instead of having thorns for protection, it had an oily phototoxin on its leaves and stem. When the phototoxin got on the skin, exposure to sun could create a horrible, blistering reaction, particularly bad in those who were sensitive.

Everyone was sensitive to the foul piles left by river otters.

How ironic that the cutest of the mammals, or, at least in the running for the Top Ten Cutest, had horrible poop. Fetid. Sticky. Stinking. I think that must be why a long-ago biologist gave otter droppings a unique name: spraints. Sloppy, fishy, squishy, spraints. If poop quality were considered in the Cutest Rankings, otters wouldn't make the list at all.

Our otter fence had collapsed while we were on our Homer adventure. Wind? Poorly installed? Neighbors? Playful otters? Who knows. Our failed fence meant that we found the remains of the otter party when we got back. Spraints coated the dock and the main decks. Otters must have been rolling in them. Their party required lots of human clean-up time, as well as time to refit the fence. Luckily, for me, Joe took on those tasks. There was sailor language involved but who could blame him, after all? I felt very spoiled. And relieved at not having to deal with it.

I was hoping the fence would work. If it failed again, the nail board would be our next choice. Living on a spraint-filled boat and boat shed was not an option. It was hard enough to live with a husband who was unhappy at work, and it was hard enough to write. Adding otter poop was a step too far. Though a nail board was going to give me nightmares—I hoped the fence would work.

Ah, the eternal tension between wildlife and human development: spraints or no spraints.

* * *

Joe opened the slider, coming home from work. "Hey, Phil invited us to go fishing with him this weekend."

I smiled at the normalcy and said, "Phil, the engineer?"

Joe nodded, "Yeah, the one that keeps a secret record on his fishing success. He knows where the fish are and what is needed to catch them."

I smiled at the thought of fishing success. Fishing was the single activity I did with my father that was enjoyable. I still remembered my feeling of success that time when I was six-years-old and caught a little sunfish. A good day of fishing can make up for a bad day of everything else, at least when you are six.

A day out with Phil also meant we could spend the day on the water, on a fully operational boat, getting to see something beyond the boat shed view.

Joe noted, "We will have to bring sandwiches. Phil expects the people he brings aboard to feed him—sandwiches."

"No big deal. We can slap together some peanut butter and jelly …"

Joe interrupted, "No. Phil expects good sandwiches."

I squinted at Joe, "I like peanut butter and jelly." Joe didn't think peanut butter and jelly were good? He had never complained.

"Phil is not going to. He is very particular."

I decided to ignore Joe's apparent opinion about PB&Js and switched to an old story, "As bad as no mayo on the cheese side?"

Joe smiled, "Yes! And, no jalapeños!"

It was a treat to share memories even if it was only my mother's odd requirement for her sandwiches: mayonnaise only on the meat side, never close to the cheese, plus no condiments, never anything spicy like mustard, or heaven forbid, jalapeños. Joe had been trained by her. She trained us all.

Now that I was thinking about my family, "This won't be like packing for fishing with Tim, will it?"

"No. Phil doesn't allow beer. And your brother's idea of 'sammies,' white bread and ham, with a big bag of chips, is not going to do it. Phil doesn't like chips on his boat—too messy."

Fishing with Tim was sounding much more relaxed than fishing with Phil.

"So, when Tim comes to visit next month, sounds like we should not have Tim and Phil go fishing together?" Mr. Particular with Mr. Whatever-As-Long-As-There's-Budweiser might not be pretty.

"Tim is likely willing to put up with a beer-free boat as long it is a boat that catches fish. Well, if they're big fish."

I nodded, then I suggested, "Breeze Inn for sandwiches?"

Joe smiled, "You read my mind."

Breeze Inn had two locations in Juneau, only three miles apart. Both were busy. Both had racks of beautiful sandwiches: cheese, lettuce, tomatoes and loads of meat filling. Choices of bread. Selection of mustard, ketchup, relish, and mayonnaise packages. It was the perfect fishing expedition shop.

The biggest problem for me was that Breeze Inn, both locations, also had beautiful racks of donuts. Donuts. Fancy glazed. Chocolate dipped. Apple fritter. Chocolate cake, with almonds. Or with sprinkles. Old fashioned glazed. Donuts were a problem for me.

If I had one then I had two, and if there were more, well, I'd have more. Stopping was a challenge. My 12-step donut addiction solution had only one step: never be around them. I learned that step the summer before I started graduate school.

Joe and I had been married for a year and I finally finished my degree at Berkeley and would start graduate school at University of Massachusetts Amherst in August. Joe had headed to Cape Cod for his dream job with Woods Hole Oceanographic. I got a summer job in the libraries at the University of Buffalo, and I decided to stay with my grandmother in her South Buffalo home for part of the summer. Nana was a donut person. She had them in the house, every single day. She bought them by the dozen so she wouldn't run out. And she loved to have family eat her food. Here I came, unable to resist the siren call of sweet fatty treats. She had jelly. Cinnamon sugar. Glazed. Chocolate cream filled. I still dream of those. Nana would order the occasional white-iced, heart-shaped pastry, just to mix it up a little. I gained twenty pounds that summer, in my first major shift from curvaceous to roundish. I never lost those pounds. Nor my donut addiction.

I risked entering the Breeze Inn for beautiful sammies. I focused on the floor as I walked past the donut racks. If Boromir hadn't looked at the Ring, I bet he would have lived.

We met Phil at the Auke Bay dock, another one of Juneau's marinas, this one feeling a touch more upscale than Aurora, based on the lack of decrepit boats. Auke Bay was small, tucked directly east of the north end of Douglas Island, south of the Lynn Canal, and with openings westward, towards the outer coast islands. The day was sunny and the water calm—ideal conditions for one who tends toward seasickness.

We found Phil's 24-foot boat. I looked at it and could see no renovation projects in the works; his boat looked immaculate. Phil greeted us, "Come aboard! Joe, you sit here. Paula, over here."

Once he seemed satisfied that we are in correct spots he interrogated us, "Those bags? Sandwiches? And what else do you have in there?"

I said, "Sandwiches. Just sandwiches and three bottles of water. And I brought my camera."

Phil looked at the bag and looked at me and looked at the boat. *Did he want to search my bag?* Finally, he said, "I've never had someone with a camera on board before."

Was he going to send me back?

Phil at last decided, "Okay, you take the camera bag up there with you, away from the fishing poles. Sandwiches go in this cooler. There isn't room in there for the water. Keep those in the bag. Don't let them roll around."

I began to understand this was to be an engineered outing, entirely under Phil's control.

Phil continued, "I'll bait the rods and put them in the rod holder. Joe, you watch this one. The one in the center is mine. Paula, you watch this one, on the port side."

Fishing on Phil's boat was rod-watching, not rod handling. I could comply but I was struggling not to sigh.

Phil said, "I don't want any lines to get crossed. I've done this with lots of people—I know how it needs to go. I'll put the bait on and release the line. We are going to troll for salmon. If you see your pole move, I'll set the fish and then you can do the rest."

Phil's version of fishing was that he brought people to do the work of bringing the fish aboard, as well as to provide sandwiches.

I asked, "Phil, when your wife is in town, does she go fishing with you?"

"Not anymore."

Phil's wife had followed him up to Alaska when he first started with the Alaska Marine Highway, after he left the military where he was a maritime engineer, a career that kept him away from home much of the time. She didn't spend long living with Phil in Alaska. She headed back south, and they visited periodically. I wondered if he had as many rules at home? Did he try to engineer the household? That would certainly be a tough transition from the solo-phase for a sailor's wife. Did she get tired of living with a sailor who came ashore?

I chose to ignore that train of thought.

Phil motored the boat to the center of Auke Bay, set the bait and precisely readjusted the poles. Then he sat and studied his notebook before setting the boat's speed and direction. Joe and I looked at each other and raised our eyebrows. Joe quietly said, "He does know where the fish are."

We started trolling, slowly moving and pulling the baited lines behind us. He told us this was the perfect speed to convince salmon to bite the bait and that he had learned this after hours of study. Phil was orchestrating all aspects of this event, or was making the attempt.

We were still in Auke Bay when the water erupted with what looked like thousands of jumping salmon. My smile felt like it would break my face. Giant wild Alaskan salmon, jumping all around us!

Phil's back was to me. I don't think he saw the fish eruption at the stern, and my rod bent so I moved to grab it. I had a fish! I started to reel it in, and Joe helped me steady the rod, letting me take ownership of the moment. I had the fish almost out of the water. Phil rose from his concentration on his notebook and noticed us. I was looking down, smiling at the biggest fish I had ever caught. Fishing success reached just as we started. I was almost as excited as my six-year-old self with a sunfish.

Phil jumped over, grabbed my pole, yelling, "No, no no! Eew, no! Eeaawwww! These are dog salmon. Eew. No, get them off. Off my boat!"

I was frozen in shock. What the heck was he talking about? Are salmon on the boat dangerous? Do these bite people? Are they diseased? What is his problem?

Joe reacted to Phil's temper by bringing up all the lines and stopped fishing to stop Phil's outburst. Phil cut my fish off the line, contemptuously tossing it back to the sea while muttering "Pftt." My mouth hung open. I had no words. A grown man just said "Eew" about having fish on his boat. A grown man who was out fishing just threw away the biggest fish I had ever caught. The world had gone mad. I looked at Joe and he just shrugged, probably thinking, *His boat, his rules.*

Phil cleaned the deck of any possible dog salmon residue, muttering, "I hate those dogs. Disgusting. I sure hope we don't pick up anymore. No more lines in until we get over by North Douglas. I had good luck there for Kings this time last year. No disgusting dogs over there. Dogs aren't even good for dog food." Phil sounded like a salmon monomaniac with significant fish prejudice.

He just threw back the biggest fish of my life, that he called "disgusting" and I didn't even get a photo.

"Pftt." Phil made the Bill-the-cat sound again. *He threw my biggest fish ever overboard. Pftt to him!* I turned away from the rods, turned my back to him, and looked forward to the wilderness ahead. I lost all interest in fishing.

Looking forward was a good move. I had begun to get queasy with the motion of the boat and watching the rods behind me. I did not want to see Phil's reaction to a seasick passenger; he might be more melodramatic than "Pftt." I knew though that Joe would calmly deal with any outcomes of nausea.

West from Auke Bay and those "disgusting" dog salmon, we headed around the north end of Douglas Island. The western side of Douglas was undeveloped, with edges of the island a dream of a future developer, or a dream of the local Tlingit people to keep their ancestral land whole. The central core of Douglas was Tongass National Forest, just like the rest of SouthEast Alaska where the Tongass makes up 90% of the land mass. To the west of Douglas was Admiralty Island, which had an embedded wilderness region inside the national forest as well as a small town, Angoon, on the far west side. Admiralty was the site of the world's densest population of brown bear. I think Joe's worst nightmare would be to land there.

Mercifully, we had no boating troubles that would cause us to land on Admiralty. Phil found a place he thought was dog-free and he and Joe fished their rods. I pulled out my camera just in time to miss a shot of a humpback whale breaching ahead of us. I sighed and slumped. It was one of those days.

Joe channeled Jacques Cousteau, "Zee wily ocean wildlife confounds ze adventuring photo-grapher once again."

I laughed, straightening, letting the gloom escape with the joke. I kept my eyes on the water with camera in hand, returning to hope: one of these days I would get the shot.

Phil was looking at us crossly; apparently we were not concentrating on fishing in the manner in which he expected. Then, his face cleared, and he said, "Oh, I guess photography would be another good activity to do out here. I should start taking notes about good places to take pictures." He returned to his notebook and left us alone.

By the end of the day, Joe and Phil had brought back two beautiful king salmon, each weighing over twenty pounds. I had zero photographs of wildlife nor of the biggest fish of my life, but at least I didn't get seasick.

About a week after the Phil fishing event, we were lounging on the flybridge after a lovely BBQ of the last of the salmon. The salmon had been delicious, especially with Phil's tasty butter, garlic, and lemon recipe. Phil was a pain, but he did know his fish cuisine. We had the canvas curtain completely open to enjoy the rare sun and to throw more light into the boat. Between the light and sitting on the open top deck, I could easily pretend this was spacious living. Our boat shed neighbor had taken his boat out, so the shed felt especially roomy.

I said, "It would be nice to take the *Pilot Project* out sometime." I didn't want to pressure Joe. There were multitudes of boat projects and his life at work was stressful, but I wanted to hear his plans on using the boat as more than a house floating on the water.

"Yes, I'm looking forward to that. I have to check out the engines first though. Kathy and Larry are going to come over. You and Kathy can hang out while Larry and I get greasy. I need Larry's engineering advice."

I was happy to hear a plan though it sounded like Phil's boat would have to be the source of future fish. Luckily, I enjoyed hamburger.

"Hey, here comes our neighbor! I had never seen their boat move before." On reflection, I rarely saw noncommercial boats here move. If the owners were state employees, their available time to go sailing was short. And considering maintenance needs of boats, well, it was a miracle anybody got to sail theirs.

Our neighbor Tom was steering and his friends were waving at us as they were coming in. Then the smiles froze. The waving motions turned towards Tom to get his attention, but Tom already saw what was about to happen. I looked at Joe and he knew it too. Tom had a tight turn into the shed and he did not make it.

His boat slammed into the *Pilot Project*.

I heard a bunch of "oofs," including mine, as I grabbed something to hold on to. Joe quietly stood there—no handhold needed for him. Tom's boat rode higher in the water than ours so what he hit was our stainless-steel railing. No hull damage, at least to our boat.

Tom reversed to attempt to dock it again and made it on his second try. Tom was apologetic,

"Gosh, so sorry! I tried not to hit! I hope I didn't damage anything!"

Joe was casual, "It's fine. A bit of a ding on the stainless-steel, no issue at all."

"Are you sure?"

"Yes, it's fine, really."

"Here, let me give you some of the halibut we caught ..."

I could see Joe was about to turn down the fish so I quietly suggested, "I think when someone offers halibut the best response is just to say 'yes, thank you.'"

Joe laughed and said, "Tom, sure, that sounds good—Paula suggested that my answer to a gift of halibut is to always just say yes. Thanks."

After Tom and his group tied up and left the shed, I turned to Joe and asked, "That boat hit ... any worry?"

Joe looked at me and shook his head, "No big deal. This is a strong hull and he just dinged us. He wasn't going all that fast and he mostly caught the railing. It's all good Paula, no problem."

That reassurance made it easier to appreciate the dinner of halibut on the BBQ, with Phil's butter, garlic, and lemon recipe and Tom's fish. Who needed to sail a boat when you could sit there on the water and have halibut delivered right to you? At least on the rare days when the state employees had time to get out on the water.

* * *

Tim and Joe enjoyed each other's company. Early on, Tim thought Joe was perfect, even-keeled, always helpful and calm. And then we had the day with the Falmouth Harbor Master and Tim learned more of Joe's complexities.

While I was still in grad school, Tim, Joe and I visited Joe's parents, who lived in a house on the water in Falmouth, Massachusetts. Joe's older brother actually owned the house, and owned the small boat moored off of it. The eighteen-foot boat with outboard was good for a short day of fishing if the water was calm and if the engine worked.

Joe's Mom asked Joe to take the boat to get fueled. It was a lovely day, at least to start, so Tim and I joined Joe, as sunny and warm made a nice day to poke around Falmouth Bay. At the fuel dock, things began to go south as the boat would not restart. Joe got angrier and angrier, using every sailor word that he knew. People on the crowded fuel dock were also not happy; too much swearing around their kids. Tim and I were silent. Finally, the "piece of crap engine" started and we headed back to the house. No more poking around Falmouth Bay. Joe's temper had not cooled; he gunned the boat, probably so he could get off it as soon as possible.

Problem was … that part of Falmouth Bay was a No-Wake-Zone. Joe was definitely producing a wake.

Just a hundred yards from the safe, terrestrial, boat-free world, there appeared in front of us the Harbor Master. He headed towards us, with flashing lights just like a police car, but on a boat.

Now, a sensible person would have slowed down.

Joe did not.

He continued pushing the engine. And, for extra measure, he drove straight toward the Harbor Master's boat.

I was white-knuckling the side of the boat, ready for a semi-suicidal, murderous crash. At the last second, Joe turned the boat, slammed it into reverse, stopping just next to the Harbor Master's boat.

It was an excellent example of boat handling, other than it was also terrifying. Other than Joe, everyone's eyes were wide with shock and surprise.

Joe calmly spoke to the Harbor Master, "Having

engine problems. Have to gas it to get it to the dock, just over there."

The Harbor Master spluttered, "You are tying it up just there?"

Joe nodded. The Harbor Master paused then waved us on. I think all four of us felt a large relief that we were getting off the water. Tim said to me later, "Joe actually does sometimes have a temper. Glad that he isn't always perfect. I like him even more."

* * *

One evening after work, I gave Joe Tim's flight arrival information. Joe brightened up and said, "Great! And he is bringing Diane and Sarah?"

"Yes."

"How old is Sarah now?"

"She's about five."

"I think they will have to get a hotel. I don't think they would be comfortable on the *Pilot Project.* "

"I think they already planned for that." Diane had heard stories of the boat. "I pointed them to that little place that has a kitchenette, might be cheaper for them."

"The Driftwood? Great idea. Diane can set up their meals there. We can BBQ on the boat, go out to Mendenhall Glacier, maybe take a tour to Tracey Arm, do all the tourist things. Paula, this should be fun!" Joe sounded happy to show off his Alaska to them.

* * *

Joe came home and I looked up and said, "Hi sweets. How was the day?"

Joe mumbled something and slammed his keys on the counter.

Not a good day.

I calmly said, "I have ham and cheese ready for sandwiches for dinner. Want some?"

159

Joe started spewing about the job, the work, the misery.

My patience was limited that night, and I snapped, "I just asked if you wanted dinner."

"I don't."

I sniped back, "Thanks for the reply." And that was the last of the conversation that night. The normality of seeing my husband come home from a day in the office was losing its luster. We could not escape from each other on the boat. Silence added an entire wall.

I glanced over at the tiny bookcase in the salon and saw my three well-read volumes of The Lord of the Rings and I suddenly drew in a breath. Paula, your relationship with Joe is like your relationship with the LOTR. You will never again have the initial glamour of its first read, never again have that first meeting with Joe. Shoreside, there won't be the anticipation of him flying in or you tracking down his ship somewhere. With him ashore, it's just the day on repeat. If I don't have anticipation, what is there?

Would I lose the enchantment I had felt in our short honeymoon periods that had made up our time together? What would this relationship be without the exuberance of initial magnetism paired with moments of intense reunions? When we didn't have the novelty and rarity of being together?

Had we floated too much through our twenty-year marriage to be able to make a real partnership?

I spent the next day at the library, immersing myself in something other than married life on a tiny boat with an unhappy husband and too many unanswered questions. I stayed away until the library closed so I got home later than Joe.

On the salon table, there was a vase of flowers and a card. "I love you and I apologize," with Joe's signature.

I asked, "What are these for?"

Joe replied, "I was a real smuck last night. I'm sorry."

We hugged. I was happy he came out the other side of the misery. The boat didn't have room for the silence barrier.

* * *

"Hey sweets, I'm home!"

Joe didn't have to yell very loud as sound traveled easily down the 33½ feet of the boat. I was in the head so he couldn't see me, so I yelled, "I'll be right out sweets," glad that he sounded bright and cheery, and, wondering why he sounded that way. It was a measure of the condition of life with my husband at that point: I was expecting him to be miserable.

When I came out, after giving him a hug and kiss, I asked, "So, what's up my love?"

"I just took three days off, for Tim, Diane and Sarah's visit. I can meet them at the airport with you and spend time with them too."

"That's great!"

And that visit was a joy as Joe and I played tourist along with Tim and his family.

We explored Mendenhall Glacier Visitor's Center together, amazed at obvious glacial retreat.

Tim managed to deal with Phil's rules on Phil's boat and caught some salmon, enough for a beach-side grill and to send twenty-pounds back home.

Sarah gave Joe a new title: "Funny Uncle Joe." She bestowed that title on him the first time he ran through his one-man play, using a folded napkin for his costume.

FALSETTO; NAPKIN AS A BOW ON THE HEAD

"But I can't pay the rent."

TENOR; NAPKIN AS A MUSTACHE

"But you must pay the rent."

FALSETTO; NAPKIN AS A BOW ON THE HEAD

"But I can't pay the rent."

TENOR; NAPKIN AS A MUSTACHE

"But you must pay the rent."

BASS; NAPKIN AS A BOWTIE

"Here, I'll pay the rent."

FALSETTO; NAPKIN AS A BOW ON THE HEAD

"Oh, my hero!"

TENOR; NAPKIN AS A MUSTACHE

"Curses, foiled again!"

Joe repeated his performance a few more times that week. Sarah giggled every time. I think I did too.

A few weeks after my brother's visit, we were back in the pattern, with Joe coming home stressed from work. His vacation days had been used up and the desk job grind was full-on. As the bank account was not responding well, we were attempting to eat on the boat more often, but it did not help that our menu choices were getting old: cold sandwiches, grilled meat and fish. I had mentioned the boat's cooking limitations to Kim, the wife of one of Joe's colleagues, and she followed through with a gift: a George Foreman grill.

"Paula, I never use it. Take it, really. Just take it. I can't stand the idea of you not having hot food on the boat. Go ahead, take it. Have a grilled cheese."

"Oooh, grilled cheese. I do love those. Thanks Kim."

Two nights later I was experimenting with hot

food via George. Joe came home and found the grill was on and partially open, with a foil bowl inside. The only room for the grill was on the front shelf in the main salon, or what might be called the dashboard, under the front window. Or what Joe might use for navigation charts. "Paula, what is that?"

"I decided I wanted some chili. I made a foil bowl to hold it. As long as the top doesn't come down and crush it, the George Foreman should heat it up perfectly."

He mumbled and I took that as agreement. He looked all around the dashboard. I think he was looking for spilled chili getting into his navigation equipment. He didn't say anything, probably willing to take the risk for the sake of hot food.

I did discover a limit to this new cooking method: it took amp power. More than once the breaker snapped—two heaters and the George Foreman overworked the 20-amp service. I had to run out to the breaker box, off the boat, out of the boat shed, to snap the breaker back. I needed to add George to my appliance list for amp oversight.

* * *

Joe came home. "Hey, Paula, guess what happened today!"

I hesitated to guess. Union strike? Captain quit? Employee complaint? New bureaucratic disaster? "You are just going to have to tell me as my imagination is out of control."

"The Governor decided that Ketchikan needs more industry."

"Okay ... ?"

"He is from Ketchikan and wants to help it out; after the mill closed, the city has been pretty depressed."

"Okay ... ?"

"The Governor is moving my office to Ketchikan."

"What?! Wow!"

"Yeah, at the end of the summer, the entire office of the Alaska Marine Highway is moving to Ketchikan."

I gawped at him. The sabbatical year of living with Joe was becoming more complicated. I was just getting used to Juneau's issues in amp management, parking lot dangers, and ramp trigonometry. I unfroze a bit and replied, "Well, I guess it's good we live on a boat."

Joe laughed, "Exactly what I was thinking. We can just sail our home south."

It sounded so easy.

9 Boat as Transportation

Float: (v) to be viable

Late July 2004

My great unspoken question: was the *Pilot Project* capable of sailing? Joe started the engine occasionally and it seemed to be fine. At least for the few minutes he ran it. It obviously could float as well—there was no water getting into the bilge. But the boat had not moved from the shed, therefore I was still unsure about the transportation aspect of being a vessel. How would she do after days underway? Would the oil and fuel pumps continue to work? Would the bilge pump endure?

Joe often muttered, "Nothing lasts in the saltwater environment. It's us or rust."

Was rust going to get us? And the decks with old, cracked teak, how would those fare after a week at sea? We hadn't taken her out and I had lots of unanswered (and unspoken) questions. Joe was especially busy. He had to do the work so I hadn't pressured him with questions. And doing a test run was not easy when the boat was also serving as a house.

We'd have to tie down all our loose household bits before sailing out of the boat shed. It hadn't seemed worth the effort for our rare weekends together to stow stuff away just to shuffle it around again hours later. Joe did not have any concerns about the seaworthiness of the vessel. I depended upon Joe's experience. I chose to ignore that his experience was on large ships with a full engineering crew.

With the news from the Governor, we knew we needed to sail her. The new office was about 240 miles south, in Ketchikan, also in the Inside Passage of Southeast Alaska, just the southernmost section. It was time to test this boat as more than just a live-aboard platform.

Joe was completely unconcerned with the trip, though the bears had him stressed a bit. He didn't want to break down off Admiralty Island and deal with brown bears. As I didn't want to break down anywhere, we were on the same page.

It was a lovely sunny day in August. Joe had just gotten home from the office, he was in a reasonable mood, and there was a loud knock and "Hello" at the shed door.

In came the visitor. My first thought was, "Wow, a bald person with long hair in a pony-tail." My next thought scattered because he started talking. He was sharing his story. He had nine kids. He fixed boats. He lived in the White Ford Panel Van and on his boat. He walked to the stern of the *Pilot Project*, still talking, looked out at the harbor and pointed to the boats he had fixed. All the boats he had fixed. His talking did not stop for more than 30 minutes. I thought at first it went on for an eternity but the clock quantified eternity for me at 30 minutes.

My thought process, when it returned, got stuck in a loop, in the part on his name.

"Hello, I'm the boat repair guy. An expert! Forty years of experience. I've done it all. Teak, fiberglass, wood, racing vessels, I can help you whatever you need, whatever you want. People call me Itchy Willy."

Joe shook his hand. Joe had met him at the White Ford Panel Van and asked him to come by to discuss a boat project.

I said, "Hi Willy, nice to meet you."

He responded, "ITCHY Willy here. I can do whatever you need."

I shook his hand, wondering if someone named "Itchy Willy" was contagious.

Itchy Willy wore blue overalls. Worn, well-greased and torn overalls with holes in random places, including high on the thigh. *Was that a flash of skin?* As he was not wearing a shirt under the overalls, I focused on his head. Itchy continued talking about himself. He had nine kids, with a "bunch of different mothers."

I was now stuck trying to imagine those women. Itchy Willy in bed with a woman. Repeatedly. And different women. My imagination was not up to the task.

Joe gently and strategically broke into the Itchy autobiography, to ask him about the main deck work needed on the *Pilot Project*.

Itchy said, "This teak here is cracked. You know, I've seen that on lots of boats this age. Teak layered on top of weak wood. Wood fails. Cracks. Crevices. Water gets in."

Joe patiently said, "Yes, I know."

Itchy Willy now started his salesman's roll about rebuilding teak decks. He has done it all, on some nice boats he can point out to us in the harbor. "I helped a guy over there with the fix. Pulled it all up, re-laid the wood. Re-laid the teak. Yeah, we can do it. Fixing teak is spendy … "

Joe intruded on his flow, "Yes, I know. What other options …"

Itchy Willy jumped in, "I can make you a smooth—smooth—fiberglass over plywood. So smooth. I'll just smooth it over, smooth it around, smooth around these edges."

Itchy Willy was walking around making smoothing motions along the deck edge. "It will be beautiful. Beau-ti-ful. Smooth. Smooooth."

I thought I was smelling the scent of marijuana coming off those Carhartt overalls.

Joe continued the conversation, trying to bring in some practical realities, "We are sailing to Ketchikan in the first week of September. Could you get this job done in a month?"

Now Itchy Willy became a bit more jittery, "Ummm, pull teak. Plywood, would need plywood. I'd need a helper. It'd take time. Time for smooth. Smooooth. One month—quick, awful quick. Need smooth job, takes time."

Joe left it with him that he should stop back with an estimate.

We never saw Itchy Willy again. Apparently, deadlines were just not his thing.

As I was having a hard time imagining Itchy Willy in my home for a month, I was relieved at his absence. Joe and I decided to do a bit of the base deck work on the main deck ourselves. We could pull up the teak and Joe could lay plywood. We could layer the top with fiberglass.

How hard could it be?

It took hours to pull up the teak. Even in Alaska, that was a hot and sweaty job. At least we could immediately see how far we had progressed; we felt pretty good after a day's effort. It was almost time for a walk to the gym for a hot shower. Before we left, Joe looked to check where Tom had hit us, at the handrail stanchion. He looked over the side.

Gravity and sweat did the rest: his glasses dropped off. Into the ocean. Gone.

We were no longer feeling pretty good.

Joe exclaimed, "I just bought those damn things—$700!"

Ouch.

"I even paid for insurance on them!"

"Great, you can—"

Joe growled, "Not great. You have to have the damn broken glasses to get them replaced for free."

"Well, that's a the deal for the insurance company."

"Yeah. Crap."

Quietly I continued, "Should we call them and have them make up a new pair?"

"Grr, no, no. I have my old ones, my backup pair. Since the Coast Guard requires me to carry a second set, I'll just use those. I'm not paying another $700."

Sometimes regulations can work in your favor though I wondered what he was going to do without an updated prescription. I assumed he would put up with the old pair until the pain of loss felt less immediate. Six weeks? Six months? Six years? With Joe, I was guessing it would be on the longer side.

The next day, I was wasting time by browsing the bulletin board at the top of the ramp. Among the multitude of "Boats for sale" offers, there were notifications involving all realms of harbor life. "Captain looking for a deckhand." "Deckhand looking for a ship." "Boat parts for sale." "Harbor regulations for live-aboards." "Live-aboards looking for a cheap berth." "Boat cleaning, $50/hour." "Dive service, $100/hour." "Hull scraping, call for estimate." I turned away, forcing myself to get back to writing when I stopped and turned back. Dive services!

I called the diver and explained the challenge, "The glasses dropped straight down, in the waters in the boat shed. No boats were moving. So, the glasses might be right down there. Do you think you could dive and find them?"

"It would be a longshot. Tidal currents might have moved them. Visibility down there will be poor, probably pitch black, muddy and silty. But. It might work."

"I'm willing to pay for up to an hour of your time; I'd like to try it."

"Sounds good. Tomorrow morning okay?"

"Great."

Over our evening wine, I tentatively told Joe what I had set up.

"Paula, that was really clever." His eyes were crinkled from smiling. "I hadn't thought of a diver. You're becoming a boat person! And the price is reasonable, especially compared to $700."

We grinned at each other; I was almost blushing with Joe telling me I'd become boaty.

Managing expectations, I said, "Hopefully he can find them."

"I wouldn't get your hopes up. They could have moved with the tide and it's going to be really dark down there."

Expectations managed.

The diver came over when Joe was at work. He introduced himself as Patrick as he looked around and set up his gear on the stern.

Patrick said, "I wouldn't get your hopes up. The current could have moved them. And I won't be able to see much because of the mud and the silt down there."

"Yes, I know. I should not expect much. My husband said the same thing. Got it. But let's try."

"Sure."

Patrick pulled on his wet suit and the accoutrements of flippers, weight belt, assorted tools and tank. This was not a pretty, perfect wetsuit. No shiny neoprene. No smooth skin. It was a working diver's suit: scuffed and patched, scraped tanks, worn-down flippers. He tested his tank, adjusted the mask, and plunged in at the stern. I pointed to where the glasses went in, which I knew from the ding Tom's boat made on the handrail. Patrick went down. He immediately came up.

"I have no visibility down there—too much muck. Can you drop a line down at the point where I should look?"

170

"I'll try." Tying a line was one of the boat skills I had been practicing. I grabbed a mooring line, tied it to the stanchion, and dropped it over. It fell straight down.

"Thanks, I'll search around here."

I watched his bubbles. He came up periodically with handfuls of junk: a screwdriver, a rusted tube, an old bottle.

The hour was nearly up.

Patrick came up and pulled his regulator to speak, "I'll try a bit more but I'm not optimistic."

"Okay." What little optimism I had at the start had been draining away with each piece of junk. So, when he came up again, I figured he was done.

He was. He handed me the glasses.

"They were in deep muck, but they were there, straight down from the rope!" He was excited too, nice to have a successful hunt!

We both grinned, appreciating the long-shot success.

I offered, "Do you want to change inside? Or use the head?"

"No need. Since I have my gear on, I'll walk the docks and see if there is another job. There usually is and the luck seems to be with me today."

"With me too."

I shook his hand and handed over the hundred, a much better deal than replacing new glasses.

I called Joe and shared the news.

He said, "Amazing. I am so glad you thought of calling in a diver. Cool! Would you soak the glasses in freshwater before I get home? That will take the salt off."

"Sure." I was not yet "salty" enough to have thought of that necessity.

Joe got home and I poured the wine as he took his glasses out of the freshwater pot. He dried them and put them on. He immediately yelled, "Ow. Damn it! What the hell?!" He flung the glasses off his head.

I took a step back and stuttered, "What?!"

"The nose piece—it's sharp. It felt like a needle was sticking me."

I gasped, "What?!"

We both leaned in to look at the glasses. The nose pieces were uneven, scalloped at the edges. The earpieces—those plastic sheaths covering the end of the arm—they were all cut up too, with tiny little scalloped marks. Same scalloping as the earpieces. The lenses themselves were okay in the center, but, along their lower edge, was a line of fine, sharp scalloping marks.

Joe said, "These were in the water for less than a week! What in the world?!?"

I looked at the location of the scalloped marks: everywhere the glasses regularly touched skin. I started to smile.

"Joe, I bet it was a crab. A crab that was tasting the oily spots, where your skin left an oil deposit. Those markings, I bet those are crab bites."

Joe carefully, lightly, put them on his head. The skin contact points lined up with the scalloping.

"Crabs ate my glasses."

"Crabs ate your glasses! Now that's a sentence I never thought to hear!" We were both laughing, and then Joe stopped laughing …

"I can't wear them."

Shoulders slumping, I sighed, "My $100 bet, won, and then lost."

"No, you won the bet." His eyes were crinkling again, "You found them so I can use the insurance to get them replaced!"

We went back to laughing.

It took two days of discussion with the optometrist staff and Joe had to finally get the manager involved, but they agreed that their warranty would indeed cover damage from crab nibbling.

That night Joe was in a fairly good mood, so during our evening wine I brought up the question. "Hey sweets, what kind of dog would you like?"

Joe sipped his wine, slow to respond. "There was a smaller poodle at my house when I was a kid; I think it was my sister's dog. That was okay. I don't want a huge dog. Not a husky. I want a dog that will listen. What about you?"

"I'm not a big fan of poodles but they are smart. I like most smart dogs. Teensy ones, especially the yappy ones, those I don't care for."

"No, me either. No yappy ones for us."

I slowly smiled. He was sounding like he could imagine a dog in our future!

* * *

During our morning coffee, I asked Joe, "How are we doing on the prep for the move?"

Joe calmly answered, "I still have to move all the wood for the cabin remodel to my car, so it doesn't get thrown around when we sail. I have made ferry reservations for our cars and arranged for someone to put them on the ferry for us. Larry and Kathy will come over this weekend for the engine check-out and our test drive, so we need to have all the loose stuff stowed by then."

"Should I figure out where the loose stuff goes?"

"That would be great. Everything on a counter, on a bench, on the deck, it all needs to go somewhere secure. It would be a big time-saver for me if you took that on Paula."

"Sure, glad to help."

I attacked the last few moldy cabinets and wiped down the others to have somewhere to put things. I might not have many boat skills but this I could help with.

Sharing chores unveiled an unexpected intensity to married life. In our previous years, by the time two months together had passed, we'd already be focusing on the upcoming separation, getting ready for our lives apart. Even in our time together, Joe would do his thing and I'd do mine, with only some sharing of daily tasks of life, because in just weeks or months we'd be doing them by ourselves anyway. Now, I was learning the richness of more depth in the details, mundane though they might seem. Partnership in chores. Partnership in meal planning. In laundry. In coffee making and grocery buying. In bilge cleanout or in otter fence repair. We didn't pressure the other to do a task and we were lucky that we each wanted to help out the other, so the division of labor was easy. Especially as Joe always assumed he'd take on the nasty boat projects such as those related to spraints.

Moldy cabinets, daily dining, and boat projects gave us riches of associations. Repeating patterns of daily interaction created connections I had never experienced. We could communicate with fewer words. Just slightly raised eyebrows could have the other laughing. We were creating treasures of shared experience, learning about each other, and discovering new facets to life on a boat in Alaska. But among the treasures were scattered perilous difficulties.

Joe's work misery too often came home with him.

He railed against the layers of a bureaucracy that prevented significant improvement. He railed against the limits and boundaries that prevented him from fixing things. Joe's job allowed few successes, few fixes, and it was weighing on him. And that then weighed on me.

We were both trying to steer our way through that morass without having the conflict come between us. We were not always successful.

I hoped the move out of the State Capital and down to Ketchikan might lighten things up. Might it give him more flexibility? Might some of the old guard who resisted change stay behind? Might Joe find a way to manage the craziness, or at least his reaction to it? The move south at least gave me some hope of a reduction of the perilous straits of mood.

Joe had purchased nautical charts for the run from Juneau to Ketchikan, as well as NOAA's *Coast Pilot* for the region. As I flipped through the book, I realized that the *Coast Pilot* was for boaters as the *MilePost* was for drivers, though with no ads. Where to dock? The *Coast Pilot* knows. Major landmarks? Just check the *Coast Pilot*. Important hazards? Great recreational stops? Public docks? Typical weather and current patterns? The *Coast Pilot* laid it out island by island, channel by channel, chart by chart. This was how sailors could comfortably move through regions they had never seen before. Sailing instructions by reading a book? Sounded right up my alley. I'd start by reviewing what the *Coast Pilot* said about Admiralty Island to see if it had any bear suggestions.

That night Joe came home and asked, "Do you want to fly to Anchorage with me? We can go visit Tracey and Vince in Homer and then go to Anchorage. I have an appointment to take my first pilotage exam with the Coast Guard."

I said, "Before we head to Ketchikan?"

"Yes, I can carve out a week out of the office due to the move."

"The timing is pretty tight, but I'd love to go."

"I should be able to get us a mileage ticket on Alaska Air—should be cheap."

"Sounds like a plan." I kept my concerns about

the tight timeline to myself, deciding we could manage, as we always did. Time did not look to be in abundant supply before the sailing deadline.

The next day, Mom called to check in. "You are going to be on that boat when Joe moves it?"

"Sure!" I chose to ignore her obvious negativity about "that boat." I had long practice with giving strong, positive responses in a light and cheery tone. That generally made it harder for her to find a crack for any disapproval.

Silent pause, then, "Tim told me that the boat needs some work. He said it was sort of ratty." She found her crack, as she so often did.

"Well, all boats need some work, unless you own a million-dollar yacht and have a giant trust fund. And it isn't too ratty; Joe wouldn't bring me on a boat that isn't seaworthy."

Mom paused again. I think I took her major argument away from her. "Still, are you sure you want to be on the water that long?"

"I'm looking forward to it." Stay steady, positive, and confident, Paula.

"Well, let me know when you go and how it goes. I'm going to be like Nana and I want to know when to worry about you."

"Sure will. I think it will be more than a month yet." I wanted to give myself a nice long window of a worry-free Mom.

"Tim mentioned Joe isn't very happy in his job." Mom must have called Tim to see how the visit went. She had no model for long-term relationship success, so she explored for signs of doom.

"Joe's frustrated. It's a desk job in a big state bureaucracy. He isn't thrilled."

"Is he going to keep the job? He's changed jobs frequently."

"Not all that frequently, and it is not uncommon for merchant sailors to switch shipping companies. Plus, those job moves were so he could build his license up to unlimited ship master, which he did." My tone of voice was moving away from light and cheery, or even steady and confident.

"But he's not using that license to sail anymore, is he?"

"He had a goal to get it. He got it. No easy feat."

She went direct and said, "Do you think he is going to stay at this job?"

"Probably not. He is working hard on getting a piloting position somewhere. I think he will stay with the Marine Highway until he gets that pilot spot."

"You have your hands full there Paula."

As my throat tightened up in defense, I chose not to discuss exactly what she meant by that. Mom and I never figured out how to have tough conversations and I was uninterested in hearing her gloomy perspective. I ended the call as soon as I could.

Later that night, Joe and I chatted about the transit.

I finally asked the question that had been popping into my head more and more often. Mom's call just added its own pressure. "Sweets, what if we break down?"

Joe replied, "No problem. We have a radio and can call. There are boats that sail around the area all the time. I have a good tow line if someone had to come get us. Or, we run aground and wait for help. That's the nice thing about the Inside Passage, we aren't likely to float out to sea and be lost forever."

Being married to a deep-sea sailor brought skills and reassurance to married life on a boat. And allowed me to sleep more easily.

Joe looked at the chart, and the long shoreline of

Admiralty, "Though I think we need a rowboat to serve as a lifeboat. It will also let us get to land if we have to anchor out. Or even to row away from a concentration of brown bears."

Here it was, the bear fear. Which became a perfect excuse to buy a new boat. *Was he really concerned, or did he just want a new boat?* I was glad to have another back-up plan if the *Pilot Project* left us stranded somewhere.

My favorite thing about getting a new boat was choosing its name. Walker Bay sold an ideal rowboat: small, inexpensive, lightweight, plastic, and easy to move on land with its little wheel on the bottom of its stern. Joe thought he could lash it to the stern of the *Pilot Project* and we could use the swim platform as the base of transfer from the big boat to the bouncy little one. Joe and I quickly agree on a name: the eight-foot rowboat would be named the *Pilot Lite*.

Another cutesy boat name brought forth into the world.

We bought the *Pilot Lite*, piled it on the roof of the car, drove to the harbor, and wheeled the rowboat down the ramp. It was easy to wheel her down the ramp at high tide, though I was sweating from the heat of the day. I never thought to bring sunglasses as they were rarely useful in Juneau.

Joe wanted to row *Pilot Lite* over to the *Pilot Project* so we dropped the little skiff into the water at the base of the E-Float. I held its line when we put it in the water, so it didn't float away. Joe climbed down to sit in it, carefully balancing in the floaty, tippy boat. *Pilot Lite* was not quite as tippy as a canoe but it was close. Joe smiled when he had settled in the boat, and I asked, "All good?"

Smiling, he said, "Yes."

And I then tossed the line to him.

He stared open-mouthed at me, still holding out

his arm, eyes wide.

He looked surprised that I just threw him the line. *Was he surprised I didn't get it wet on my toss? That my toss was good enough for him to catch?* I was feeling pretty satisfied about my toss but the look on his face … ?

As he floated off the dock, he said, "Paula?!?" I then realized he was surprised because he did not yet have the oars.

I had just tossed off his only connection to land and left him with no way to navigate. No way to row. No way to power his vessel. He needed a lifeboat to escape the lifeboat.

Joe silently pointed at the oars. I quickly grabbed one and held it out to him. He was just within reach. He pulled himself back to the dock.

I was glad it wasn't a windy day. He would have been blown off and lost at sea in an eight-foot, non-powered dinghy.

One of the things I liked about Joe was that he had never yelled at me, even when I released him to sea in an unpowered vessel. He calmly handed me the line again, and, being a very brave man, said, "Paula, hold this line, until I ask for it. Okay?"

"Okay! Got it!"

He picked up both oars, attached them, tested their functionality, then politely asked, "Now Paula, now I'd like the line please."

I again successfully threw it to him.

He smoothly rowed the *Pilot Lite* to its new home, on the stern of the *Pilot Project*.

Joe lashed the *Pilot Lite* to the stern, to securely fasten it in place, and giving quick access if needed as a lifeboat. I liked the concept but like much in life, there was a trade-off. It blocked most of the best view on the boat. Off the stern, with the shed's curtains open, I would watch the harbor and get a glimpse of the breakwater and Gastineau Channel. This was BBQ Grill Central, where we had our evening wine and watched the water. Now the only good view was blocked by the *Pilot Lite*'s hull.

I focused on the benefits: safe transit to shore and safe transit away from bears. Plus, Joe could now propel me on romantic turns around the Aurora Harbor, dancing around the busy commercial fishing ships, in our eight-foot, bouncy rowboat.

Sadly, only once did we find time for a romantic paddle. Our deadline to move south was tightening our schedule.

September was getting close. That's when Joe needed to be in the Ketchikan office and we needed a week to sail south. There were loads of boat projects, especially as the *Pilot Project* had not been out of its shed since Joe had owned it. I think Joe's optimism about what could be completed in the time available verged on fantasy. But I knew, like the toilet install, it would happen, one way or another.

Joe mentioned over our evening BBQ, as I silently glowered at the *Pilot Lite*'s hull, "Hey, I ran into Chris's grandfather in town today."

"Great, you bought the boat from him, didn't you? How's he doing?"

"He's doing well. I told him about the move south and we talked about what to do with the boat shed. He'll take it back after we sail. One more move item off the list!" Joe paused before continuing, "He also said that will be the first time the boat has moved in seven years."

I slowly turned to look at him, blinking in confusion, "Seven years! What!!"

"Yeah, he had not taken it out in all those years."

"Why?"

"Well, it was getting a bit hard for him to handle alone …"

"I get that, especially with a left-handed screw." I loved having nautical knowledge.

"I think it was having only a single screw that made it hard for him."

Dang, I preferred having the correct nautical knowledge.

Joe continued, "He said the decks might leak a bit."

"A bit?" I decided not to mention this uncertainty to Mom.

We had completed dozens of boat maintenance projects as the sailing date got closer. While it was mainly Joe who did the work, I enjoyed the Royal We of married life. We replaced the water pumps. We reattached the water pump raw water strainer to keep those pesky clams out of the engine. We replaced fuel filters and fuel filter lines and fuel filter petcocks, using special little parts apparently only found in Britain at a cost of $3 plus $50 shipping. We replaced part of the leaky stern deck, leaving the rest of the main deck and upper decks untouched. With Larry's help, we overhauled the engine. We made sure the bilge pump started automatically as it was crucial when water flowed into the boat it flowed out without the need of human intervention. In six months, we had put in a new toilet, new MSD, new water tank, new bed platform, and new mattress. The *Pilot Project* was a twenty-five-year-old Chien Hwa Marine Trader, a boat model known to have maintenance needs over time. We thought we hit the "time." We were pleased with ourselves and with the boat. We thought it was all going so well.

Our maiden voyage was just two weeks before our planned departure for Ketchikan. The trip included Larry and Kathy; Larry for engineer backup and Kathy for moral support. We had one of those perfect Juneau days: sunny and windless. Kathy and I lounged on the stern while the guys drove the ship from the flybridge between visits to the engine room to see how the machinery was behaving.

Joe said the *Pilot Project* sailed like a dream, smooth, responsive, easy to maneuver. The boat dealt well with waves and the engine restarted immediately. But Larry and Joe discovered a few more maintenance projects to be addressed before sailing south. Leaky windows needed to be replaced, but as that was not going to happen in the time available, they would be caulked before departure. Old batteries had to be pulled off. Fuel lines that leaked when the engine ran had to be replaced. We used oil absorbent pads to catch the diesel drips, but they cost a dollar apiece. It was pricey for a fancy piece of paper towel that made me want to start singing the SpongeBob SquarePants song. It was time to fix the oil problem. Overall, Joe and Larry thought the first trip with the boat went great.

I wasn't 100% sure that forty-five minutes on a beautiful sunny day with flat seas close to the harbor was the best example of what it would be like for a five-day trip with uncertain weather, sailing into wilderness. I was 100% sure the trip would be a real-life adventure. I was hoping it was one we would all survive.

10 Countdown to Ketchikan

Floater: (n) drowned dead body

Late August 2004

I had learned a great deal in my months on the boat with Joe. First, I picked up more sailor talk. Things like 'bilge' and 'scupper' and 'flemish the lines' along with less polite sailor words. Second, I could cook almost anything on a George Foreman grill. Third, I learned that there is no such thing as having too much Damp Rid to control the moisture in the closet. The moisture in the cabinet. The moisture in the head. I was also finding limits to my optimism: I insisted on emergency backup batteries for the marine radio. When you have to call for help, it is not the time for dead batteries.

We had to be efficient to fit in all our plans before sailing south. The local marine electrician would replace the marine batteries. Joe would fix the fuel lines. I'd take a shot at the window caulk. We'd fly to Anchorage, drive to Homer for pilot training and head back to Anchorage for the USCG pilotage exam Joe had scheduled. He wanted to lock in that first exam as validation that he was on his way to his goal. We were filling life and operating in problem-solving mode to get this all accomplished.

The Homer trip went well. Joe and I both raved about the roadside pull-off at the bluff just above Homer—neither of us had ever seen a more beautiful vista, from glacier to volcano, Spit to bay to ocean, mountains and lakes, all in one view. Breathtaking.

I visited with Tracey and her kids while Joe picked up a pilot observer trip for Cook Inlet. The clear day on the drive from Homer back to Anchorage gave us the beginning of fall colors: the mountainsides were bright, green of spruce, gray of rocks, yellows of fall willows, with yellow, rusty stains coating the mountaintops. This was how I imagined the boat trip to Ketchikan would be, but with no traffic, no cars, no road. Just the boat skimming through quiet waters, surrounded by wilderness just touched by the start of autumn.

During the four-and-a-half-hour drive from Homer to Anchorage we chatted about the move to Ketchikan. Joe would be again surrounded by his office colleagues, but it would be a quieter office. Only eight of the 42 staff members were making the move south.

I guessed it wasn't as easy for everyone to haul their home 240 miles away.

Before we caught the evening plane for Juneau, Joe was set to take his first Coast Guard test for pilotage, to demonstrate his knowledge of the Vessel Traffic System in Valdez. He was a tad nervous.

I reminded him, "Joe, you always do well on exams."

"I know, I know. I'll be fine if it's a multiple choice. But if I have to write it out …"

I scrunched my forehead. "Write out the whole Vessel Traffic System? No, no way, they wouldn't do that. Would they?"

Joe frowned and said, "I doubt it, but I don't KNOW how the exam works. I've never taken a VTS exam before."

His anxiety was high. This was standard for Joe doing something important for himself, especially when he had no previous experience doing it.

He entered the exam area and I looked around to decide where to wait. The Coast Guard office in Anchorage had an odd location. Boston's Coast Guard office was on the waterfront, on tarred and oily dock works with the sound of boat horns and mast lines. Seattle's was also on the waterfront, facing Puget Sound. San Francisco's was on the waterfront, facing the Bay. Anchorage's was housed in a mall: two floors above an indoor skating rink, one floor above the pet store.

I wandered the stores for a bit and sat down at one of those uncomfortable mall benches: no back and a slightly curved seat. Did anyone really think anybody's butt would fit comfortably in those? Or was that the point, to keep people walking and therefore shopping? I pushed off my shoes and sat partial lotus fashion, legs crossed, balancing a book. I nearly finished the book while waiting. After an hour I frequently looked up for Joe. After two hours, the book was not keeping my attention, as every few minutes I wondered, "What's taking him so long? Did he have to write it? He only studied for an hour. There's no way he can write that whole book by memory." I struggled not to worry though the line between wondering and worrying could be quite short. I started to chew on my fingernails.

At the two- and one-half-hour mark, I started to wander. The pet store had no dogs; their furry creatures were just weasels, rats and rabbits. After my third time in and out of the store the pet store owner asked, "Can I help you with anything?" I nodded, "No thanks" and headed back to the painful bench.

I pushed the worry aside and settled back down. The next time I looked up, there he was.

We smiled at each other from across the skating rink. My tension level immediately dropped.

He walked over to me, smiling the whole time. We hugged and kissed.

I asked, "So, how'd you do?"

Joe, shrugged his shoulders and, with a little grin, "Oh, 100%."

I paused with open mouth, then stammered, "Excellent! But—it took you three hours? Did you have to write it out?"

"It was multiple choice. It took me all of five minutes, plus talking time with the Coastie."

"Five minutes? And so, you talked for nearly three hours? What was so interesting?"

"When I brought the exam back to the Officer, he smiled like he was pitying me, asking 'You have questions?' I told him, 'Just one. Did you give me the right answer sheet? I am assuming A equals true and B equals false, and, for question 17, that there is a choice F. The answer sheet provided doesn't reflect what I think are the correct answers.' The officer looked at my test and realized he had given me the wrong answer sheet. "

My cheeks were stretched from smiling, "And so what did you do with the rest of the time?"

Joe said confidently, "He wanted to talk about ideas he had, about pilotage training and grading exams. So, I listened."

"Hey, time well spent ... 100% score and good schmoozing with the man who grades all of your future tests."

Joe replied, smiling as he took my hand when we left the building, "Exactly. What a great weekend."

We were in a lovely happy place, enjoying each successful accomplishment.

And then the cell phone rang.

It was his boss at the Alaska Marine Highway, informing him that someone thought Joe shouldn't be taking pilotage training and observer trips. They charged him with an ethics violation.

FLOATERS

The good weekend was at its end.

* * *

We flew back to Juneau, in high irritation, ranting together for most of the trip. How dare those @#$! jerks accuse him! His boss had no problem with him going for pilotage, on his own time! Why didn't his boss get this cleared up before it got to this point? He's not getting paid for the trips, how can it be an ethics violation! He's using his own time, his own travel money! If this means he can't take any more pilotage trips, then he might as well quit! And not move south to Ketchikan! How dare those @#$! jerks …

This venting was not healthy, but we kept feeding off each other's anger.

We calmed down a bit as we cycled through the rant. Neither Joe nor I were good at staying irritated for too long, though Joe's irritation time was about quadruple of mine.

Our normal mood started to re-emerge after the two-hour flight. We convinced ourselves that the ethics violation would go away. It was just another way for an unhappy crew to pick at the Marine Highway administration. The vent cycle had ended. I felt my heart rate settle down.

Then we got to the boat.

We expected the boat to have its new batteries installed and its old ones removed. Marine batteries are about twice the size and weight of car batteries, and about four times as expensive. We'd need functional batteries otherwise we'd end up in the middle of Southeast Alaska wilderness with no way to start the engine. Rowing the *Pilot Lite* to the next port, which might be 150 miles away, did not sound like a desirable back-up plan. The solution: fix the batteries, even if it was expensive to hire a professional marine electrician.

Our timing was not ideal as our professional had

to fit us in his crowded schedule, which was while we were away in Homer, just before we were due to sail. He knew we had to be on our way, and he had been willing to spend two weekend days getting it done.

When I saw the post-it note on the boat's door, my expectations sank. And my heart rate started back up again.

The note said: "You need to build the battery boxes now. Call me. Ray. 324-3456."

Joe ranted. "What the #@$%*&*! What does he mean?" As he spewed sailor talk, he tore off his clothes and put on old ones. "I'm going down."

Down was the direction of the engine room. "Engine room" was a misnomer. "Engine closet" would have been more accurate, or better yet, "Engine coffin." The only way into the engine compartment was down. And unless the floor of the salon was pulled up, a thirty-minute exercise filled with frustration, the only way in was to crawl. And you had to crawl over batteries with open, acid-covered terminals. Through nasty, oiled soaked teak mesh decks, dodging the occasional rusty nail found at prime handholds. No, "engine room" just didn't suffice.

I clearly heard Joe's rant while he was below. "What is this supposed to be? He hasn't even connected the new batteries. What the #@%&*#@! I have to get this boat moved to get to work!"

We still had battery "issues." Our professional left us the wrong battery and didn't finish the installation.

Our professional marine electrician had let us down, though he gave Joe the opportunity to practice his sailor talk, something this boat provided Joe in abundance.

I wondered if SWAPA would appreciate Joe's vocabulary? Probably not.

Spending a week in Homer before finishing the

boat projects may not have been the wisest choice. Time was running out.

On the day we had planned to sail, Joe called the electrician and spent half the day in voice mail hell. He tried to control his tone, but it was clear he was not pleased. He was in that horrible conundrum: you want to scream at the guy, but you also want the guy to do something for you. Joe tried to keep us in play.

Joe glowered at the ceiling, took a deep breath, and relaxed his jaw enough to say, "I need the batteries installed. I understand you need the woodwork done to support the batteries, but the way you left them, the 200-pound battery is in my way. I cannot do the woodwork until your stuff is hauled out."

Joe's eyes squinted shut while the electrical shop guy talked.

"The electrician will call me back or come over today to move the gear, so I can work?"

Joe's teeth were clenched when he hung up. I was not optimistic about seeing the electrician.

Joe built the battery box by moving the whole arrangement. Rather than wait for the professional electrician to show up, I pitched in as unskilled labor. Joe didn't really want me to have to help, but I'd rather do it then experience the frustration of waiting. I helped push hundreds of pounds of acid-filled electrical hazards around. Joe did 90% of the heavy lifting and together we got the work done.

In his next call to the electrical store, they assured Joe that the marine electrician would show up the next day to finish the job. Depending on our professional marine electrician was not relaxing for either of us. We pushed off our sailing plan by a day.

"Hey Paula, let's go to the Breakwater for dinner."

"Great idea." I think we both wanted off the boat though it was just one more hit to the budget. Part of the upper floor of the Breakwater had a bar and restaurant, overlooking the harbor, which would be a good perspective change. Getting off the boat let us both ignore the boat projects for a few hours. Joe's deadline to move south was looming as was his ethics violation. If dining out could relieve that pressure for a bit, it was the right choice. We'd make up the money someday.

The next day the electrician called at 8 a.m. I thought that might be a good sign. He said, "Yah, I'll be over first thing. I want to get your guys on your way. I know you need to go. I just have to stop at the shop and then I'll be over."

My optimism ended when he hadn't shown up by 10 a.m. Joe headed out to do last minute shopping errands. Our professional finally appeared at 11 a.m. to "do the final work."

I was planning to complete the stow. The food, the tools, and the dishes all had to be stashed, otherwise, when the boat moved, they could fly off and crash against our heads. I couldn't stow with the electrician working. He'd taken off all the engine room hatches, leaving the floor of the salon open. The final stow wasn't going to happen until I had a floor to walk on.

I switched to emptying out the boat shed.

The shed had become our garage equivalent: the resting place for stuff that had no home. Moving time meant we could procrastinate no longer. It was time to decide. Where did the snow shovel belong? Keep or toss the extra length of garden hose? Save the leaky crusty bottle of boat wash or admit it had passed on to that state of garbage? What to do with the old brass window that Joe was sure we could use somewhere. What to do with all the lumber that Joe pulled out— he was sure this too would be useful again. After moving three times in less than a year, from a 2,400 square foot house to a 33½ foot long boat, I knew everything could go, but Joe needed to find that out for himself.

Joe came back and we started filling the cars. Not everyone was lucky enough to have a Subaru Forester and a Ford Explorer as movable garages.

One of the other boaters came by and chatted Joe up. Guys who want something from other guys, they don't get cozy, they don't get close. No shaking of hands. No meeting of eyes. They just start talking about the other guy's project.

The Boat Guy, while looking at the timber, said, "That looks like a lot of work there."

Joe, while loading a wheelbarrow, replied, "Yeah. We have a Chien Hwa Marine Trader trawler; they're known for plywood rot."

Boat Guy, glancing into the boat shed, continued, "Aye, I used to have one of those. Takes some work to get it fixed. Looks like you are making that effort."

Joe, still loading, said, "I pulled out all the rot. And I took out the good, interior teak. I'll put it all back together again sometime."

Boat guy, watching the wood Joe was loading, "You're sure doing the hard work. I've been doing a bit of teak re-work on my boat too. Yep, you have to stay on it to keep it in shape, especially on these older boats."

"Yeah, you gotta do the maintenance."

"Are you throwing away this bucket of wood bits?"

"I won't be needing those, too small for the cabinets I have to replace."

"I've been looking for a piece of teak. If you aren't going to keep that, can I take it? I have a small corner on a cabinet in the aft cabin to replace."

"Go for it. Good luck with your project."

He replied, "Aye, that's what boats are all about, ongoing projects," as Boat Guy walked away.

Somebody had a project that just took a small piece of teak? A project they could do in an afternoon? I could not imagine.

It took us the rest of the day to load the cars. What kind of an effort will it take to puzzle all the lumber pieces back together? It didn't matter. There would always be another project to do. They would each take more time than expected.

I was learning: boat ownership was like all long-term relationships, you had to keep working at it to get anything out of them, or they sank into the muck.

Heading back into the shed for one last load, I asked Joe, "Are we taking the Styrofoam step?"

"No, that stays with the boat shed."

That was fitting. I asked, "How are we going to step up to the boat?"

"We can use the milk crate in the forward cabin. Or any of the Rubbermaid totes. Should not be a problem."

A solution, and at least the shag rug would be out of my life.

The electrician left about 4 p.m., saying, "What time do you folks want to leave tomorrow? I need to replace the voltmeter and check out the alternator."

Joe, whose jaw must have hurt from the tension on his teeth, said, "We wanted to leave by late morning."

Professional marine electrician replied, "I'll be over first thing so we can get you on your way."

We planned for another delay.

Joe and I lugged stuff up and down the dock for hours. I hadn't been that tired since we lugged 100 pounds of gear on our bikes thirty miles down the Natchez Trace Trail in Mississippi. I could barely move without creaking. I was not looking forward to the walk to the gym for a shower. Joe suggested a hotel that night so we didn't have to clean the tools off the bed. He did know how to fix things!

FLOATERS

We checked into the Breakwater and enjoyed a long hot shower before heading to the restaurant. We almost fell asleep over our dinner drinks as we chatted about tomorrow's route. It was warm and cozy overlooking the Gastineau Channel from the comfort of the Breakwater Inn Bar. *We were going to sail south down those waters!*

I did wish the weather report was sweeter.

Miracle of miracles, the electrician showed up early and finished before noon. With the salon floor back in place, Joe and I stowed the food and all the loose gear. I felt someone step onto the deck and then heard a knock at the ship's door.

It was Joe's boss, John.

Joe opened the door and said, "Come on in, John, what's up?" I could see the new tension in Joe's jaw line.

John said, "Hello Joe. Hello Paula. Good to see you both. Shed looks like you are just about moved out."

I sat back in the corner of the salon, wondering what John was here to drop.

Joe nodded, still containing his tension.

John continued, "Joe, I wanted to let you know, before you left Juneau, that as far as I can see, the ethics violation charge should not be any big deal."

I could see a bit of muscle relaxation in Joe's neck.

John continued, "We will go through the steps, deal with the process. I have your back and I will testify to the truth: you followed all the rules. We just have to go through the steps and I expect it will all go away. You did nothing wrong."

The rest of Joe's body relaxed as Joe said, "I appreciate that John. Nice of you to come over before we left."

John said, "I wanted to relieve at least some pressure off you before your trip. I cannot do much, but I wanted to do something."

Joe nodded and shook John's hand. I wished they could hug each other but I had to settle for them sharing a good stiff handshake, in theory as a *bon voyage*.

I hugged them both as John left the boat. Life as an administrator with the Alaska Marine Highway had a large dose of bureaucratic pain and suffering. They could use more hugs.

I think Joe believed John was doing his best, and that John hated aspects of his job as did Joe. I believed John was desperate to keep Joe, to have Joe show up in Ketchikan. Going from a staff of forty-two down to a staff of eight while maintaining ferry service was a daunting proposition. John was both trying to help Joe while helping himself and his operations. I appreciated that.

By 4 p.m., we finished lugging, tying, and stowing. The prep was done. We could sail.

Meanwhile, the weather had, in sailor parlance, gone to crap.

The wind was screeching. White caps were all over the harbor, even inside the breakwater. Rain was pelleting down. We could no longer see the mountain tops. We could barely see the sides of the mountains. Everything was disappearing in a cloud of clouds.

I said to Joe, "We could wait another night, no problem. John isn't going to fire you for missing a day or two."

Joe the stoic said, "No, we can go. Visibility isn't too bad."

By four thirty, visibility was abysmal. We could barely see across the channel.

Once more I suggested, "Another night at the Breakwater?"

And Joe returned, "No, we are ready, let's go."

After a final check around the boat shed and the decks, Joe turned the key. The engine started. As I looked out at the weather, I was not sure if that was a good thing.

Joe untied us and climbed up to the flybridge, reversing out of the slip and out of the boat shed. I had a firm grip on the railing as I pulled up the fenders. The *Pilot Project* was moving, departing on a 240-mile trip.

We found out later that John's wife Kim was frantically calling John. "Joe and Paula aren't leaving in this, are they? It's horrible out there."

She was right, it was horrible out there.

The rain was coming down in sheets—heavy, thick, flannel-like sheets. We left the harbor, into the Gastineau Channel, and the wind hit. The wind drove the rain. It bit when it hit my face. I went inside. Chaotic white caps surrounded us. I had never seen white caps of any kind in the Gastineau Channel. I started a mental chant: *Joe's a professional. He's fine with this.*

Joe preferred driving from the flybridge because he could see further with the flybridge's elevation and no walls to obstruct his view. But the flybridge was open to the weather. Once we cleared the docks and the harbor breakwater, Joe came down. In the five minutes he was up there, he was soaked through to the skin. His rain jacket didn't keep him dry. He began steering the boat from inside. Visibility was so poor it didn't matter where he drove from as he could barely see anything.

Joe handled the boat smoothly, easily moving us through the wind and the waves. He was, however, swearing at the lack of a working depth finder. And that he had to get the radar mast up. The mast was too tall to put up while in the shed. I don't think he thought he'd need it immediately upon leaving the shed, but the visibility was so poor, radar was now necessary. He was also grumbling about the chart being too small—too zoomed out—to see important details such as where shallows lie.

These seemed like major issues to me, but I just kept up the mental refrain, *Joe's a professional. He's fine with this.*

He saw that one of the five huge cruise ships began to move from its berth at the city docks. He slowed and told me he'd ride in its wake, "Ships that size make great wind blocks, and are visible even through this rain."

If we followed them, we knew we wouldn't run aground. Just a quarter mile out from our quiet, dry boat shed, we weren't sure of our exact location, as the weather blocked our view of any landforms.

Then I noticed the first leak.

Water was dripping into our forward cabin, the V-berth, the food storage area. Water was coming through the hatch. I yelled this information to Joe. He asked, "Is it bad enough to stop or turn back?"

Did I really know how to answer that? I finally responded, "Ummh, no, I guess not. Not yet at least."

We continued.

I returned to the main cabin.

Joe now noticed a different leak through the forward window. He said, "It's a slow one."

I nodded, while sticking paper towels into the window frame. I had no idea where this adventure was going to lead us, but five minutes into it, the experience was looking soggy.

Joe said, "I need to get the mast up. It's bouncing around out here too much for me to raise it here. I need some flatter waters."

The thought of him falling off the *Pilot Project* while raising the mast wasn't comfortable, so I asked, "Do we need to have the mast up?"

"No mast then no radar. No radar and we will hit

something in the night. Or if we lose our cruise ship guide in this weather. We need the mast."

"Oh, got it." Joe was going to have to go out and up to the flybridge and put up the radar mast. I was going to have to manage my anxiety of having Joe going up to the flybridge and put the radar mast up with high winds trying to blow him down.

Joe continued, "We will lose the cruise ship, but it can't be helped."

I nodded, sadly looking towards the big white box that was no longer going to be our windbreak.

Joe said, "I need flatter water. Douglas Harbor, the one nearby to where we played softball, we should be able to get there and it should be out of this wind. Should be calmer. I've never sailed into that harbor, but we should be able to find a spot to tie up. Too bad the boat shed wasn't taller so I could have done this in there. Could you hang the fenders? I'll tie us up. You don't have to be out there for too long."

"Sure, that's easy for me."

In the thirty seconds it took me to hang the fenders, I was soaked. Dripping. Glasses fogged. Pants sticking to my legs. But by that time, we had even more problems.

Joe had gone to the aft cabin to get a third line to secure us in the wind. I heard his swearing.

As I went to see what was going on, I stopped and gazed open-mouthed. There was a steady stream of water coming in the salon's starboard window. My caulking attempt had failed.

Joe stormed up from the aft cabin, "Leaks are all over the damn place. Through the bulkheads. Under the friggin' windows. Along the portside of the deck."

I forced myself to ask, "The mattress?"

"Getting soaked."

"Crap."

"Yes, a giant load of crap."

We didn't have enough towels to get dry. We didn't have enough caulk to stop all the leaks. I hadn't bought rain pants, just rain jackets, as I had thought, "How wet could it be?" I learned. Wet. Drenched. Sopping. Soaked. Very very wet. In less than an hour.

Joe continued, "And I don't know if the batteries are getting a charge off the engine."

I froze. Head down. Just stared at the floor. We could be without power at any time. No flushes, no lights, no recharged radio, no emergency contact.

Joe's stream of sailor talk started, interspersed with swearing about why he ever bought the boat. It was clear that my mantra no longer applied: *Joe was not fine with this.*

I was staring at the floor, numb, cold, wet, unable to move, silently wondering how we got to this point, wondering what I should be doing to fix this. I had no idea. I felt like Frodo must have felt in the Dead Marshes. I did not want to be there. I also felt useless. Maybe it was Bilbo I was channeling. *I get it now Bilbo. No one wants to be carried around like a sack of potatoes when all you want to do is help.* I was doing a poor job of managing in a sailing adventure that hadn't gone much more than five miles. My brain was as frozen as my skin.

I don't know if Joe had picked up on my state, or if he had sufficiently vented, but he returned to his problem-solving mode.

Joe started, "We need to have the deck replaced and fiberglassed in."

Problem-solving began to unfreeze my brain. I began to mirror his reasoning, and stammered, "Yes. That one piece we fiberglassed isn't leaking."

Joe continued, "We can fix some of this."

I warmed a bit more, "We just need to replace more of the deck."

Joe took the next step, "If we go back to the shed, we can do the work."

I carried on, "The shed is dry. We could lay down more caulk there."

The plan was building as Joe continued, "We could leave the boat in town for a few weeks, pulling up all the old deck and laying down the new. I'd have to fly up every weekend …"

I filled in, "Hey, it's only money."

Our tones were lightening. This no longer felt like the trek into Mordor. I said, "Sure, we can maximize the boat shed time here, because there won't be one in Ketchikan. "

We both thawed enough for a small laugh and each said at the same moment, "Sounds like a plan."

Joe untied the *Pilot Project* and we sailed back to our dry boat shed. My head fell back as the tension flowed out of my body. This sailing adventure was coming to an end, just hours after it started, and I was not sorry in the least.

Joe was certainly not boring me. But I was discovering my preference for not being bored had limits. Variety, excitement, and discovery: I now knew I liked them balanced with safety, security, and a dry place to sleep.

We were trying to move to a land where rain was measured in feet, not inches, and we needed to shore up the leaky bits of our floating home.

11 The Inside Passage

Float: (n) a vehicle in a parade

September-October 2004

The boat was too wet to live aboard. It had been out of the boat shed for less than an hour and it had become unlivable.

I broke out those phone numbers of people who had offered their spare bedroom. It was a great thing to have people you could count on to take you in. The first I called, Lora, was happy to help with a dry place for me and Joe to settle into while we worked on the next phase of the boat project.

While I called Lora, Joe called to cancel the ferry transport for my car. He'd have his car go south while mine stayed in Juneau until we sailed again. Joe then called John to give him the update.

John told him, "Kim will be relieved. She parked near the Douglas Bridge saying a rosary for you. But she couldn't see you. That weather was really bad."

Joe nodded in full agreement.

We moved into the warm and dry extra bedroom in Lora's place and made plans. Joe still had to get to work in Ketchikan, so he'd fly down during the week and back on the weekends. While not a cost-effective commuting style, it was our best option as the boat had to get to Ketchikan and its decks needed some care before it would make the journey through the temperate rainforest. I spent my mornings writing and my afternoons doing fiberglass lay-up.

The sabbatical was providing a large range of new skills for me to learn.

Before Joe left, he had ripped out the old teak from the main deck. My first task was to put in a layer of fiberglass before we'd lay new plywood and then top that with more fiberglass. After a morning of counting new, completed pages, or sometimes just new, completed paragraphs, I found it satisfying to see the fiberglass going down, inch by inch, layer by layer. While I laid down the fiber, I dreamt of a cozy, dry boat life. That helped erase the soggy nightmare of the last boating effort.

The next week, I met Joe at the Juneau airport, giving him a big hug.

He asked, "How did your week go my love?"

I answered, "Great! I got a whole chapter drafted up and I got about half of the starboard deck fiberglassed in."

"That's amazing!"

He stopped and took my hand, "You know Paula, I couldn't do this without you."

I blushed and replied, "It's fun, it's new and I enjoy seeing each new inch of protected deck."

"You are sweet my dearest, sweet! Shall we go down to the Breakwater for dinner?"

I responded, smiling, "Absolutely." Commuting by air and dinners out meant we had to pull more cash from our retirement accounts, but I didn't care much at that point. We would figure out how to restock it or we'd both just keep working.

After the relaxing Friday night, the rest of the weekend was spent running to the hardware store or working on the deck. While we hoped to get the deck done before the end of September, we'd have to start moving much faster to make that deadline. If we missed that deadline, it was not only more cash outlay but also moved us closer to the start of Alaska's winter.

If we had successfully made the trip in August, even late August, we would have had fourteen hours of daylight in temperatures well above freezing. September cut our daylength to eleven and a half hours, but still likely kept us above freezing temps. A delay into October would mean only nine hours of daylight and occasional freezing evenings. November ... I didn't even want to imagine sailing through wilderness in November's conditions.

The deck repair meant days gooping down fiberglass and the plywood deck pieces, pieces Joe fit where he had pulled the old teak. *Gooping* = applying goop. *Goop* = nasty, foul smelling fiberglass resin with hardener. It was a timed puzzle: if I didn't goop quickly, the goop hardened the brush into an unnatural, permanent shape, wasting both brush and goop, and requiring another run to the hardware store.

Goop required respirator use: uncomfortable rubber masks with canisters stuck to the side. The canisters absorbed the toxic fumes before they reached our delicate noses and our even more delicate brains. We also wore white Tyvek suits to keep the goop off the skin as skin absorption was a significant threat. We looked like space invaders, waving hardened, goop-filled brushes around.

After a few weeks, I would have preferred alien abduction over a day of gooping.

We bought out all of Juneau's supply of *Bondo* fiberglass resin and had to find another brand. We were nervous about mixing different brands, but the new version had some truth in advertising (*Evercoat*, *"easy to apply"*). It was much faster to "lay down"— gooping—into the fiberglass fabric. *Bondo* had taken more repeated effort to get it to soak into the glass cloth. Using *Evercoat*, we were able to gloop down all the boards in one day. *Gloop* = past tense alternate of gooping.

Like the plywood, the fiberglass mat had to be cut to size for each deck area and placed into goop. These were large, sticky puzzle pieces that released toxic fumes. I was covered in shiny glass pieces from cutting the mat, which could have made a new fashion style if it wasn't so itchy.

Was this how Itchy Willy got his name?

Once installed, the fiberglass and goop-coated boards hardened in place. The gaps along the deck and the house or between boards had to be filled with bits of fiberglass and more goop. Then, a final layer of fiberglass fabric and more gooping to solidify.

We had been gooping for five weeks just to finish the main deck. With the main deck done, we worked on caulking the windows and hatches. Joe, conscious of the shortening days, decided not to even try to replace the flybridge and middle decks; he covered those with tarp that he tightly stapled down. I kept hoping the result would be a relatively water-proof salon.

We did not make our end of September sailing deadline.

The summer warmth was gone. We bought a boat heater that could keep us warm when detached from shore-side electricity. As our sailing date moved into late October, the heater could play a valuable role in keeping us alive and unfrozen. The boat heater cost $1,000. This fit our Boat Cost Unified Theory of Pricing (BCUTP): all things purchased for the boat cost either $50, $250, $500 or $1,000. To date, all our purchases fit the BCUTP. Joe's boat acronym, Bring On Another Thousand, continued to be correct as well. I had hoped his pricing theories were wrong, but they were, sadly, proving to be accurate. The retirement fund took another hit.

It took Joe two days to install the heater but once installed our aft cabin would be cozy warm, even without an electrical connection. No more worrying about amps with this heater! The heater had its own pump to bring the fuel up from the tank in the engine room and the heater had a window, showing the flames of the burning diesel.

"Joe, this is like a fireplace on a boat!"

"Yeah, I thought you would like it. I love seeing the flames—really makes it feel warm."

We enjoyed the visual warmth for about ten minutes, until the window sooted over. The soot meant we had to figure out the proper oil:air balance for the heater.

The heater instructions, all twelve pages of them, were in desperate need of an editor—preferably an English-speaking one as neither of us could quite figure out the instructions to fine-tune the burn. Even without the view into the firebox, the heater was warm. And we knew when the pump ran because it made a *pock-et-ta pock-et-ta* sound. I hoped I'd learn more about the heater after I cleaned the soot out of it a few more times.

We were ready to sail her again, more than six weeks after our last attempt. The main deck was now solid, caulk liberally applied, the heater installed, an extra supply of towels stowed, and rain pants purchased. It was again time to leave our safe and dry boat shed.

We checked the weather forecasts this time and found a gale was heading towards Ketchikan later in the week. That gave us about three days to do a four-day trip. The math was not looking good, but Joe said we would figure it out along the way. "The weather changes, Paula. We should have a few good days and we can always anchor up."

This was another item I would not mention to Mom.

It was late afternoon on a Sunday when we finally headed out as it took hours to complete the stow. Packing all the loose material into secure spots in a 33½ foot boat is just not quick. The weather was rainy and gray. Lora said, "You guys leave at the worst time."

We had looked at the weather and thought we'd get a good Monday and Tuesday though Sunday was not great. This might have been an optimistic read on conditions; I didn't have enough sea time to really tell.

My sea time was measured in minutes. And Joe was used to sailing on big ships that sailed in just about any condition, so I was not positive that he was the best judge on this either. The weather was better than the last attempt, that I was sure of.

Visibility was good leaving the boat shed. Sailing south in the Gastineau Channel was calm, just a touch of a chop, a bit of rain and a trace of wind. We easily docked up at the Douglas Harbor to raise the mast. No drama. While we didn't have a cruise ship to try and follow this time, we could see where we were going, as could the radar. I was almost able to relax. Almost.

About two hours south of Juneau, the Gastineau Channel opened into Stephens Passage, which was five times as wide. The seas had picked up. Literally. The boat was being picked up and set back down. Stephens Passage ran north and south, with Admiralty Island to the west and the often-uninhabited Alaska mainland to the east. If I had read the *Coast Pilot* (I had not gotten to this section before the gooping event), I would have known about the various currents that could affect the Passage, that could create tidal rips and swells. That plus the weather system explained the rough ride we were having.

We didn't have a chop, mostly large, rolling waves. The further south we went, the worse the roll, the worse the random motion. Waves were over five feet, then over seven, rolling chaotically. Joe and I were both in the main salon. I was using two hands to hold on, having already picked everything up off the floor.

"Paula, I told you those would fall off the counter."

"Yes, yes, you had. Apparently, there are some things I needed to experience firsthand." Like rough seas while sailing in the dark.

Night had fallen but the full moon suddenly peeked through the clouds, hitting the waves. I wished it hadn't. Viewing seven-foot waves was disturbing. It was bad enough feeling the hit they made to the hull. Moonlit waves hurtling toward the boat—my knuckles were white from clenching.

Even though the rain was ending, the seas weren't calming. One of the Passage's currents came from the east, from the Taku River, off the Taku Glacier, through Taku Bay. The Taku winds that froze me on the boat last winter were now indiscriminately pushing me and the boat around. I was feeling unwelcome in the neighborhood.

Joe was working the wheel, to keep us on an efficient track, if efficiency was even possible in these seas. The waters tossed us side to side, up and down. As we got near the mouth of Taku Inlet, the waves got worse. Now even Joe was holding on, though only with one hand. The *Pilot Project* was rolling. Back and forth, back and forth, then front to back with some side to side, plus up and down with the seven-foot waves. Joe was trying to explain to me the different nautical terms: pitch and yaw, heave and surge, sway and roll. The lesson wasn't getting through.

I was just trying to keep my stomach from hurling and my grip from failing. All my muscles were clenched working to keep me upright. I didn't think Joe expected his wife to fall off the deck like an unstowed coffee pot. I know his wife did not wish for that outcome.

The seas were bad. I was wondering if I should get Joe his Mustang—his float coat, designed to keep a body tossed into the ocean warm and floating. I was visualizing having to swim to shore when the boat tipped over all the way. I also began to wonder why I didn't have a float coat. *I don't think he bought a life insurance policy on me?*

Was Joe hugging the eastern shore, not sailing in the middle of the channel, because it was a shorter swim? Even though there are bears over that way?

I finally asked him.

He laughed, "No, Paula, the waves are calmer

over here because we have some protection from the Taku current with the shoreline."

He turned to me and looked entirely surprised at my pale face, "Are you worried? Nothing to worry about. These seas are really not very bad, just seven or eight or so. The boat is riding just fine."

Well, I learned something new—seven-foot waves were "fine." I should have thought about what this sailing adventure would mean to a deep-sea sailor compared to a complete newbie. One person's terror was another person's normal day. *Okay, Joe wasn't concerned by this.* I returned to a mental mantra: *it's fine Paula, fine.* I tried not to remember that more people die in Alaska from hypothermia than from bears or moose or probably even car accidents. Everything was "fine."

I would try and channel Joe's perspective and get mine out of the morbid hole it had fallen into.

The boat moved slower than expected, only getting 6-7 knots, which I learned was about 7-8 miles per hour in non-boaty terms. Therefore, we reached our first harbor after dark, twenty-three miles south of Juneau, Taku Harbor.

The moon had disappeared, and the drizzle had returned but at least there was no danger of a freeze. Joe had to use a spotlight to find the state float, trying to light up a distant shore on a rainy, cloudy night, a shore with almost no human footprint, while standing on a moving surface. Luckily, the smidgen of human presence, signs from the State Marine Park, reflected enough for Joe to find his way to the dock.

There was a shoreside cabin, a short dock and there might be people (and therefore lights) during the summer, but in late October, it was dark and deserted. We had no idea what the place looked like when we tied up at the dock about midnight. I was hoping the Taku winds were not going to add more pain to my authentic Alaskan boating experience. We headed immediately to sleep, in the aft cabin cave whose mattress had largely dried out from the last sailing attempt.

The Taku winds were kind and I had a solid night's sleep. In the morning we woke up to sun and a magnificent view. Taku Harbor was gorgeous. Still, calm waters surrounded by spruce-covered mountains. It was like floating in a green bowl, with green hillsides all around. A small jut of land protected the Harbor from the swells of Stephens Passage, which helped my stomach settle down. I was becoming fond of still waters.

Joe used the BBQ to heat water for coffee and he poured the rest of the pot in a thermos so we could have a cup later without having to go out onto the deck and try to grill hot water.

We shared the joy of our observation that the decks weren't leaking. I did not mention that I smelled the slight odor of goop out on the deck. The thought that the goop might not have fully hardened, and therefore would fail, was too difficult for the fine morning. I refused to spend time worrying whether the rain was dissolving the laminating resin, resin we hadn't topped with the final waxy layer. Did the resin not cure and therefore not solidify? I refused to think about it. I chose to focus on decks that weren't leaking, on my good night's sleep, on the shining sun, and that I was not pukey—a good start to the first full day of the adventure.

While my night had been restful, Joe's was less so. There was a slow leak from the window, just over his side of the bed in the aft cabin. Just one window leak. Joe woke up to it, as it was the window over his head. He got up three times to caulk it "dry." I slept through it, but, for Joe, random water drops landing on his forehead did not make for a restful night.

With calm seas and dry skies, we sailed all day to our next stopover, Hobart Bay, at the southern end of Stephens Passage. This was another uncrowded (census population: 3), beautiful place with otters ten times more plentiful than humans. The river otters came up on the dock and looked at our stern deck. I think the only reason they didn't jump aboard is because we were there.

Why do the otters of Southeast Alaska like boats so much? Or did they smell the spraint of their Juneau friends? I'd hate to think the spraint smell survived the main deck replacement, but, who knew? Humans have so little knowledge of the secret world of smells. Were otter noses more finely attuned? Without a doubt.

Hobart Bay was also spectacular: snowy, glacier-topped mountains around a calm, peaceful harbor. Joe cooked steaks and we sat enjoying the sunset in the quiet world, watching the otters play on the dock. We reminded ourselves to walk around the spraints on the dock when we would untie the next morning. That night the *pock-et-ta pock-et-ta* sound lulled us to a warm, cozy sleep. Even Joe got a full night's sleep— nothing to fix.

My otter theory looked right as in the morning there were a few piles of spraints on the stern as well as on the dock. Joe kindly washed them down with a few buckets of ocean water.

Once out of Hobart Bay, I was queasy again. But I could ignore my nausea: the wilds of the Inside Passage were visible all around. Sharp blue sky balanced against gray-green waves, all framed by white-topped and green-clad mountains. Joe pointed out whale blows, columns of moist air just above the surface. I stepped out to the deck, and with a hand on the railing, I saw the magic: not whales in the distance but porpoises, swimming with the boat.

They were Dall's porpoises. Almost like small orcas: black with a large white patch on their sides and running on their undersides but their dorsal fin was short compared to orcas. Unlike my childhood porpoise, Flipper, these didn't have much of a beak. Their head was small and their body was thick. They played in our bow wave, swimming and jumping ahead of and next to the bow, not just for a minute or two but for nearly an hour. I couldn't pull away from the sight. *This was it! Authentic and real!* A dozen black and white porpoises swimming, diving, jumping just an arm's length away.

After about an hour, I began to notice how cold I was. As I slid open the door to the salon, Joe said, "I like having you aboard my love. I like seeing how much you are enjoying the ocean I've worked on for decades. I think I've gotten a bit cavalier about all the wildlife out here. Thanks for reminding me of it."

My smile widened even further, and I hugged him as he steered the boat. I pointed to the porpoises in our bow wake, "This happens a lot?"

"It's not unusual. Depends on the waters but if there are swimming marine mammals around, they often like to swim with a ship. I think the pressure wave at the bow is fun for them. I think I told you the story about the whales near the Woods Hole ship ... ?"

"You did but tell me again, I love your sailor stories."

"It was just before I met you in Acapulco—"

"Gosh, I loved that trip!"

"On that Woods Hole ship, we had a pod of humpback whales swim with us, along the port side. Just behind, a bit beyond the stern, was a pod of orcas. And behind them, was a school of sharks."

Even though I had heard this story a few times, I gazed at Joe as he told it, imagining the lineup of animals swimming next to his ship.

"A humpback was giving birth and she was swimming just next to the hull near the bow. There were two humpbacks to her left and about four just behind her. As soon as the baby was born, the ones behind helped the infant get up to the air for its first breath."

Whales watching a birth!

210

He continued as I pictured the marvel, "We thought the orcas were hanging around in case the young one did not survive, or in case they could grab it, but the humpback pod wasn't letting them get close. The sharks hung out for the afterbirth; it was a pretty big meal for them. Those humpbacks hung around the ship for hours, using the hull as protection against the orcas. The baby survived and the orcas went hungry."

I beamed at him and said, "For me, to see these porpoises, in this wilderness, sharing it with you—I feel like I could burst with joy. It's been completely worth all the effort, all the work to get the boat ready, even worth all the nausea. Thanks for bringing me along."

"Of course, my love."

"And next time, next stop, remind me to include Dramamine in ship stores." We both laughed.

I made us a few sandwiches for lunch, appreciating the tiny salon as I could keep one hand on the counter to steady myself while I used the other hand for sandwich making. Counter, refrigerator, sink, utensils, all were within reach of my one arm without taking a step.

With the weather still kind, on the third full day of the trip, we made it to Petersburg, "Little Norway," about halfway to Ketchikan. This stop had people. Shops. Restaurants. Bars. All within walking distance of the harbor. Joe radioed into the Harbor Master and got a transient slip for a week.

There was a gale on its way. Tying up in Petersburg until the weather improved looked like the right move. The boat could stay until we had a three-day weather window for the final push to Ketchikan.

Joe had to get back to work so we planned for me to stay aboard while Joe returned to his commute via Alaska Airlines, as they had jet service between Petersburg and Ketchikan. I was now comfortable enough on the boat to stay aboard alone for a week. I mostly ignored my internal trepidation to feel pride in my growing boaty-competence.

This was going to be my first time alone on the boat overnight. Days alone. I prepared. I had my caulk gun to deal with any stray leaks. I knew where I could find a hardware store that sold a variety of tarps. Before Joe left, he went through a list of things I should check occasionally: the bilge, the bilge pump, and the lines. I took careful notes. Before he left, he covered the after-cabin windows with tarps, to keep the occasional drips off my head. We were prepared.

Petersburg was a marvelous little town, having at least three espresso cafés, two bookstores, and a choice of bars. The harbor, filled mostly with commercial fishing boats, sat at the center of town. I adapted to most aspects of the noisy harbor, particularly the 1,000s of gulls fighting for scraps at the seafood processing plant. However, there was a noise that kept me extra attentive. Huffing and puffing from just outside the boat. Not from the dock side, but from the water. Noisy huffs. Huge, wet puffs. Mixed with loud wet sneezes. Coming from the sea. Not joggers. Not fishermen who had smoked too much. Not angry harbor masters. Petersburg Harbor held a noisy marine mammal. A sea lion. The big one: The Steller sea lion.

Weighing over two tons, this big male hung out in the harbor, watching for the stuff dropped by the commercial fishing boats. I was happy that we had not been fishing on the *Pilot Project*: my boat had limited tasty smells. But he kept swimming around, looking at me, hoping for a fishy treat. Steller sea lions had been known to take a tidbit out of the boaters' flesh rather than out of the fishers' catch, but only if a person was foolish enough to hang over a railing near the giant marine mammal. I had no plans to become a tasty bite.

I hoped they didn't like to lounge on the boat like the otters did—they'd be harder to clean up after, and Joe was not around to do marine mammal sanitation.

Life aboard the boat gave me neighbors,

including some of the human variety. I could see people as I sat in the salon. Neighbors I could watch having their first cup of coffee on their boat while I was having my first cup on mine. In Juneau, the boat shed gave me privacy, other than the single neighbor who only came around on rare weekends. Here, I was going to have to be a bit more cautious. A Petersburg fisherman saw me while I was brushing my teeth in my 'jammies on my second morning aboard. He quickly looked away, head down. He may have blushed. Shy Norwegians in Petersburg, Alaska. From then on, I used the aft cabin head for my toiletry routines.

Now that I was alone on the boat, I learned how much I depended on Joe. About 11 p.m., the gale arrived. Winds gusted to 60 knots, meaning occasional winds of nearly 70 miles per hour. Rain fell sideways. The tarps over the windows flapped constantly. Joe had used 2x6 lumber to hold down the sheeting. The boards pounded the deck and threatened the windows. It wasn't restful. Someone needed to tie down the tarps. Joe wasn't there. He was the natural choice for this job. He wasn't there. It was up to me.

Over my 'jammies, I pulled on my new Helly Hansens—Alaskan raingear: rubber raincoat, hood, and bib pants—in a fashionable bright orange. I slipped on my Alaskan slippers, *XtraTuf* boots. I found some extra line and I went out into the storm. The wind blew my hood off but I persevered. I'm not sure what kind of knots I tied but they held the lumber away from the window. It took me twenty minutes until the lines were snug enough. It then took me another twenty minutes to dry off and relax from the excitement, but I managed a good night's sleep.

Sitting in Petersburg, I learned about functional clothing. Helly Hansens and Juneau slippers were just the beginning. In the movies, guys on the waterfront often wore caps, watch caps. Wool caps without brims that lay over the forehead or over the ears, usually black.

On the Waterfront guys or Mickey in *Rocky*, whose gym was close to the waterfront. Most any TV detective show with a harbor murder had someone wearing a watch cap. In the real world, it was a favorite of both Jacques Cousteau and most submariners. I had never thought about that stock wardrobe choice before, but now I understood. It can be cold on the waterfront. Damp. The watch cap was the first order of protection. Mine was red and, while it clashed with my Helly Hansens, it served. Warm. Coziness. Heat retention. Crucial when you were living on a boat, in Alaska. Especially when you have a cold.

Two days after Joe left, I got a cold—fever and cough. Luckily, I had plenty of food aboard. I curled up and kept the heaters on high. Petersburg's harbor had a hotspot—wireless internet access readily available on the boat. Every day I could get some online book research done and check the weather forecast. I'd email the forecast to Joe as we searched for a window in the weather.

Once my cold was gone, each day I enjoyed a morning walk around the harbor, staying away from the huffing monster. Each time on and off the boat I'd check the lines—were they secure? Then a stroll looking at the other boats: scuffed-up wooden trawlers, long-liners with multiple booms, aluminum tenders edged with fenders, and the occasional sailboat, probably docked for the winter. From the harbor, I headed to the coffee shop and then a browse through the bookstore, before going back to the boat for some writing time. Most evenings I went back to town for a beer and a sandwich. I didn't mind the drizzly weather and was glad ice season had not yet arrived.

About a week after Joe left, we found our window: three days without gale force winds. Three days with seas under five foot. I called Joe to see if that window could work for him. He planned to take the ferry from Ketchikan to arrive in Petersburg about 2 a.m. on Friday morning.

It was that day that I learned how much I really did depend on Joe.

That Thursday I went shopping to stock up for our two-day voyage, stowed all the food. And in the evening, I went back to the Harbor Bar for one last visit: an Alaskan Amber and a pizza for dinner. On my way back to the boat, I took care around stray lines and massive marine mammals. I was my normal perky self when I went to bed. I woke up about 11 p.m. My normal perky self had departed.

Every muscle in my body hurt. My head was pounding and there were no wind-driven 2x6s to blame. I was both burning up and freezing. I was nauseous without rough seas. I was as miserable as I had ever been.

By the time Joe came in at 2 a.m. I was softly moaning, "Joe? Joe? Is that you?" He got home just in time to supply me with a bucket as the nausea progressed to retching. I continued to retch, on and off, for hours, though my stomach had long been emptied.

It was a long night, for both of us.

I'd toss, knotting the bed linens, moaning, with Joe softly asking, "Can I get you anything? Can I do anything? Do you need the bucket?" He felt bad for me, but I felt worse. I had never been that sick.

He wanted to take me to the hospital immediately, but I didn't think it opened until 8 a.m. The Petersburg hospital was just a small-town clinic. At 7 a.m., I started putting my clothes on. I could barely stand. Each movement was trembly and off-balance. Sliding each limb into my shirt or pants took Joe's help. I was lethargic and weak and had to sit down periodically to continue. An hour after I started, I was dressed. I could not have managed it without Joe.

I would not have made it up the few steps in the cabin or down onto the dock without Joe carefully handing me off the boat. He held me firmly as he led me down the dock. He was sweet, repeating. "Are you okay? Can I do anything? Take your time. Keep a hold of my arm."

I needed that arm to make it along the dock and to the street.

He called for a cab at the harbor master's office. When the cabbie heard the destination, he said, "The hospital is only two blocks away. You can walk it."

Joe almost yelled, "She's not walking it. She needs the ride. I'll gladly pay your fare, doesn't matter. She's not walking."

The cabbie got the idea.

I was pitiful. The clinic's secretary wanted to give me a bed right away. Even the nurse was making pitiful sounds, "Oh, you poor dear. Tsk tsk tsk."

I had never before heard anyone say *tsk tsk tsk*.

My blood pressure was extremely low (80/40) and my heart rate was extremely high (110). I was dehydrated and could barely hold up my head.

One listen to my lungs and the doctor knew. I had pneumonia.

They had a shot for pneumonia. I hoped the miracle of antibiotics would kick in fast.

I couldn't bear to return to the boat, as every slight motion hurt. Joe checked me into a Petersburg hotel, just one block from the clinic. He had me settled in and we thought that he'd take the boat south while I caught a flight later that afternoon. I wasn't sure about that plane ride, but I had a hotel room and I thought I could get on the plane with a few hours of antibiotic magic.

Joe left the hotel but was back within the hour. He decided not to leave me alone. He said he saw an omen that said he should leave the boat where it was and stay and take care of me. He hadn't been able to move the boat. There was a huge Steller sea lion blocking the stern.

Apparently both Joe and I made a connection with that immense floating creature.

I was a bit relieved with his decision as the antibiotic magic was not working as quickly as I hoped. I was also pleased to have someone to fetch me ice water at any time I wanted it.

We stayed in the hotel for two days until I was feeling well enough to take the plane.

The weather window was still open for the boat move to Ketchikan. Joe put me on the plane, and he sailed her while I flew south. Kim and John met me in Ketchikan and opened their home to me, giving me a warm, stable spot to recover.

All tucked in Kim's quilts, I fully relaxed when Joe crawled in to join me 24 hours later. He had sailed straight through without rest to get the boat to its new home, and to get back to me.

I mumbled, "Sweets, you made it. The sea lion left you alone?"

Joe hugged me and said, "Yes my love, no marine mammal problems. Boat is all tied up in Refuge Cove. Go back to sleep my love, rest and get better."

I was sorry to miss that leg of the boat adventure but was glad for the comfy warm cocoon of Kim and John's guest room, especially with Joe to share it with me.

Over the next two weeks, Joe and John headed in to work early and returned late. It didn't take but a few days for Joe's relaxed mood to drain away with the demands of the office. He'd get back from work just in time for dinner and would be monosyllabic for dinner conversation, unless he and John got going on a work topic, and then Kim and I heard the angry rants. Kim and I attempted to make the dinner table a No Work Zone, but we realized it was useful for both the guys to be able to rant a bit to each other while out of the office. We gave up the No Work Zone.

In the mornings, Joe was up and out before 6 a.m. to attempt to deal with the daily onslaught of managing a ferry system with only 20% of its normal administrative staff. His crazy job had become even worse with the move to Ketchikan.

The one positive thing about the Ketchikan move: John said it was fine for Joe to be free of the necktie-requirement. Joe no longer had to wear the clothing accessory that reminded him of the middle-management doldrums before he even left for work.

After two weeks in Kim's haven, I was well enough that it was time to go back to life on the boat.

Joe drove us from town to the boat's new marina, located north of the city, near his office in Ward Cove. Ketchikan, like Juneau, had one main road running north and south, the Tongass Highway. While Juneau was on the mainland, water and ice isolated it from other mainland communities. Ketchikan was fully isolated by water on Revillagigedo Island. Much of the human development was rooted on the east side of Revillagigedo, bordered by Tongass Narrows. Tongass Highway ran over 30 miles north and south up the eastern edge, paralleling the Narrows. Like Juneau's Gastineau Channel, Tongass Narrows separated the city from the nearby islands, Gravina and Pennock, with the larger islands of Metlakatla and Prince of Wales a bit further away. Ketchikan is Alaska's southernmost city, with Canadian waters just sixty miles south.

Ketchikan reminded me of another city: Buffalo, NY, my hometown. Not in landscape as Ketchikan has complex topography of mountains and hills while Buffalo is just flat. Not in population, as Ketchikan and its surrounding borough has under 14,000 people while Buffalo and its metro area has well over a million. The similarity is their industrial remnants.

Buffalo had been a rust belt town, filled with working middle class folks and industry that kept them employed. And then the industry went away. Buildings weren't maintained. Factories were shuttered. Real estate prices took a hit. Buffalo spent decades to get back on its economic feet. Ketchikan wasn't a rust belt city but a wood belt one, entirely dependent on wood supply from the US Forest Service in the Tongass National Forest. The Ketchikan Pulp Mill was the major employer. When its wood supply largely ended in 1997, the Mill shut its door and Ketchikan got hit by the same sort of economic loss as Buffalo had. Ketchikan's rebound was underway, but the scars of deficient maintenance were visible on buildings all over town. It didn't help that Ketchikan's climate was not kind to the built environment.

On the drive from Kim's, the windshield wipers were getting a workout. When we got to the Refuge Cove parking lot and marina overlook, in the heavy rainfall, it took me a second to find the boat. Joe had covered the entire boat in tarp, gray tarp, enormous gray tarp covering the top of the mast to below the main deck. The boat's live-aboard condition had not fared well and Joe had to tarp her to give us a dry place to sleep. The lovely lines of the *Pilot Project* were hidden.

Looked like the *Pilot Project* shared Ketchikan's maintenance deficit.

Home was now under a tarp. A gray-covered world, in a gray-covered town, with Joe working a job that turned his moods dark, dark gray.

I paused before going down the ramp to the boat. I was pretty sure I was going to miss the cocoon at Kim's.

12 Life in the Big Top

Floater: (n) sewage treatment plant: buoyant human waste

November 2004

Our deck fix had failed. All those weeks of fumes, goop and glooping, all mostly wasted. Joe did think that we could save the plywood and the goop under the plywood if we kept the deck dry. The upper layer had washed out. The great Evercoat goop (*easy to apply*) may have been too easy to apply. The deck covered with Evercoat, which was all but the starboard corner, had dissolved. In two weeks out of the boat shed, the rain and the seas dissolved the resin. Maybe it hadn't hardened properly because it was too cold when we applied it. Maybe we hadn't put enough on. Maybe it needed a top gel coat to protect it, like the can said. Whatever the reason, it was gone. We now had to protect the plywood from more moisture or chance losing that too.

Protecting a boat deck from moisture was easy in a boat shed—just pull the curtain closed. Out of a boat shed, it was a trickier problem. Lay the tarp flat but wind would shift it and rain would soak underneath. Protecting a boat deck from moisture was an especially tricky problem in Ketchikan.

Most US cities have thermometers measuring donations to the United Way. Ketchikan had a giant thermometer, taller than a building, denoting annual rainfall, measured not in inches but in feet, which they named the "Liquid Sunshine Gauge." I was not convinced by the city's effort to rebrand torrential rain.

Ketchikan may be the only city in the world which closes steep hillside streets when there is even the slightest chance of ice. And the steep streets are particularly tricky because of all the rain, rain that supports the growth of mold and algae on the streets themselves. Shoenbar Road in the center of town even has a sign letting motorists know if it's open or closed due to weather.

How to protect a boat deck when rain falls an inch or two at a time, when it rains more days than not, where fourteen feet of rain a year is not unheard of? When sunshine was the unusual condition? When we still needed to live aboard her? The answer was a hanging tarp. It wasn't a good answer, but it was our only choice.

Take a 33-and-a-half-foot long boat. Add a 12-foot-high mast with a 12-foot boom (the horizontal bar attached to the mast.) Tie a line from the bow to the top of the mast and then down, to the end of the boom, just off the stern. That is a structure from which to hang tarp. Rolls and rolls of tarp. Hundreds of dollars' worth of tarp.

Duct tape could hold the tarps together. So could zip ties. Wire line. Nylon line. Polypropylene line. Whatever line was at hand. These same materials could tie the tarp to the boat rails. Joe threaded these materials through grommets, some of which he had to create. Luckily, hardware stores sold grommet-making kits. Until this trip I had known nothing of the grommet-making world. One more skill to add to my sabbatical year. We had to have a supply of tie-down gear to replace those lost after every 60-knot blow, or about once every two weeks in Ketchikan.

On a sunny day, the tarp arranged as above would look good—well, would look not too bad. It would look like it could keep the deck dry. But it was not as functional as it looked.

A tarp covering a boat that size became a wonderful sail in the slightest breeze. Wind gusts combined with loose tarp edges expanded the cover, tearing tie downs and pulling deck rails with a strong breeze. And, if it was raining, which it mostly was, then the decks got wet. Which was not the point.

To make the tarps fully functional, Alaskan-winterized, Ketchikan-ready, the boat cover needed one more thing: milk jugs. Or one-gallon plastic jugs that held any liquid. Once the containers held liquid (freshwater or seawater, or even orange juice), the jugs were tied to the lowest tarp border. Joe used any of the tie-down materials to connect the heavy jug to the lowest, tarp-edge grommets. The jug's weight would hold the tarp from fluttering, if there was enough tension kept on its tie to the tarp. It was best if the jug also floated in the ocean, so that the jug wouldn't always bang against the side of the hull with the wind. The jugs kept the tarp from blowing too far and kept the water off the deck, if there were enough jugs.

Joe had to keep adding them and then keep refining the tension on the juglines. Sometimes there was too much tension and the grommets blew out. We spent weeks improving the jug-hanging craftsmanship. I even added a few myself, feeling very sailor-like as I became a grommet-creator.

Sometimes jugs had to be added in the middle of the night. I was happy to let Joe have the nighttime jug installs.

By early December, we had ten hanging jugs off each side of our 33-and-a-half-foot boat. Our tarps were gray. We had yellow and white lines holding the tarps down, along with black or white or yellow zip-ties. Some grommets were black, some were silver, some were brass. We had plastic milk jugs, clear water bottles, and two orange juice containers hanging off the tarps. The *Pilot Project* was not going to win any design awards.

I just wanted functional—anything that kept water from dripping on our heads in the middle of the night was highly desirable. We hoped the tarp would remain in place and keep us dry until we could figure out how to get the deck fixed.

Life under the tarp was not like life in the boat shed, cozy and private. We could hear everything folks said as they walked past the boat. As the boat was moored at the bottom of the only ramp in the marina, everyone who came down the ramp saw the tarp-covered mess that was the *Pilot Project*. More than once, I'd be inside writing, and listened to their commentary about the boat.

"Someone lives in there?"

"What kind of a boat is under there?"

"Really, they live in there?"

"They did a nice job on the jugs holding down the tarp."

I always appreciated the compliments. There weren't many.

We had to assume most folks could hear us as well. The tarp not only didn't give us the privacy we'd like but it transmitted the weather all too well. Rain as a pitter-patter of drops echoed inside the boat. Rain as a torrential downpour blocked most other sounds inside the boat and we'd have to yell to speak to each other. This, along with Joe's job pressures, meant we had few conversations.

When we heard water drops, we had to consider: were those outside rain drops or was the tarp leaking somewhere? These were not restful thoughts.

Gentle winds pulled at the tarp, which then slapped against more tarp. With stronger winds, the tarp flapped in the breeze. Gusty winds and the jugs banged against the hull. More than once we woke up to make the calculation: was the banging bad enough that someone had to go out and do something with a jug or a tarp line?

The weather gave us lots of practice to get better at identifying sounds and reacting appropriately, though we paid the price in sleep.

One of the worst things about the tarp was that

the diesel fireplace-like heater could not be used. No more *pock-et-ta pock-et-ta* sounds to go to sleep with. No more cozy warmth. The heater exhaust was under the tarp. If we had fired it up, the exhaust by-product of the toasty warmth would have killed us.

I was trying not to be miserable. Maintaining my mood was hard living in a gray cocoon that was neither particularly warm nor particularly cozy nor particularly restful. On cloudy days it was the best, as the outside weather was much like the inside weather. On sunny days, it was bad, just bad. The bright yellow sun rays became rays of gray inside the boat and the lovely golden teak in the salon turned into a pukey, washed out, dim, sick-yellow color. On cold days, I was sad when I looked at the unusable *pock-et-ta pock-et-ta* heater.

The tarp also meant we couldn't take the boat out. No sailing. No exploring. No fishing trips. Just life under the gray. And Joe coming home each night from a job he hated.

I did appreciate the better amperage in Refuge Cove Harbor—30 amps. No more having to switch breakers on or off. Though the downside was that I stayed under the tarp for longer periods of time and had less break from the gray.

I'd been meeting the neighbors, but only when I emerged from the tarp. They often didn't realize I was under there. Dale lived in the boat just ahead of us. He was concerned about our tarp acting like a powerful sail. The wind would push the *Pilot Project* off the dock and, in the process, it would pull on the dock structure, the same dock that Dale's boat was tied up to. I think he worried that our sail would destroy the dock and take out his boat too. We had to trust the quality of the Refuge Cove Marina pilings and hope they were deep and strong.

Life under the big top was not restful even for those not living under it.

Dale asked, "You living under there?"

I nodded yes.

Dale continued, "Nope, I couldn't do that."

This was from a man who ran a cattle ranch and lived in a wilderness cabin on Admiralty Island, who coped with the highest density of brown bears in the world, alone with his wife and the bears for seven years.

I guessed the gray was too much for some people.

There were a few bright spots. The Refuge Cove ramp was longer than at Aurora Harbor and Ketchikan's tides were a bit less extreme making a more favorable trigonometry for low tide ramp excursions. Boat life and Joe life were mixing in my sleep. I woke Joe up one night, telling him that he had to wake up because of the small bathroom rule. Did I have any idea what that meant? No. Did Joe? No, but he thought it was cute.

Mostly though, it was gray or black.

There were a few other liveaboards in Refuge Cove and all their boats looked better than ours. Other than Dale and his wife, there was Matthew and Claire with their two-year-old son. I could hear their diesel heater making the *pock-et-ta pock-et-ta* sound so I knew they were cozy and warm. On the outside edge of the dock, there was a fancy sixty-foot yacht that had sleek lines and perfectly fit, tight canvas work. The owner was a vice-president for a local corporation. He and his wife of fifty-plus-years appreciated the flexibility of living on a boat. She gave me a tour once—they had an onboard washer and dryer. I stopped and stared at the luxury.

In Juneau, I combined grocery runs with shower runs. In Ketchikan, it was laundry runs with shower runs. A year ago, I was looking forward to the change from my regular life in Central Pennsylvania; I never expected to learn to keep plenty of quarters on hand for a shower to be one of the changes. In towns and villages without gyms, laundromats often included coin-operated showers to go along with their coin-operated washing machines. These gave boat people a place to get clean in exchange for about ten quarters. While using public showers was not my favorite experience as it was always odd to get naked just a wall away from random people hanging out in a laundromat, it was a good way to get the chill off.

At least there were no Taku winds in Ketchikan, just torrential downpours and frequent gales.

But even without Taku winds, on cold days, with every electric heater going, the inside temperature did not get much above 40 degrees Fahrenheit. Forty degrees inside. In Celsius that would be 4. In Kelvin, 278. As I ran the temperature conversion in my head, I wondered, *Did any of these numbers help me feel warm?* Maybe Kelvin. It helped with the horrible reality of the quantifiable cold.

I headed to the laundromat for a long, hot shower to escape the quantifiable chill. I walked past the washers and dryers, two spinning without oversight. I entered the back, looking for signs of life or signs of dirt. Neither being found, I slowly opened a door that led to an individual shower stall, slowly in case anything jumped out, intent for signs of life. Scaring a naked showering stranger was not on my to-do list. Hearing no screams, I opened the door a bit wider, assessing the floor and walls for any unpleasant leavings from a previous occupant. Breathing more deeply I could catch the scent of bleach. *Okay, linoleum is safe. Clothes hooks are empty.* I locked the door behind me. *Shower floor mold-free? Yes.* Shampoo, conditioner, and box of bar soap went on the floor inside the shower. I hung the towel on the hook just outside the shower curtain and made sure it had no contact with the white plastic drape. *Is the bench dry?* The bench would be home to my folded clothes. *Do I have enough quarters?* I counted twelve quarters and stacked them on the edge of the bench. *Will the shower spray get anything wet? Can I reach the towel without freezing?* Once I was satisfied, I quickly stripped, keeping my clothes off the floor. I picked up the quarter stack and stepped in, about to start sliding in the coins, feeling each quarter so not to lose one, when I paused.

I stopped my deliberate shower procedure. I looked at the coins in my hand, at my toiletries, at my folded clothes distanced from the towel. I then closed my eyes and started laughing at myself.

In my focus on this coin-operated shower, I suddenly knew. This was authentic. This feeling, this intense reflection on the moment's events, this was part of an authentic life.

Focus, the deliberate action, mind and body engaged on the moment: that intensity of experience was what I had yearned for at the start of my sabbatical. Here it was in the laundromat shower stall. I thought the wilds of Alaska and life with my husband would provide the intensity of 'real life.' And it did, sailing with the porpoises, watching the Steller sea lion, exploring the old growth forests. But here, naked in a freshly-sanitized rental shower stall, I realized authentic had nothing to do with where I lived, nothing to do with rural or urban, wilderness or suburb, wild or domestic. Authentic was how I thought. How I focused. How mindful I was of my environment.

Here, focused on the immediate, on the process to get warm and clean, this was authentic. It didn't need any special travel, location, friend, or love. It didn't need the most unique landscape nor the most dynamic environment, nor even the perfect romantic marriage. It just meant being present in the moment.

When I had been in either wilderness or dense human cities, those environments forced that immediacy to me. I had to think about where I was in relation to the place and the surroundings. The moments of meeting Joe in a strange port brought me that consciousness of the instant in time, the smell of the port, the challenge of language, the color of the bougainvillea. It took the Ketchikan coin-operated shower for me to discover that mindful engagement was under my control. I could live in the moment, in the present, wherever I was.

I finished sliding in the coins and soaked in the warmth from the hot spray, closing my eyes and feeling the pressure of the spray against my face and chest. I grabbed the soap and focused on the frictionless slide of the bar. My heart felt like it was keeping time with the drum of the water. I took the shampoo and rubbed it into my scalp and then worked it down the length of my hair, feeling each strand, connecting to my head, to my shoulders, to my toes. A full rinse and a sense of warmth, deep, even into my toes, and the shower was done, with a few seconds on the timer to spare. *Paula, this focus on the now, you need to keep practicing.*

I smiled thinking that my husband would be home after work, and I could chat with him about my laundry-shower enlightenment. Sharing the news of the day was a tiny daily treasure of cohabitation.

Sadly, he was in no mood to chat when he got out of the office. I decided I did not want to focus on the moment of having the disgruntled husband home for dinner.

I chose to focus on a new trick that I had not used in Juneau: make water for tea in the coffee maker. Or skip the tea and make the hot water. The steam added heat to the air and just watching it warmed my core. It also added moisture, but as the boat was already damp, moored in the land where rain was measured in feet, adding steam for warmth made little difference in the damp. Water heating gave me a toasty moment or two to enjoy.

One of the great things about Refuge Cove was its proximity to Ward Lake, a National Forest area with a walking trail encircling a lake, through old-growth forest, close to areas that had been logged. Driving through the stubble of logged forest, it was always a joy to come to old growth, to see the forest similar to its ancestral form. I imagined this was the transition described in *The Lord of the Rings*, from the orc-ravaged forest outside of Isengard to the Ent's Fangorn wildwood. Giant straggly trees, dressed in layers of multiple mosses and lichens, complex arrangements with trees' ages ranging from youngest to oldest and deadfall as habitat for all sorts of birds, mammals, and insects.

Joe and I would take lunchtime walks around the Lake. At first, it only took about a half-circuit of the walk before his work rant stopped. On bad days, the rant continued for two full circuits. Walking in the woods had become much less tranquil when Joe was on a long rant. I stopped walking with him on what looked like bad days, excusing myself, "I'm deep in writing, go on your own, and I'll see you tonight." This did not bode well as walking in the woods had always been a fundamental way for us to connect.

One evening when Joe's stress was not too extreme, I started, "Now that we are back on the boat, I think it's time."

Joe studied me, "Time for what?"

"Time to get a dog."

Silence ensued.

I pushed as much as I ever did and said, "This is our first year of living together. It's the best time for us to get a dog. You like dogs. I've seen you with them."

"I hate those little yappy dogs."

"I do too. There are other kinds of dogs."

"If we get a big one, it won't fit on the boat."

"I'm sure we can find one that will fit, the perfect, boat-sized, non-yappy version. Tomorrow, let's go see what the pound has."

"You go. I have to head to the office."

While he did not sound exactly like an

enthusiastic dog-finding married-couple-partner, I took it and went to the pound. I had expected to be smiling when this moment happened, but Joe's unhappiness was sticking to me.

When I got to the pound, it was out of dogs. Totally empty.

I was not smiling on the return trip either.

When Joe got home, I told him about the empty pound. He seemed relieved.

"That's probably for the best. In February you are heading to India and France for a month and I have to travel for pilot observer trips. We can wait until you are back in March to get a dog."

March. I froze and my head dropped. March. That would leave only three months left of the living-together-concept. I took a deep breath and sighed. Even my exhaled air looked gray.

* * *

Joe was again on his daily rant about work. I had enough. My quiet, calm demeanor, my silent body language, my deep breathing exercises were not working. I lost my composure and snapped, "I'm getting tired of this rant as our evening conversation."

He paused and tensed up, "I can't stand this place! That job!"

And then it was silence. No conversation at all. For the rest of the night. No smooching. No interaction. We walked around each other without touching, which was no easy feat on a 33½ foot boat. We had voiced a conflict but had no experience on what to do with it once it had begun. Now it was silent tension, which was slightly better than the verbal rant, but not much. The tiny, cramped living quarters magnified the silence. Then, no warm cuddles in bed. My last thought before sleep, *Did we have the skills to problem solve this one?*

After work the next day, I said to the air that had him in it, "I'm going for a walk at Ward Lake."

Joe spoke, "Do you want me to come?"

Words!

"If you want to, you are more than welcome."

"I'd like to go."

Communication had started. Even though it didn't address the fundamental conflict, we might have found a way through the tension, at least for a time.

On the walk we talked about trees, other walkers, the ice, and the geese. By the end, our silent tension had dissipated.

"The walk was a good idea. Thanks for bringing me along."

"I love you Joe and I generally like being with you."

"I'll try and be a better partner."

"Thanks my love." And I could breathe deeply again, my core had relaxed for a bit. That night we got to enjoy the other benefits of being relaxed enough to actually touch each other, another lovely tension reliever. I hoped this time it would last for a while.

Three days. That's what we got before the next work insanity took over my husband. Just three days. This living together thing was not working well.

Joe and I had a spat. He came home from lunch all irritated with work.

Someone did something. He couldn't get any work done. What were those idiots thinking? He hated the job.

Just the normal whine. I could stand it but when he turned the whine on me, my patience ran out.

"Do you have your keys?" I asked, trying to be helpful, but knowing I might be irritating for asking such a basic question.

He gave me that look—that look of irritation for asking such a basic question.

I responded, "Well I won't try to be helpful anymore." And now I was in a huff too, becoming passive aggressive and irritated which was not where I wanted to be.

Was that his plan? If he can't be happy then I can't be either? Or was that my plan? An excuse that something caused me to be miserable, rather than me facing my own issue of mirroring his mood? Rather than trying to fix the conflict?

I was mad, mad at getting dragged into his emotional state, mad at him, and mad at myself. I was beginning to hate this moment I was living in.

My tolerance had found its limit. I had no way through this conflict and my dream of life with my husband had shredded.

I spent the day off the boat, thinking of getting a hotel room, thinking of leaving entirely. Wishing the road out of Ketchikan went anywhere. Roads on an island were useless. I would have to take a ferry to drive someplace else. The only way out, even by plane, required a boat ride. The "Bridge to Nowhere" was actually a Bridge to Somewhere: the Ketchikan airport, and away. But the bridge didn't get funded. There was no easy escape from Ketchikan. I wasn't in the mood for another boat ride. I didn't want to have to take a ferry to get away. I had lost patience with everything maritime.

Romance had disappeared under a gray, gray tarp, under gray, gray skies.

I spent three hours sitting in the Ketchikan airport parking area, frozen, considering my choices. I felt like Sam, as he looked down at Frodo's lifeless body wrapped in Shelob's web. I was desolate and it was hard to decide what to do next.

I was tired of it all. Was it dead, this life together? Like the wildlife in the museums, did I have to kill a full-time marriage and stuff it into shorter periods to save it?

Marriage was beginning to feel like the Ring, a burden of pain and responsibility. Should I fly off? Could I leave this burden behind for a time? I'd have to tell all those practical friends that they were right, that having Joe and I living together, combined with the stresses of "regular life" was a mistake. Joe could work this kind of job or find something better and I could live elsewhere.

Our marriage would be only honeymoon sandwiches? That was sounding like the next step, to get rid of the rot that had set in.

The tears were going to make it hard to drive.

13 New Discoveries

Float: (n) a tool used by masons to smooth cement

Winter and Spring 2004-2005

After staring at the airport ferry for three hours, fully dispirited but unwilling to depart and leave my year with Joe, I headed back to Refuge Cove. Joe got home a half hour later. He was quiet. I was quiet. We slowly started talking about mundane things that we could both deal with neutrally.

"The dome light went out again."

"Um, it must be the switch."

"Thanks for the toilet paper purchase."

"No problem—I hate to run out too."

"The heater seems to be working well."

"Yes, cleaning it off was the trick."

Through these small steps, we again found a bridge to communicate.

About an hour later, having firmed up the bridge, Joe put it to use. He found a way into conflict problem-solving.

He asked, "What do you want out of life, Paula? Where do you want to be?"

Twenty-some years of married life and we had never talked about these big questions. We sailed through, letting ship and college employment transport us to wherever they took us. We never had a solid discussion of what we wanted—it was always about what could work. We flexed around any conflicts. We problem-solved our way through life. I mirrored his moods and interests and that worked for the short bits of time we were together. He followed my career choices and moved where academia took me. We supported each other's goals and adapted to those needs. We floated with the opportunities of the moment.

The float method wasn't working anymore. This was a conversation long overdue.

I faced him and spoke without a smile, "I'd like to feel at home somewhere, some sense of belonging. I'd love to end up in Homer. That's the kind of location I could imagine spending my life in, with loads of good friends and amazing landscapes and close to wilderness." I was fully focused on him as I continued, "Would Homer be okay for you?"

He nodded carefully, "Yes. I like the outdoors stuff there, boating, fishing, hiking."

I had to be clear, "This time on the boat has made me want a home, a permanent home, one that we stick with for a while. I don't want to have to sell off another house and most of our possessions."

He agreed, "Yeah, I'd like that too. We have moved around every few years. That's getting old."

He got quiet for a second and then said, "But what about your tenured job at Juniata? You worked so long to get tenure. And you are waiting on that promotion. Are you okay giving it up? What would you do for work? That was your dream job."

"Juniata will decide this Spring whether they give me the promotion to Full and I'm hopeful I'll get it. If I do, that fulfills my goal. Just like you wanted to get your Unlimited Masters, it didn't mean you had to sail on that license forever. Same with me and Full Professor rank—I'd like to get it, but I don't want it to tie me down. I could give up tenure and find something at the local college in Homer or in Alaska somewhere. If an Alaska university job didn't open up, I'd love to try writing for a living. This pilot job of yours, it would give us the financial leeway for me to have a career change, and that's exciting."

I took a deep breath and spoke through a strained voice, "But, if we are going to settle in a place, a place we'd build a home that we'd keep, a place we build roots, it has to be a place where you do a job you like. If you work a shore-side management job like this port captain job, then …"

I paled and looked at my hands, this was the hard part and my eyes were filling with unshed tears, "I cannot imagine living with you full-time."

I couldn't look at him as I said, "I'm sorry …"

I was telling the love of my life that I didn't want to live with him under certain conditions and it was killing me. I felt a sliver of the grief Arwen must have felt at Aragorn's passing. I couldn't breathe …

Joe bridged my pain, "No, I get it. I don't want to live with me in this job."

My stomach unclenched enough for me to take a sudden deep breath and look up at him. My eyes began to clear. We were both breathing now. I could see a bit of lightness in his face from our sharing of heartache.

Joe quietly spoke, "Sweets, remember what I used to say about the red scarf?"

"The red scarf?"

"Yes. That if we ever separated, all you'd have to do would be to send me the red scarf you wore on the day we met, and I'd come back. I still feel that way."

My eyes were watering again as I took his hand, "Thanks for the reminder my love. Hopefully, it won't come to that." *Tears for his love? Or tears over its loss?*

It seemed some of my more rational friends were right: living with my husband full-time was not going to work, at least not with the unending stress of his current shore-side job. My cohabitation "experiment" had limits. I breathed deeply as I admitted this truth.

Ms. Realism was a sadder persona than Ms. Optimism.

Joe replied, "Love, I will work on getting us to Homer. And into a job I will like. The independence of a pilot job, that will work for me, truly."

That night, we did not pressure each other with planning and dreams—the bridge was too fragile for that. I was relieved to have communicated my limits. We had faced the conflict and I had not turned my husband away.

Three days later, it was another stress-filled evening, with more tension and more silence, and plenty of sailor talk as Joe fixed a line on the tarp. Even when Joe was off the boat, I'd just sit and stare at my computer, trying to remember a positive perspective. Words did not flow in the gray.

I needed an escape. I was walking through Mordor with the weight of the ring around my neck and there was no Mt. Doom in sight to end the misery. But there was a break coming up. I had planned travel before I ever left Pennsylvania: to teach in two international programs. I had a way to escape the tarp world, at least for a month. I just had to hang on until then.

* * *

It was late December and it was pouring, Ketchikan-style. At least it was not a sideways-pour, just a straight-down dump. Joe had to go to the SouthEast Alaska Pilot Association office. Was he exploring another pilot group? SWAPA had been slow to have another vote. Or was it a work-related visit? I had gotten to the point of not even asking about his work or his day. We were running out of conversation topics and the end point of that trajectory was heart-breaking.

I picked him up at lunch time.

"Paula, let's skip lunch and go to the pound.

Maybe they have something."

Eyebrows raised, I turned to look directly at him, "What? Now? Now you want to look for a dog?"

"Yeah, I think we should."

I don't know where that idea of his came from, another strange, unusual Joe idea. But I briefly smiled for the first time in days.

It continued to pour. We entered the city pound, located at the southern end of town, directly next to the city cemetery. The pound door led into a narrow, dank hallway: cinder block walls, cement floor, all worn from years of chlorine bleach applications.

The only staff person, a middle-aged, sad, serious woman, came out, and softly said, "Can I help you?"

I asked, "What dogs do you have for adoption?" Our backs were to the line of kennel cages.

"Just one. She came in over a week ago."

We turned and looked. There were about nine cages, made of chain-link fence and cement slabs. Only the center cage was occupied. The dog sat in the middle of the cage, as far away from the chain-link as she could get. She looked at the staff person and not at us. She did not move, just stared, frozen.

She looked like a middle-aged dog, with peppered white hair, and extra weight around her middle. I did not know what the breed was. She did not look at us at all. Her tail was still. She simply sat there.

Joe and I turned to each other; we didn't smile. We raised our brows and we might have frowned. There was no enthusiasm anywhere in that cement block building, human or canine.

The staff woman said, "Her owner died suddenly. You might have seen the story in the paper?"

Joe looked quizzical and I said, "Oh, the lady who died on the boardwalk downtown … drugs? Alcohol? Sounded sad."

"She had three dogs but the other two were not adoptable."

Not adoptable was Pound Code for "badly behaved and euthanize at first opportunity."

"Precious here—"

"Precious?"

"Yes, her owner named her Precious."

Dog three was Precious. I felt like more sadness was at hand.

"Precious has been here for more than a week. She only has a few days to go."

More Pound Code, "Only a few days to go" meant "future euthanasia." I asked, "What kind of dog is she?"

"She's an Australian Cattle Dog, a heeler."

The words were foreign to me. I looked at Joe and he didn't look like he knew anything about the breed.

At the same time, Joe and I started a slight shuffle, a lean, a move towards the exit, away from that sad, overweight dog who just sat there, a breed we had never heard of, frozen with an unnatural disposition. It was not the dog we imagined. We turned more towards the door to escape the coming sadness.

The sad woman pulled out a leash from her apron pocket and held it out at us, "You could take her for a walk."

We stiffened.

She continued in a quiet voice, "She'd like a walk."

Neither of us moved to take the leash.

"You can walk her through the cemetery. She'd appreciate getting out."

We looked at the leash and we looked at each other and we looked at the dog. The dog had not moved. She did not respond to seeing the leash.

Joe and I turned to each other and we both shrugged. Joe said, "OK, we will just take her out for a walk." I was thinking that at least she would get a final walk before the code words took effect.

The serious woman went to the cage and the dog stood up, still staring at her. She clipped on the leash and handed it towards us. After a pause, Joe took it. Low, low energy, all around.

"Just out the door to the right. There is a cement path."

We would do this, for the dog. We headed out and into the pouring rain. We turned to the right, up the hill. The dog followed on the leash.

It was gray. It was pouring. Joe and I stopped and glanced down at the dog, who sat between us. She began to focus on us.

We looked at the dog.

The dog looked at us.

Joe and I looked at each other.

We walked through the cemetery, two unhappy people, in the rain, with a depressed, soon-to-be-killed dog. Gray had settled onto all of us.

Joe said, "Well, she's not a little yappy dog."

I paused, quietly, "No, she is not that."

"She is not what I expected."

"No, she is not that. What were you thinking of for a dog?"

"Maybe a mid-sized, poodle-like dog."

Poodle. Shudder. Maybe we should have had this conversation earlier. I said, "Me, I was thinking more like a medium-sized lab-type dog, one that was a bit goofy."

There is a wide range between poodle and Labrador retriever. We looked down at Precious, who was staring at us. Nothing goofy about Precious.

Joe mumbled, "Maybe she is okay?" He was staring at her.

"Ummmm." *I was waiting my whole adult life for this dog?* I had a hard time imagining that.

Joe whispered, "It would be hard to leave her."

It took me a moment to respond but I finally agreed, "True, it would be hard."

We watched the dog. She sat and watched us. No wagging tail. No happy smile. No emotional responses anywhere. We were all getting soaked.

Joe noted, "She does not look like a 'Precious.'"

"No." I paused then slowly added, "Maybe a *Lord of the Rings* Precious?"

"Ummmm, hopefully the Smeagol version."

"Eew, right."

"She would be the right size for the boat."

I eyeballed the wet dog, "Well, I guess."

Joe took the leap. "Let's take her. It is too hard to leave her."

I regarded my husband. Mirroring his moods had not served me well recently. I considered the dog. I don't know if I was reflecting Joe's attitude or if I just couldn't leave her to her doom, but I finally said, "Okay."

Enthusiasm continued to be in short supply but there was enough for us to make the decision. I was already regretting it.

The Pound Lady gave us a towel. I wasn't sure if it was for us or for the dog but all three of us used it. She smiled slightly when we said we'd take the dog, a bit of sadness relieved.

I said that she didn't much look like a "Precious."

She shrugged, "You can change her name, find something that rhymes or has the same number of syllables or—"

"No," Joe interrupted, "She has already lost enough. She can at least keep her name."

After buying dog necessities, we headed back to the boat. Joe carried the dog aboard as he didn't know if she could make the jump. *Were we going to need a doggie-ramp for the boat?* She sat on the main deck until Joe opened the tarp and slid the door open. He then picked her up and carried her down into the salon. She laid on the teak parquet and just stared at us. We fed her. Then we had our wine and dinner. The boat was silent except for the sounds of the rain. *Well, she wasn't yappy.* After emails and my writing time, we headed to sleep.

Joe carried Precious down the two steep steps to the aft cabin; he didn't think the slow, overweight, depressed dog could make it on her own. He arranged a blanket on the deck at the foot of the bed and directed her to lie down. The dog lay down. Joe and I got into bed. We looked over: Precious was still staring at us. Joe and I looked at each other, and we finally fell asleep holding hands.

In the morning, the dog we thought we had adopted disappeared. Instead, there was a joyful bundle of energy. A night's sleep, a night out of the Pound, and the genuine Precious emerged.

She greeted us with wild tail wags. She bounded up the steep steps, never again needing to be carried, jumped off the boat, no doggie ramp needed, with her tail a blur from the speed of its wagging.

She rushed up the marina ramp. I said to her, "Go pee!"

She peed.

From the dock by the boat, Joe yelled at her, "Come!"

She ran down the ramp and went to him.

I pointed and said to her, "Sit."

And she sat on the dock, wagging her tail at the same time.

Joe and I looked at each other and we both burst out laughing. When I regained some breath I said, "We have a dog that knows commands!"

Joe's smile filled his face, "She listens!"

"She likes us!"

"And she's happy!"

Joe grabbed a tennis ball and tossed it to her. Precious caught it. Joe pointed to his hand and said, "Ball." Precious trotted over and dropped the ball in his hand. He said, "She may be smarter than we are!"

That was the start of learning—about Precious, about life on a boat with a dog, and a life with less gray.

* * *

I called Mom. "Hey Mom, we got a dog!"

"A dog? What?! Are you crazy? A dog with your lifestyles? You two are nuts!"

"I always wanted a dog and we figured it was finally time."

"It lives on the boat?"

"Yes, she jumps up to the deck from the dock with no problem."

"But where does she do her business?"

Ah, euphemisms. "We take her out for walks. And she lets us know when she needs to go out."

"Well that's good. What kind of dog is she? A little one?"

"She is an Australian Cattle Dog, also known as a blue heeler. She's about medium sized, about

Nicky's size."

"I never heard of that kind of dog. And I always thought Nicky was big." Nicky was my sister's childhood dog.

"She's about 45 pounds which is not really big in the dog world." I didn't say that she thought Nicky was big because she had limited experience with dogs. A tiny chihuahua would have been a big dog in her world.

"Paula, you and Joe, you two. You are always surprising me. I never know what you are about to do. I used to worry about it. I'm going to stop worrying. You end up figuring it out, even if they are crazy things like driving the Alcan alone or owning a dog on a boat!"

"Thanks Mom." I didn't expect she would stop worrying but her criticisms might slow down. I expected to hear that her lunch ladies laughed hysterically of the story of her crazy daughter getting a dog while living on a boat.

* * *

I was procrastinating packing for international travel, largely because packing for Alaska, France, and India in one February trip had me a bit flummoxed—too many climates to deal with. Plus, I had two entirely different courses to teach, in two countries with dramatically different climates. This meant I needed notes, handouts, shoes, clothes, and books, in a suitcase I could easily haul around the world. The time on the *Pilot Project* had at least taught me how to live minimally. Less stuff. More layering. I'd layer my India clothes under my France-in-February clothes. I wasn't quite the miracle packer that my sister Lisa was, but I managed to get it reduced to one suitcase.

Joe was not getting up quite as early as he had been, having begun to realize there was only so much he could do in the job. And he liked to take Precious out for her morning walk. I had more mornings with him, so I got to hear more of his morning ramblings.

"Worm and parcel with the lay turn and serve the other way."

"What does that mean my love?"

"It's how you wind line around cloth to stop chaffing friction."

"And you remembered it now why?"

"Just popped into my head."

I smiled at my uncommon guy.

He'd take time in the mornings for a ball toss with Precious, bouncing the ball off the rocks at the neighboring beach. Precious bounded up and over. She'd easily catch the ball, always returning it to Joe's hand. If I joined in the game, she'd return the ball to me, if I asked.

The dog was consistent. Under the tarp, every time someone walked down the ramp, Precious became Gollum. Insane barking would ensue. We could not calm her down until the noise ended or until we let her out of the tarp. When she laid outside on the dock, she'd stay quiet as people walked by. She'd let Matt and Claire's young son pet her. There was no sign of Gollum when not hidden under the tarp.

I understood her perspective.

Joe drove me and my luggage to the airport ferry and said he'd ride the ferry over with me. I said, "You don't have to do that my love."

He shook his head, "I will drag your bag up that airport ramp. You don't need to do that. Plus, it gives me more time with you." He turned and took my hand, "I am going to miss you."

I squeezed his hand and tucked my head under his chin. This moment was different from past separations, from past transitions to the solo phase. We had become much more engaged in life together.

More attuned. For better or worse. This separation plucked at our emotional connection.

We hugged, standing on the ferry's deck, watching Ketchikan slide away from us.

We hugged again as I left him before airport security. His last words to me were, "The boat will be better when you get home." I wasn't sure what that meant but I liked the concept.

I left Joe to problem-solve. How to take care of Precious, the boat, the tarps, his workday, and his pilotage training trips. He'd deal with it all. I put it out of my head and headed to Paris. My break from boat life, sabbatical, and my husband began.

* * *

First up was my week-long course on watershed management at the Université Catholique de Lille, in their multi-cultural, English-intensive week. Faculty were from the US and Great Britain. I lucked into this project when one of my Juniata College colleagues couldn't attend. It was a great experience, both in teaching and in eating.

The students developed case studies of French watershed management after I presented conceptual outlines. Faculty taught for 6-8 hours each day. Then faculty ate and drank for 3-4 hours each night. One food and wine tasting was organized by the agricultural engineering students. Most of these students grew up on family vineyards and farms and they liked to share their favorites with visiting faculty. It was exhausting and fabulous and there were no boats in sight.

The course content aligned with my sabbatical project. I spent a few hours integrating the French case study concepts into my notes for the book. In the middle of the week, I realized these sections of the book could be used immediately in one of my classes back at Juniata. *Success Paula! Your sabbatical project is going to produce something! Even if it isn't a completed manuscript.*

I did find time to go shopping. It was, after all, France, and Tim's daughter Sarah would love a new French dress. She'd finally get a gift from Aunt Paula that was free of moose-motifs.

During my previous Lille teaching adventure, at the end of the week, the Lille staff took us to Paris for a final dinner at the 56th floor of the Montparnasse Tower in the *Le Ciel de Paris* Restaurant. That year, Joe flew in to join us. He arrived in Paris before I did, and explained to the hotel desk clerk that he was my husband and he was meeting me in the room.

The clerk responded, "Ah, a rendezvous!"

Joe laughed, "Oui, exactement!"

This year, on my last night in Lille, I was alone. The other faculty had departed and the class was over. The waiter came over to my table in the corner, looked down and shifted his notes, and said, *"Bonsoir."*

My tongue stumbled as I said, *"Bonjour,* no, sorry, *bonsoir, Monsieur, bonsoir."*

The waiter was now wincing.

I continued, "Sil vous plait. Une bière."

He stopped his wincing, controlled his eyes before they rolled to the back of his head, and said in perfect English, "Yes Madame, you would like one beer. What size? A pint? A half pint? What kind of beer? Amber? Blond? Dark?"

"Yes, thank you, a pint of the blond please."

"Very good Madame."

My head flopped down and my eyes closed. Then I straightened and picked up my novel. My Lille class was done, my book notes were packed away, my French students gone. I started reading the novel then sighed. I had not comprehended a single word. I dropped the book and sighed again.

I was wishing for a rendezvous. My memory of living with an irritated husband was fading. I missed him. And the travel was giving me time to reflect on my errors of married life. I had too little communication on difficult subjects and too much mirroring of his moods.

I mirrored his bad moods, turning myself miserable. I mirrored his good moods, ignoring my own state just to merge with his. Reflecting his good moods wasn't so bad, but it meant I ignored the conversations that needed to happen. I mirrored instead of addressing the conflict. I had to work on this.

I wished he was here so I could start, plus, I would have the benefits of a hotel rendezvous. Feeling lonely in France is like regular loneliness times ten. France is just too dang romantic to be alone.

The next day, I got on the Eurostar for a fast train from Lille to London. This was the first time I experienced the Chunnel, and it made the trip across (under) the English Channel much more pleasant than my first experience (on top of) the Channel. I was sixteen then, traveling with my Mom on my first European trip. I puked my way across the Channel as the ferry was bouncing on strong seas. The Eurostar was smooth and easy, with no queasiness. I spent the trip wishing I could be sharing it with Joe, relieved that the gray had not formed a permanent stain.

I connected by train to Heathrow for a British Airways flight to Chennai, Tamil Nadu, India. Chennai used to be named Madras which explains the airport three-letter code of MAA. Leaving Customs at the Chennai airport, I had to watch for a driver who would take me to FERAL (Foundation for Ecological Research and Advocacy Learning) that was somewhere south of Chennai.

It was about 1 a.m. I was exhausted and there were hundreds of drivers, holding up various signs and waving them back and forth. I searched for fifteen minutes before I found him. It was during that search that I realized the only contact information I had for FERAL was an email. I didn't know exactly where the place was, only that it wasn't far from a spot called Auroville. Finally, in the crush of drivers, I found one whose sign read, "Welcome Dr. Paul Martini. FERAL."

I was not entirely confident, but my options were limited and I was tired enough to assume he was my driver.

I went with him through the crowds to his car.

I tried to speak with him, but received no words in return, just energetic head bobbing. It did take a bit of faith to travel in a faraway land with car and driver set up by other people. After getting in the tiny white car, the driver spent some time to figure out how to fit my large suitcase into the small car. While he worked, I started thinking about what my mother would think about getting in a car with an unknown driver who didn't have my correct name nor share my language. In the middle of the night. Going to a place that I only knew through emails and a website. I silently laughed, thinking of my grandmother's reaction. Nana would have been screaming at all the drivers in the waiting area and she would have never left the airport. Though in truth, she would have never made it as far as India or even onto a jet plane.

Before I began to mirror my family's paranoia, the driver sat down in the driver's seat, having managed to fill the backseat with my suitcase. He handed me a letter. I looked at him in surprise and took it.

FERAL was the return address and it had my correct name on the front of the envelope. It was from a FERAL colleague. He had written to prepare me for the upcoming three-hour drive, and my destination of an Auroville guest house in an isolated, rural area, where he'd come pick me up the next day.

I turned to the driver and smiled. He bobbed his

head and I bobbed mine in return. And then we were off. I relaxed into the seat, appreciating the FERAL folks for their consideration of a travel's discomfort and glad that my hopeful nature had won out.

I didn't know it at the time, but I was heading to an experiment of hope and work.

* * *

Thirty years ago, the Auroville landscape was desolate and hardpan, baked red earth, gullied and bare. The forests had been taken down. The agricultural land overworked. The annual monsoons eroded off more topsoil, leaving hard, cement-like ground behind. Each new monsoon cycle would worsen the erosion and runoff. The land produced less and less, and the people became poorer and poorer. Survival had become chancy.

An unusual group of immigrants came to Auroville, following a local guru, The Mother. They came from across the globe and shared a vision for a new collaborative that would renew the land while living in an open, international society. Today, 3,000 people from across the world have made Auroville their home, their community. And they did renew the land. Lush, diverse forests, including nut crops and orchards, now fill the landscape. Scattered among them were artisan shops, creators and producers, and spiritual retreats for visitors and residents. They built a gigantic structure to honor The Mother, amidst the larger tribute of the transformation of hardpan to forest. They renewed the soil. Legumes, other nitrogen-fixing plants, trees, and plants aided the soil's rebirth. They caught and controlled the monsoon rains so the water wouldn't sweep away the soil and young seedlings. The local people thrived with the new economic activities, education, and health care. Water runs off hardpan while it would soak into functional soils. And less runoff meant more water for agriculture and fewer destructive floods.

I would use their story in my sabbatical project.

And as a lesson for marriage as well.

Sitting in the Auroville guesthouse, I thought about how the story of Auroville's soil applied to a couple. Desolation was not a friend to life nor to relationships. Love too needed the right ground so that it could sink in and not run off.

After a day of rest, Anu, the FERAL project lead, phoned and made plans for her to pick me up and to have lunch at an Auroville café before heading back to the FERAL office.

At the café, Anu found us seats on the veranda. The students sat together while Anu and I had a table next to them. The students suggested I try their favorite beverage: a fresh lime soda, so Anu ordered one for me. I was glad to be outdoors, under shade. The reforestation of Auroville meant more humidity, and in southern India, well south of the Tropic of Cancer, sitting on a veranda helped cool me down in the thick, moist air. Plus, I got to watch the street from my seat.

Auroville traffic wasn't too dense by India standards. The cars and three-wheeled auto rickshaws kept to one lane, only occasionally passing and creating a lane that the road builders had not planned. A few scattered large trucks zipped by. Pedestrians filled the sidewalk and sometimes spilled over into the road. Sidewalks and roadways were dynamic, morphing into one another. Clothing choices ranged from men in lungis, women in saris or in salwar kameez, either sex in Oxford-, tee- or polo-shirts. In Auroville, the mode of dress had little to do with the wearer's ethnicity. Indians might be wearing dress pants and European males might be wearing lungis, though the Europeans often topped their sarong with a plaid button-down shirt.

After ordering and getting our drinks, Anu began to fill me in on the plans. "The rest of the course should be peaceful, Paula. Hopefully, no more drama."

The start of the program had gotten off to a rocky start as it was the year of the Boxing Day Tidal Wave. Students were supposed to fly to India on the day the tsunami hit. Revi and Anu were the on-the-ground communicators who were key to making decisions about the program's future. While the student program was important, it was more crucial to be sure the program would not in any way hamper the needs of the community that had just been devastated by the tidal wave. Revi and Anu balanced it all perfectly and, after a delay, the program was able to start.

Anu continued, "We will have a week here, based at FERAL. There will be time for you and the class to visit the Kaliveli watershed, if you'd like. You wanted to take them out to an aquatic habitat?"

"I would like to, but I have only read about the Kaliveli area. Will I have someone who knows the lake and wetland area?"

Anu grinned, "Oh yes, Revi wants to go along. He can be your guide."

I nodded in relief. I did not want to get a student lost in a thick, tall grass, tropical swamp. Or lose myself for that matter.

Anu was reading my reaction, "Paula, do not worry. Revi will take good care of you and the students."

I nodded, unable to say more because a truck horn blast interrupted the conversation. I drank the rest of my fresh lime soda. I hoped the tart yet sweet drink might keep me hydrated since I was sweating profusely in the humid, 90 degree heat.

When the noise abated, Anu asked, "Paula, would you like another? You are looking a bit warm."

I nodded yes. "The climate shift from Alaska then France and now southern India ... it is a bit warmer here."

Anu laughed, "Yes, I imagine it is. We will make sure you have plenty of water during your stay."

I nodded, appreciating her care. I said, "What is the plan for the second week?"

"We have a small bus that will take you and the students. First you will go to a few different universities. You will stay in their housing and visit their marine science programs. We have checked with them after the tidal wave and they are fine with the visit—the campuses were not damaged. It has been arranged for their faculty to speak with the students about the research activities in the program."

"Sounds great. Will Revi be along for this?"

"No Revi. I will be along for the first part, for the majority of the trip, but I need to return back to FERAL early. One of the FERAL staff, Rajat, will stay with you and with the students for the whole time. The second part of the week you will visit a tiger reserve in Periyar. I wish I could join you for that; it is a wonderful place. Rajat knows about all the arrangements for that visit."

I said, "I appreciate you setting up all these logistics—they sound good. I will plan my lectures with the students to include topics related to the field sites we will visit."

Anu said, "They should enjoy that. It should be a peaceful, smooth rest of the year, Paula, nothing for you to worry about."

Anu was right, it was peaceful. Except for the elephants.

* * *

We made it through the Kaliveli swamp. I was unable to cope with the noon sun, so I depended upon Revi to guide the students through the tall grass and shallow waters as I stayed in the shade. I had long ago learned that field trips were best when no one passed out from heat stroke. Especially the professor. The students would bring me samples and we'd discuss the ecological processes involved with the organisms in a brackish water habitat. Revi finished the day with a touch of sunburn. But no one passed out.

After Kaliveli, it was rather enjoyable to sit in cool classrooms and to meet various Indian faculty. Anu left the group just before the drive to Periyar.

There was a good deal of quiet time in this phase of my travels. Students studied at night and I holed up in my hotel room, alone. Quiet time meant reflection time. I faced life with my husband. I had to stop mirroring him. I also had to rethink my attitude about boredom. Life in our old leaky boat with a miserable husband was not boring, nor was a life married to a blue water sailor. But "not boring" did not necessarily mean "desirable."

Like that conversation Joe and I had, we had to get down to what mattered. What did we want? And, what did I want?

Moving along from one adventure to another meant I didn't have to dig into those questions. Floating along meant there was no conflict within my world. I'd just flex. I could just keep pressing ahead as the jobs took us, believing movement was progress. But it might just have been random motion.

As Joe settled in one spot, as we shifted less often, I needed to rethink my approach to staying engaged in my life. Waiting for the next adventure was not going to work anymore. I remembered the feel of those cold laundry shower quarters moving through my hands and I smiled. *Work on living in the moment, Paula.*

The way to Periyar sent us through diverse human-scapes of the India states of Kerala and Tamil Nadu: industry, farms, townlets, and mile upon mile of garbage-filled ditches. It struck me that a culture had existed here for 1,000s of years, and for all that time, dumping garbage was fine. The goats and cows ate it. The heat and the moisture of the rain helped the microorganisms decompose it. Garbage a hundred years ago would not last long in the monsoon tropics. And then came plastics. The goats were uninterested. The bacteria and fungi were uninterested. The waste no longer disappeared. India's ditches were now filled with plastic waste, the worst being thin plastic shopping bags. White, pink, green plastic laid in the ditches, scattered with plastic bottles and the occasional banana skin. The thin bags created a water barrier between the air and the soil, yet the ditch network was a key avenue to recharge groundwater with rainwater.

Farmers depended upon those groundwaters, through pumping of water from wells. The ditch's plastic liner of plastic garbage reduced those key water supplies. Instead of sinking into the ground, the water ran off, creating bigger floods in the process. It was as though India had accidently tarped over its groundwater recharge areas.

Ditches not only let water sink into the ground, they also helped prevent floods by moving waters away from homes and farms. Non-decaying garbage meant the ditches filled up and could hold less water, could move less water, and local flooding worsened. This was a tough combination: more flooding yet less groundwater. Driving through Kerala and up into the Western Ghats to Periyar, the poor condition of the drainage network was obvious.

The irony struck me during the ride: the *Pilot Project* soaked up too much water from leaky decks while the ground in India ran off too much water due to impenetrable garbage.

There is an ideal range, the right balance between what is taken in versus what is let go.

* * *

I had not brought the right shoes.

Having the right shoes on a trip is crucial to the success of an experience, or at least crucial to the amount of foot pain felt during the experience. A packer should consider shoe needs for the main expedition as well as the side expedition. I failed. For the weekend at the Periyar Tiger Reserve, I failed to bring hiking boots, water-repellent shoes, or even sneakers. What I had packed were my dress "professor" shoes, and a pair of flip flops. Flip flops. They turned out to be a less-than-ideal choice.

We spent the first afternoon at Periyar on manicured trails and on a boat trip on the lake, looking at wildlife. Buffalo were common and the guide told us elephants were in the Reserve, but we saw none. The guide explained that tigers were around but that they were quite shy. I wondered if that was code for the "tigers are extinct, but we still want visitors to think they might be here." I said nothing of my pessimism to the students.

The next day, we had an early reservation at the Reserve for a guided hike. I figured this hike was going to be a bit of a challenge wearing flip flops. For a moment I flashed on "I Love Lucy" where Lucy did something stupid and embarrassing. *Was I going to be Lucy in this footwear?* I considered having the students and Rajat go without me. I was supposed to be discussing conservation biology with the students while in the Reserve and Rajat did not have a strong background on that topic, plus his English may not have been up to the task. I needed to go, flip flops or not.

I chose to not mirror Lucy.

Two rangers guided our hike; they both had limited English. At the start, the rangers handed out knee-high, yellowish-beige, stained, heavy canvas socks. We all looked at each other. *What?* Knee-high, thick canvas socks, with a calf-high, draw-tie to hold them in place. One of the guides said something in Tamul and the FERAL staff person translated it to us, "Leech socks."

Leech socks.

Of course.

As I looked at the socks, I was wondering what I was going to do with thick canvas socks and flip flops. How could I get the thick canvas at the toe of the sock through the toehold of the flip flop? One of the students, a student with an occasional contrary streak, stridently complained, "I'm not putting these on!"

Okay, we had a student revolt. The other students were now thinking of skipping them too. I could not force the students to wear the socks, but I attempted to motivate them via shame, because if the professor wearing flip flops can put on canvas socks, so can they. Role Model time. I worked the socks onto the flip flops and said, "Do you think they'd give us these if we didn't need them?" Three students looked at each other and began to put on the socks. Fear, a marvelous motivation. My role model behavior did not affect the contrarian, but the rest of the students put on their canvas knee-highs. I took it as a win.

I wanted to know why we needed them; I was hoping that would somehow become clear during the hike. It would be a good class discussion once we got a bit more information.

Be careful of what you hope for.

The start of the hike was easy—standard dirt trail. And then we came across a pile of tiger scat. The students and I smiled, pointed, and looked at the trees around us. The possibility of tigers in our midst was very exciting. I hoped the guides didn't plant the scat to prove their Reserve had tigers, but it did look like cat scat. I also hoped any tigers would leave our group alone.

The tiger scat was the high point for the first hour. It was a nice walk through woods and meadows, but no tigers, no buffalo, no elephants, no quadrupeds of any sort. We stopped in an open meadow. It seemed the guides were discussing which way to go: to the right into a side valley on an underused path, or continue straight through the meadow on a well-used trail. The guides conferred, in soft voices. One said, pointing to the side valley, "Here." And off we went, on the path less traveled.

Once into the valley, the rangers again conferred and we shifted, to go up the forested hill that formed the left side of the valley. Trees and bush were thick. We were in a single-file, one guide at the lead and one at the end. I was at the end, both because I was slow in the canvas sock-flip-flop combo, and because I was chatting with a student about an insect on a flower. Suddenly, out of the corner of my eye, I saw the lead guide running downhill, with the students behind him. I caught a glimpse of one of the students' faces as she looked at me as she passed: big eyes, raised brows, pale face.

Scared, she's scared. No. She's terrified.

And then the noise hit.

Trumpeting elephants. Elephants! And very close. I felt the ground tremble through my leech socks. The sound of the trumpet felt like it was crushing my lungs, smashing my ear drums.

I didn't see the elephants, but I was running, as were the rest of the students and the last guide. I was now last in line: flip flops, leech socks, an extra fifty pounds and an extra twenty years. I was desperately trying not to trip. Being trampled by an angry elephant was not a desirable authentic experience.

We got off the hill, out of the side valley, and back to the large meadow. The guides stopped. With shaking hands, they both pulled out cigarettes, lit up, and took a deep drag. They looked pale.

Students were catching their breath, bent at the waist. I was huffing so much I could not speak.

When I finally had air, I went up to the first guide, "Why didn't you say anything?" I was shocked that he just ran past without speaking to us, that he took the lead to run. My voice was a bit loud and sharp.

He shrugged, "You understood."

I gaped at him. Then I began to slowly nod my head in agreement. There are certain acts natural to mirror, such as running away from a trumpeting elephant. When the ranger was running and the elephants were trumpeting, no words were needed.

Elephants were excellent communicators.

We slowly walked back, as the main trail looped back to the ranger headquarters. My flip flops had stretched in the excitement. They barely stayed on my feet, but the thick canvas leech socks provided some protection.

We stopped in shade under large trees. Someone yelled, "Monkeys!"

The American students and their professor stood under the trees, looking up with big smiles. The guides and Rajat had not stopped directly under the canopy but to the side. When I noticed, I thought about it for a second, and then followed their lead and suggested the students might want to do the same. Monkeys had been known to both drop and throw things at humans below. Their excrement is usually what is available for them to throw. Or rotten fruit. I'd rather the fruit. No, I'd rather nothing, nothing at all.

We walked on; the guides were saying something about leeches, but it was hard to understand. They weren't stressed so I didn't worry about it.

It turned out the long grass under trees with monkeys was ideal leech habitat. Back at headquarters, at the end of the hike, as we took off the leech socks, we found the proof. Two or three leeches, each as long as my index finger, were crawling up the socks.

Almost as a group, without words, all of us turned to look at the contrarian. She had at least five leeches attached to her calves. The guides shook their heads. The student complained, "Why didn't anyone warn me?"

I shook my head. A leech sock from a local guide was plenty of warning. I was glad she had followed the running ranger as I wouldn't have wanted to explain to her parents about her death from angry elephants. Their warning was clear even if it was in the language of a different species.

Clearly, there was some mirroring that was helpful to survival.

A guide pulled the leeches off her legs using his strong fingernails. Leech saliva includes a pain killer, so the student didn't feel any of it. The bites bled for a bit but finally stopped as the leech saliva anti-coagulant washed out with the blood flow. The student was quiet headed back to the van and I hoped she had learned something that day.

On the ride back to FERAL, it struck me. I stared out the window so my students couldn't see my stricken face. The elephant lesson, the need to listen to the warnings. Joe had been communicating with me. Yet I ignored it. I was not fully listening. I needed to heed his message. Directly respond to it, no more gliding around.

* * *

On the way home, I saw a Cathay Pacific cargo plane; it was huge. A giant plane with no windows other than the two tiny ones up front for the pilots. What did it hold? Where was it going? Where had it come from ? Who was paying for the cargo? How did they load it? Who made the stuff? Who was going to use the stuff? Even after a month of travel and nine months on the boat, I was still curious about the world's intricacies.

My next mystery: would Joe meet me in Seattle?

Joe said he might, but his offer was a bit vague.

Did he want to? Could he get the time away from the office? Was he on a pilotage trip? When I got out of airport security and he wasn't there, I worked to contain my disappointment.

I headed over to baggage claim. There he was, collecting my bags. I could only smile. Then I rushed over, my arms open wide, for the hug and kiss.

We smiled and laughed all the way back to the hotel, where we had our typical homecoming. Then I dug out the gifts, showing him the stuff I bought for others, giving him the little bits I found for him, just chatting about the trip. Then he updated me with the SWAPA: they were going to vote! We talked about how many votes he might have, how many he might not have, what the plans might be, future hopes, future dreams. We went out for a great dinner, eating sensibly and having a few drinks, both of us pleased to be together again. I glowed hearing the routine details of daily life that I had missed.

I got the dog updates: how smart she was, how athletic, how funny. She loved balls and would chase them for hours. Joe took her to work and kept her in the car; he took regular breaks to throw the ball with her in the parking lot or walk her at Ward Lake at lunch or after work. Precious had bonded with Joe. If Joe moved, Precious was behind him, heeling her human. *Ah, the source of the breed's name!*

Joe was pleased to share his big news on the boat update. He had professional fiberglass experts replace the main deck. It took more than $10,000 of savings but there was now a solid main deck with topcoat, done correctly so it looked like a boat deck. Joe joked that Itchy Willy would have liked the outcome, "It's smooth, smooth, all smooooothhh."

And the best boat news of all: the tarp was gone. Gone. Not ripped off in a windstorm, not lost to disaster, but deliberately taken down. No more gray life, other than the natural climate of Ketchikan. We talked about the places we could sail her to, with the boat free from its tent. Joe said Precious didn't bark much at people walking down the ramp now that she wasn't inside under a tarp. Boat and dog topics kept us away from talking about work insanity, for awhile.

The "while" ended when we returned to the hotel and Joe hooked up my computer to the internet—time to check emails. Time to be irritated with the latest insult, the newest challenge, the latest craziness. We started talking about his work and I tried not to vent along with him, to keep my cool. I decided it was time to show I had really listened to him.

I moved the conversation to the real topic that I had been ignoring all this time. I had to address it directly.

I took his hand and said, "Joe, you really hate this job, don't you my sweets?"

Joe squeezed my hand firmly as he said, "Absolutely."

"Let's talk about the plan to get you out."

He tensed up and looked at me carefully and said, "I'm going to stick around through your sabbatical. I did promise!"

I nodded and smiled, "Yes, I know, and I appreciate that tremendously. I know it has cost you. Let's plan for the next steps: SWAPA or what else? We need a plan. You need to see the way out of this craziness."

He started relaxing as he said, "I promised John I'd give him a year in the new office in Ketchikan—then, I'm done."

"Can you make it in the job until October?"

"I'm going to give it a shot."

"October—"

Joe interrupted, "Paula, if SWAPA doesn't happen by then, I'm not going to stick with this job."

I beamed at him, "Yes, I get that. And I'm glad."

He carefully scrutinized me, then gave me a hug and said, "Good, we are on the same page. I'll find something, but I'm going to try my best for SWAPA."

I relaxed into the hug. He needed to hear my expectations as much as I needed to hear his. We had found the balance again.

I pulled out of the hug and said, "While you search for the next career move, we can figure out something with finances, even if we are down to one salary while you are unemployed and looking. Our savings will see us through for a couple of years if it comes to that."

He nodded and smiled, "We will figure this out."

I think we were both relieved to talk about these future choices, to see potential paths, to make a path forward together, that worked for both of us. There may have been uncertainties but at least staying in the crazy job had a clear limit, even if we drained our retirement savings.

The next day, work insanity was the first topic of conversation. I switched to talk about the dog ... time to break the old pattern of mirroring the rant.

* * *

Back at Refuge Cove, I stopped suddenly on the ramp heading toward the boat. I raised my arm and pointed, not quite having the breath to speak. Finally, I croaked through my smile, "Wow!" I turned to Joe and hugged him, "It's really not a circus tent anymore!"

The golden wood curlicues were shining in the sun. I could see the entire boat, from her gently upturned bow to her flat stern deck, with the *Pilot Lite* tied to the swim platform. The new main deck was beige, with sand embedded for traction, and a white overcoat around the smooth edges. I heard Itchy Willy's voice in my head, *Smooth, smooth, smooth.* It almost looked like the yacht it was. Almost. If you didn't look too closely. I chose to ignore the old teak on the upper decks and the dried caulk spilling out of the side windows, to focus on the positive changes.

That positive focus worked until about 2:00 a.m.

Lying in the aft cabin, Joe and I both woke up. We had drizzle in the aft cabin. Outside it was pouring. Inside, we had raindrops on our heads. In bed.

Joe said, "This is the first night it has rained since the deck work was done."

"Ohhh. This was the first chance for leakage to happen?"

"Yes."

The leaks were coming in from above, on the decks that had not yet been repaired. Joe got up and spread old tarp on the mid deck and flybridge deck. It looked like the windows next to those decks were also leaking—there hadn't been enough money or time to have those repaired. Joe spent about an hour tarping the upper decks, to attempt to stop the interior rain, keeping the tarp horizontal rather than the previous, upright tent style. He used staples to hold it down. No more milk jugs, no more orange juice hangers, no more circus tent, just a lot of staples. While he did that, I moved our pillows and blankets back to the salon. The inside drizzle had made the mattress a damp sponge. The table was going to be our bed again.

The next morning, over coffee, I continued my effort at improving my communications with my husband, even on difficult topics. I commented on how well he problem-solved the dripping, with no sailor language and no angry venting, even though we had interior rain at 2 a.m. while lying in bed.

Joe paused, "I have to apologize, my love. I hadn't quite realized how bad I could seem. Precious helped."

I turned to him and squinted, "Precious? Precious helped?"

"Yes. While you were gone, I was fixing something in the aft cabin. The dog had been in there with me, like she always is, a shadow at my side. I was swearing and yelling because the project wasn't going well. You know, my typical sailor vent. When I looked up, Precious wasn't there anymore. I went up and she wasn't in the salon either. I found her curled up in the forward cabin."

"The forward cabin? I never saw her go in there."

"No, me neither. She was trying to get as far away from me as possible. I felt horrible. Since then I've tried to tone it down around her. I always knew you understood my frustration when I'm in sailor-talk mode, but she can't. She doesn't know what's going on. So, I am working to keep my frustration under wraps."

I looked at him and looked away as I worked to process this information. My emotions were jumping between relief and anger, between pleasure and resentment. Relieved that he was managing his irritation levels. Angry that he did it for the dog but not for me. Pleased that life with Joe on the boat was likely to be more pleasant. Resentment that he was more concerned about what the dog felt than what I felt.

I worked through the emotional puzzle, landing on acceptance. He did recognize my ability to think it out and deal with it, an ability that the dog did not have. He recognized I could cope. As I was always proud to be competent, relief and pleasure won out.

Over morning coffee, Joe mentioned, "Sweets, I got you a late Christmas present."

"What is it?"

"Well, maybe I shouldn't call it a present for you, just something I did for the boat, for us."

"The main deck work that saved our glooping efforts, that was a great present."

"This one will make life aboard the boat a bit nicer."

I had a whole list of things going through my

head, loads of projects would have filled that goal. "What is it my love?"

"You know that natural gas/plumbing shop that I walk by on the way to work each morning?"

"Yes?"

"I had them come over and check out our gas lines for the stove. They all checked out and they put in a propane tank. We now have a working stove."

"Wow!" I could cook on something other than a George Foreman grill. I didn't even like to cook but I was excited at all the new options.

Joe continued, "I know I used to say that propane will add moisture inside the boat, but I learned that just doesn't matter in Ketchikan. Every time we open the slider door we are adding moisture."

"Thanks, my dearest, great idea!" Now I could boil even more water to warm up the place.

Our walks in Ward Cove now included the dog. There was almost no venting about Joe's work as we both focused on the dog's antics. When Joe grabbed a tennis ball, she tracked his hand, intently watching the ball. Joe would throw the ball and it would bounce off a large tree and Precious would catch it on almost any bounce. She would jump and run and dash to catch the ball. When Joe put away the ball, she'd explore the woods, drink out of the streams, and chase the geese, sometimes swimming out to try and get them. Walking the circuit, with Precious off-leash, once in a while we'd stop. We had lost the dog. She was out of sight. One of us would ask, "Where's the dog?" And then we'd find her, in our blind spot, directly behind us, as she herded us along the trail. These hikes relieved stress by creating joy rather than releasing anger. Precious was great at reframing the moment.

My writing was going well without the gray. Unlike in the boat shed or when under the tarp, now when I looked out the window, I could see sky and forest and something other than the junk in the boat shed. I think the Advanced Procrastination Therapy session should include something about a positive, engaging work environment.

One aspect of the boat life that had worsened was the sleeping arrangements. We were back to sleeping on the table. The aft cabin mattress was too damp, and we could not stop the window leaks into that cabin. It wasn't a lot of water coming in, but any water onto the pillows and comforter and a foam mattress was too much. The aft cabin was officially unlivable. It did turn into a good place for Joe to set up his tools, making the salon tool-free. And I no longer had to wake up to the hideous stained fiberglass, instead I had the golden glow of the salon's teak. The table bed was even cozier than before because Precious was now sleeping with us. Not only did I have my husband to warm up my feet, I also had a dog. I couldn't turn over in bed very easily, but I was warm.

One day, when Joe had already headed to work, I opened my email and found out Juniata had approved my promotion to Full Professor. I glowed with the result and called Joe to share the good news. He said, "That's great my love! You worked hard for that and you deserved it! Let's go out to dinner tonight to celebrate."

At the restaurant with our first drink, Joe saluted and said, "Here's to the new Full Professor Martin! Congratulations!" I smiled at him and took a sip of my cocktail, feeling the joy of the moment in attaining a long-held goal. We talked about Juniata and the helpful cushion of the additional 10% salary. During dessert, Joe put down his fork and asked, "Love, now that you have the promotion, do you really want to leave Juniata for Homer?"

I put my fork down as well and looked at him, then said, "Joe, if you have a pilot job, where you will be settled in one place, working a job you liked, where we could live together, then, yes, I'd leave Juniata for Homer. Easy choice!" I took a sip of my drink, "I'm just glad I fulfilled this ambition to reach Full Professor before I had to choose between goals." I looked at him intently, "I do not intend my title of tenured Full Professor to be a chain around my neck to hold me in place."

He grinned and we both picked up our forks.

* * *

We had a rare and magical moment in Ketchikan: a sunny weekend.

"Hey sweets, there are a bunch of ferries coming in and going out at the docks today."

Dang, he was going to have to go to work on this spectacular weekend?

He continued, "Do you want to sail the *Pilot Project* and go watch them shift the ferries from the water?"

"Wow! That sounds great." A boating adventure that involved moving the boat sounded like a great change.

"And Precious would enjoy it too."

I said, "Precious would enjoy anything with her people around."

Joe laughed and kissed me, "Yes, very true."

We sailed down Tongass Narrows and did a couple of loops close to the ferries. I felt small and fragile next to those big steel ships.

"Hey Joe." He nodded and I continued, "That Coast Guard boat is looking at us, I think it's coming towards us."

"Yes, they are probably out training, doing safety boardings. And, I expect we look suspicious going back and forth like this."

Suspicious. After 9-11, being suspicious could be dangerous. We were up on the flybridge and as they got closer, Precious started barking like an insane dog. She entered her Gollum mode to protect us from that orange thing that was getting close to her people. Precious clearly thought they were the suspicious ones.

We got a radio hail.

"*MV Pilot Project*, this is the US Coast Guard. Channel 22-Alpha please. Over"

Joe responded, in his best captain's voice, "Roger, 22-Alpha." He continued the conversation after switching off the emergency channel and onto 22-Alpha, "This is Captain Martin, Port Captain of the Alaska Marine Highway aboard the *MV Pilot Project*. Over."

There was a bit of a pause at the other end.

"Ah, Captain Martin. This is Petty Officer Smith." Another pause. "We would like to board your vessel for a safety check."

"Roger that Petty Officer Smith. Be aware we have a dog aboard."

"Copy that Captain Martin."

Precious continued her insane barking until their boat came alongside. Then, she quieted, and stood behind Joe. Uniformed people coming aboard from an orange and black boat, wearing orange suits and carrying weapons—even Precious knew to be cautious.

Four came aboard and climbed up to the flybridge, with the lead officer explaining their purpose. "We go out to do safety equipment inspections. Today we have two junior officers who we are training on the process. I hope you understand if we take time to explain the safety regulations in this inspection."

Joe responded, "I understand the need for training. Take all the time you need."

They discussed what they wanted to see. Joe said, "If you'd like, Paula could show below decks? Meanwhile, I can show the life vests up on the flybridge."

"Thank you, Captain, that sounds good." The officer split his team: two below and two above.

I took the two down and into the salon where the senior officer pointed out the placards Joe had placed next to the steering wheel, saying to his trainee, "Look at the safety check-off sheet. This vessel requires placards for plastic, oil and garbage. See these three? These signs are exactly what are needed. They are all here. Please check them off." Turning to me, "Could you show us the head please?"

I took them down to the aft cabin, letting them go through to the head. The senior officer pointed out all the required waste collection equipment listed on his safety sheet, telling his trainee, "Check all those off the list." The Coast Guard was also interested in boats having functional toilet arrangements—less pollution over the side.

With the below-decks review done, we went up top. Joe and the officers were chatting comfortably, with Precious curled up at their feet.

The senior officer said, "Captain Martin, thank you for your time and your patience. When I heard it was you on the radio, I almost decided not to bother to come aboard—you have way more safety training than the rest of us combined. But I knew it would be a good training experience for my people. I appreciate it."

Handshakes all around, and the team left.

I turned to Joe, "This went much better than the Cape Cod Harbor Master experience."

Joe laughed and gave me a hug.

Sailing back to Refuge Cove, my smile was about to break my face. This had been a dream of a day. I knew it wasn't going to be like this every day, but days like this could make up for the more challenging bits.

And we were about to have another challenging bit.

Coming back to Refuge Cove, Joe was driving from the flybridge. He slowed, as the entrance to the marina was tight. Once in, he had to make a sharp left turn followed immediately by a sharp right turn to get to our slip. I had no idea on how Joe could pilot her in: too many sharp turns and only one propeller. It seemed impossible to me but then I found parallel parking to be overly challenging. If I was alone, I would have never left the dock. Joe? Joe had no problem maneuvering the boat. He spun the wheel and depended upon the engine, using forward and reverse, to sharply move her around tight corners.

Just into the channel entrance, just when Joe had to start maneuvering to make the first turn, the engine died. There was no way to control the momentum of the boat.

We were headed directly into the stern of another boat—a fancy, expensive-looking, well-maintained, yacht-like boat.

I was on the main deck to manage lines. Joe flew down from the flybridge, skipped the steps, jumped straight down to the main deck, grabbed a pole, and went to the bow. Hitting a fancy, yacht-like boat would be expensive. Joe was going to try and man-handle us from hitting. I imagined Joe was going to break his arm in the process.

While he headed to the bow, I stepped into the main salon, at first just to get out of his way. Then I looked at the controls and thought to take the chance.

I put the boat throttle in neutral and tried to start the engine. It started. Immediately, I put her in reverse. Once our forward momentum ended, I put her back in neutral. We had stopped in the channel entrance. The yacht was safe. *Pilot Project* was unharmed. And Joe's arm didn't break. I then looked at Joe.

He was still standing at the prow with the pole. He had a giant smile on his face, looking at me.

"Paula, you saved it—nice job! Really, great, you

saved it. How did you even think of trying the engine?"

"Well, I did not know how else I could help, and, I figured our only help was the engine, so I gave it a shot."

"Great job! You are becoming a good sailor!"

"I wouldn't go that far …"

"Much improved from the day you threw the line to me on the *Pilot Lite* when I didn't have the oars."

"Hey, I can learn."

He hugged me, "You really saved the day, my love."

I smiled all the way back to the dock, while we tied up and while Joe went off with Precious for some ball time. I watched them, feeling a warmth deep into my heart and down to my toes. Joe mirrored my positives, my successes and accomplishments, and that echo strengthened me. I realized I could count on my mother to mirror the negative, the inadequacies and missteps. *No wonder I don't tell her everything.* Still smiling, I shut my eyes and tipped my head up to the sky.

I had learned even challenging bits of relationships could be joyful. The honeymoon flavor of my marriage sandwich didn't disappear with time together, it instead got richer, more complex, more sophisticated, and more challenging. Sort of like adding lettuce, cheese, peppers and condiments to a plain turkey sandwich—the additions made it more interesting, and sometimes, gave a sharp bite from an overly spicy addition.

It was good to find the right balance, as long as the mayonnaise was not on the cheese side.

14 Did the Happy Couple Make it?

To Float: (v) to move gracefully

August 2005

Returning to Pennsylvania, I felt a bit like the hobbits returning to the Shire at the end of *The Lord of the Rings* (the movie version, not the book). Life had changed and home didn't look quite the same. I saw the comfort here that I had missed when I had concentrated on the sameness. I saw the stability that comes from a solid roof. My dreams of "authentic" had widened to include the potential of each moment in life. I now knew the richness that could come from sharing the details of life together. And some of the challenges associated with that sharing.

I never thought to experience the run from trumpeting elephants while wearing flip flops and leech socks. There is no National Geographic show with scientists who made poor shoe choices. Living closer to the natural world had amazing joys but also a fair amount of muck. I never thought life with my husband would require me to mirror him less and communicate with him more, using a dog as a translator. And who knew a silent dog was the perfect communicator?

There was a dichotomous range in a marriage, balancing conflict, much like the tension between humans and wildlife. It was best not to ignore either end of the range.

Life with Joe was much like Joe: uncommon, surprising, and mostly joyful, at least on good days. Joy could be found in a warm cup of water, a jumping fish, or a silly poem recited by my husband at 5 a.m.

Even the mundane could be rich.

I felt the loss of daily life with my husband. I hugged Precious and then tossed a ball to her. I could see she felt that loss too.

I watched her run through the woods filled with small straggly trees, trees fighting against vines and prickly underbrush. This patch of forest was far from Alaskan old growth. Its tree trunks were barely six inches in diameter. The central Pennsylvania hills had been cut and recut, timbered and cleared multiple times in the past 300 years. If people left this wooded patch alone, a few of the trees would live for a hundred years or more. But people were not likely to leave it alone.

Having seen the straggly black spruce of the north, I had a new appreciation for these disheveled Pennsylvania woods. This was no Fangorn forest of Tolkien, with Ents immersed in its long growth. This patch of woods still lived, returning and growing even after centuries of repeated human disturbance. Clear-cuts. Acid rain. Old road cuts. Houses that came and went. Life still managed to emerge even if it was less majestic than a forest primeval.

As Precious ran around, while she didn't have any giant trees to bound against, she did have a maze of branches and bushes to run between. She had chipmunks to chase and the old road surface to race upon.

Joy was what we made of it.

* * *

I had gotten to *Mimi's* early, just after opening, to take my favorite seat at the bar. From behind me came, "Paula! You're back!"

I turned to see Bonnie, just in time for her to grab me in a tight embrace.

"We missed you!"

"I missed you too, Bonnie."

"So, how was it? Was it great living with Joe? Was life on the boat amazing? How was Alaska? I can't even imagine."

The rest of the *Mimi's* crowd was now filling in, behind and around Bonnie, more yells of "Paula!" "Welcome!" "Welcome back from sabbatical!" "How was it, life with your husband!"

Bonnie quieted them, "I just asked her that very thing."

"The landscape was beautiful. Amazing to be in a place where people had less of a footprint. Though I did learn that I liked certain human comforts and that I had limits to how much precariousness I wanted in my daily life. The boat was one adventure after another. Not always fun ones …"

"What, Joe had you in a boat with problems?"

I laughed, "Yes, problems. Leaks, lack of a real mattress, more leaks, often cold, often dark. But we managed. Southeast Alaska was spectacular. We had whales and otters, Steller sea lions and eagles, oh and the porpoises! Amazing …"

Someone in back said, "Sounds like an adventure! You sure escaped the ordinary world around here."

Should I tell them that ordinary had a certain joy?

Bonnie interrupted my thoughts with, "Paula, Paula, what about married life? Life with Joe, I know you teach that environment stuff, but I want to hear about how it worked out with you and Joe."

"You know how I told you before about otter control?"

"Yes! They pooped all over your deck! And you had to keep them away."

"Yes, that's what I learned about living with my husband."

Quizzical faces looked at me.

"When things get bad, fence it off. Limit the smell. That way you can still appreciate the adorable otters ... or husbands. Try not to use nail boards to cause permanent pain. Spraints will be spraints so deal with it. Living together can work but build in space, have fences, give each other boundaries. Watch and listen to what's really going on and plan to solve any issues that arise. I had to figure this out. I think Joe did too."

"Gosh, I think my husband and I figured that one out a long time ago. It took you two twenty-years?"

"Yes. And isn't that great?"

After the sound of laughter died down, Bonnie said, "Will you do it again?"

I paused, "I don't know."

The crowd got silent, ready to be sad.

"No, no sadness here. Joe's job situation is up in the air. His current job drives him nuts so he will be giving it up; his last day will be in early October. But we don't know if he is going to get into a pilotage job or something else. Joe and I are back to our traditional life: we see each other when ships and semesters allow."

"Well, that is sort of sad Paula. Do you want to live with him again?"

With a big smile, I said, "Absolutely."

The crowd relaxed.

I continued, "But maybe in a larger space than a 33½ foot boat. Or at least a boat that stayed a bit drier and warmer inside."

The crowd laughed. Someone yelled, "Paula, I want to see photos."

"Well, I have excellent photos of trees and forests."

"What about the boat?"

"Well, most of the boat pictures are pictures of broken bits being worked on. You probably wouldn't appreciate them."

"How about wildlife? Otters? Eagles? Whales?"

"Sorry. It turns out I'm better at looking at them than taking a picture of them. No photos of wildlife. But we got a dog. I have photos of her."

They all appreciated how cute Precious was. I didn't share with them how Precious helped Joe and I build our comfort zones together; the bar was a bit too crowded for that depth. The conversation turned to the start of the semester stuff, and I turned back to my drink. Bonnie quietly leaned over, "You miss him?"

"I miss him." I felt a bit like Sam after Frodo went to the Gray Havens, though my love would be coming back sometime.

* * *

I was back from campus where I spent most of the day deciding which parts of the sabbatical book project I could integrate into my syllabi and use with my students. I had a few chapters, but I was a long way from a completed manuscript. I did have enough to provide a deeper educational experience to my students, and I was satisfied with that. Finishing the book was going to be a long-term project.

Precious was curled up on my lap, as we both sat in the only comfortable chair in my tiny, furnished apartment in Huntingdon. She was heavy but we were both happier with her there. My cell phone played the theme to *The Lord of the Rings*.

Picking up, I heard Joe say, "Hi sweets, how are you? How is Precious?"

"We are both good. You should see her chase chipmunks! It is the best thing about this new apartment: no shortage of chipmunks. There is one thing she doesn't enjoy so much …"

"What?"

"I cannot throw a ball nearly as far or as fast as you. She looks at me entirely bored with my ball throwing."

"See if the pet store has one of those ball launchers; I think they are called 'Chuckits' or something. She might prefer that."

"Great idea!"

"Hey, I have some news for you."

Breathe, Paula, breathe. "Okay, what's up?"

"I have a going away party set for October 3 here. They will send me off with a big blast. Want to come up? Gail has offered you mileage tickets."

"Wow, that'd be great! How sweet!" I'd get to see Joe in just a month or so. I didn't know when the next chance might be, but I was pleased to have a date for my next Joe-sighting.

"One other thing," his voice had gotten serious, "SWAPA voted."

My breathing slowed. My stomach clenched. I stopped petting Precious.

"I'll be starting as a pilot trainee on Oct. 5, just two days after leaving this job. I'm moving down to Homer—that will be my base, my new home."

Once my breath returned, I may have screamed into the phone.

Precious jumped down on the floor and started barking. "You did it my love, you did it!"

Joe got in!

His plan to try for pilotage while working a full-time port captain job worked out. Just two days after his last day with the Marine Highway. He still had his knack for timing.

My future shifted. Once he was through the training program, life would be with my husband and my dog, in the same home, in the same place, in the most beautiful place on the planet. A new place I'd get to learn about. The financial hemorrhaging would stop. His work would no longer drive him crazy. I had tears in my eyes as I closed out the call with our traditional smooches.

Then I hugged Precious for a good joyful cry.

I didn't know what my career plans would be, but I had no doubt I'd figure it out. I would happily exchange the gold and diamond ring of a tenured full professor for a grand life with Joe as a pilot, living in Homer, together with Precious the dog.

I would write or find a job at a local college to satisfy my ambitions. I'd have a new landscape to explore, with attention on my immediate world and not just the float to the next landing. I had already fulfilled the big dream of being a professor and with that success I felt free to expand my professional goals.

Life with a sailor had provided me with an abundance of unexpected adventures, and our year had delivered a richness even with its less than pleasant moments. We were going to share our next chapters in a beautiful, magical place, putting down roots, roots intertwined between me and Joe and the landscape, giving us the chance to live in the moment, together.

We'd have the time to explore our new home state, build more richness of time together, and hopefully, without more leaky decks raining on us in bed.

My cheeks were sore from smiling, anticipating the future, living with my husband fulltime. And with a dog.

***

The End

Acknowledgements

Odd how a memoir can both be a solo effort and entirely dependent upon others. The words would not have made it to these pages without the fuel of other voices. Friends and family wanted to hear the story of Paula and Joe and life on the boat. Those words of encouragement kept reverberating in my mind, energizing me to return me to the project after fits and starts, after months and years.

Special thanks to my colleagues at Juniata College. Some wanted to hear more about Cap't Joe. Others (yes, Donna Weimar, that would be you) wouldn't let the project lie and made it a topic of conversation every time we met. I appreciated the motivation—if they wouldn't let it die, I wouldn't either.

More thanks to the folks who provided critique as this work developed. I truly feel for the early readers! Floaters improved with time and effort, and particularly after input of my first editor, Sarah Cypher of The Threepenny Editor. Sarah didn't word-smith, she idea-smithed. She thought about story and flow, about audience and intent, about story arc and scene, and her ideas helped me to see how to improve upon my earlier draft. And also special thanks to my final editor, Gwen Gere of Gere Tactical, whose careful and thoughtful eye caught many errors before they become permanent parts of the text.

Reader, be certain, any flaws, errors, misstatements, or poor writing are entirely mine. Editors, early readers, and friends-with-suggestions are entirely innocent. I take full responsibility of all errors.

Reader, also note that I did not record the conversations written in the text at the time they happened. Therefore, I relied on the poor tool of memory to fill in the details. The conversations, stories, scenes, and timeline within Floaters is as accurate as memory allowed. The events in Floaters happened and I've recorded them to the best of my ability. Other events also took place. A memoirist has to pick and choose what to include and what to leave behind all while depending on that weak link of memory. Floaters is my representation of those times. Forgive me for any omissions.

Finally, let me acknowledge Joe Martin. It takes a strong man to watch his wife write about their life together. He never critiqued the activity, the process, or the product. When I told him I was struggling a bit about how much I should describe, he said, "You write what you want, don't worry about me. It is what it is. I'll be fine." Thanks my love for the freedom to tell our tale.

About the Author

PJS Martin has nearly completed her metamorphosis with the completion of her travel adventure/romantic memoir, *Floaters: The Professor and the Captain*. With its publication she will have made the switch from entomologist/professor of environmental science/college administrator to being a full-time, published author.

Next up, her writing schedule will turn to fiction: an environmental cozy mystery series starring Rainey Collins as the scientist-sleuth. After that, she will decide whether to continue in the world of cozy mysteries or switch back to nonfiction ... maybe a book on Water? Popular science? Or the adventures of university field trips? She is enjoying the flexibility of choosing her way.

She is from Buffalo, NY, still dreams of the Buffalo Bills winning the Super Bowl, and currently lives in Alaska in a town that gets less snow than Buffalo did. She shares the home with a dear husband, and the rescue dog that came with a rescue cat.

You can connect with PJS Martin through Facebook PJSMartin Books or her website: pjsmartin.com. Sign up for her newsletter at pjsmartin.com to find out what route she decided to take next!

Coming Up

IF YOU ENJOYED FLOATERS, there's more to come from PJS Martin, but this time some fiction, a new kind of mystery, combining fiction and science: an environmental cozy.

There is No Away

The main character is Rainey Collins, a professor who just wants to teach her students and relax in the rural peace around her small private college. But her students and her colleagues keep pushing her for more. She ends up deep in an environmental disaster that risks everything. Will she be able to step up to protect her peace? To protect her students? To even protect herself? Watch for the first of the series, due out in 2022.

CPSIA information can be obtained
at www.ICGtesting.com
Printed in the USA
LVHW030312261121
704454LV00005B/687